A
FITCH FAMILY
HISTORY

English Ancestors of the
Fitches of Colonial Connecticut

by
John T. Fitch

Library of Congress Catalog Card Number: 90-061535

ISBN-13 978-19978114180
ISBN-10 1978114184

Printed in the United States of America

First edition 1990
Second edition 1994
    second printing 2002
CD edition 2003
Paperback edition 2017

For John[12]

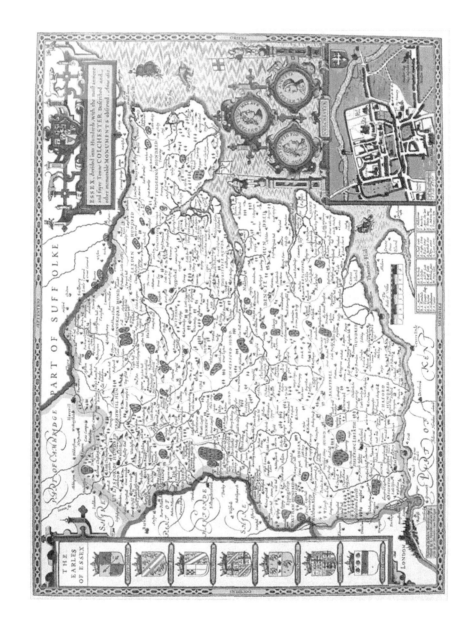

Preface to the Second Edition

I t's hard to believe that it has been more than sixty years since the only major Fitch genealogy and family history was compiled and written. But it was in 1930 that Roscoe Conkling Fitch published his two volume *History of the Fitch Family*.[1] There have been other, shorter pieces—booklets and pamphlets mostly— each written with a narrow focus. Back in 1886, John G. Fitch published his *Genealogy of the Fitch family in North America*[2] which can still be found on the genealogy and family history shelves of many libraries. Those shelves often also hold typewritten manuscripts about various local Fitch families, whether in Connecticut, Ohio, or elsewhere. And there are collections of notes—organized and disorganized, fact and fancy, useful and useless—that can be found under the heading *Fitch* in the New York Historical Society, the Connecticut Historical Society, the Rutherford B. Hayes Presidential Center, and many other libraries. And, finally, there is one, carefully researched genealogy of Fitches in America by Lucius Barbour in the Archives of the Connecticut State Library.[3]

But, there is nothing remotely like the R. C. Fitch *History*.

For all its shortcomings (and I believe it has many), it is still the only work to attempt to trace the forbears and descendants of the four Fitch brothers, James, Thomas, Joseph, and Samuel who came to America in the first half of the 17th century.

1. Roscoe Conkling Fitch, *History of the Fitch Family: 1400 - 1930* (2 vols. Haverhill, Massachusetts: By the Author, 1930).
2. John G. Fitch, *Genealogy of the Fitch Family in North America* (Olmsted, Ohio: By the Author, 1886).
3. Lucius B. Barbour, *Fitch Genealogy* (Hartford: Archives, History and Genealogy Unit, Connecticut State Library, RG 74:36 Nos. 96, 97).

Whether by luck or genius, R. C. Fitch started off on the right foot; he contacted the College of Arms in London and asked them to prepare a certified pedigree for the family. He was put in touch with the then Portcullis Herald or Pursuivant of the College, Mr. A. T. Butler, a first-rate genealogist. Much of their correspondence is reproduced in the first volume (right down to the invoice for work performed!). From Mr. Butler's letters, we can obtain a clear picture of how genealogical research should be undertaken. The College starts, of course, with a considerable advantage over other researchers, in that they have access to records not readily available to others: namely, their own. Going back to 1558, they have been responsible for the "Visitations," the on-site compilations of pedigrees and coats-of-arms of the "gentlemen and esquires" throughout the kingdom. And despite the fact that these documents have been widely copied (and modified, as Mr. Butler points out), the College still has the originals.

At the behest of R. C. Fitch, however, the College went further than simply consulting the old Visitation records; they went to the other—and more reliable—source of information, the manor court rolls. These records are literally rolls of parchment, detailing the business of the manor courts. The courts, held by the lord of the manor, handled matters of probate, real estate transactions, appointment of jurors, and a wide variety of minor infractions of the law. And, fortunately for us, many of these records—some going back to the 13th century—survive in county record offices and college muniment rooms to this day. As a result, the College of Arms, by consulting the appropriate rolls at New College, Oxford, was able to provide R. C. Fitch with citations that showed the succession of generations of the Fitch family from about 1400 to the time when the Fitch brothers left for the colonies. The College did its job so thoroughly that nothing that I am aware of in the way of research since has changed anything of significance in their work of 1929. The pedigree of Fitch stands now as it did then.

Unlike the R. C. Fitch *History*, however, this book will not be an uncritical hagiography of ancient Fitches, nor will it be a "mug book" (as they are so aptly if indelicately called) of fulsome sketches of well-known Fitches of the present. Rather, it will trace only one slender thread from 1400 onward, pausing at each generation to try to understand what these people were like, where they lived, what they owned, and what motivated them to act as they did.

Some of these people we know a great deal about, because they left copious records for us to peruse. Others—the farmers particularly—we can see only dimly. We may have records of their births, whom they married, and who their children were. But, that's about all. In every generation, we tend to know less about the distaff side of the family. In several cases, we don't know the woman's maiden name; in one case, we don't even know her first name. In many cases, our only knowledge of the woman comes from the fact that she is mentioned in her late husband's will (women didn't often leave wills of their own).

There are many people I would like to thank for their generous help. Dr. Marc Fitch was most generous in allowing me access to his remarkable collection of research accumulated over a period of fifty years. Unfortunately, I must sadly report his passing in April of 1994 at the age of 86. Mrs. Joyce Pease Fitch of Hatfield Peverel, Essex, the lightning rod in England for all questions about the Fitch family there and custodian of the Marc Fitch collection, was an extremely helpful and generous guide and friend. I also want to thank Canon John A. Fitch of Great Yeldham, Essex, and the late Mr. Bertram W. Glover of Thorpe Bay, Essex, for allowing me access to their work on the very early Steeple Bumpstead Fitches. I would also like to thank my sister, Mrs. Edith Fitch Swapp, for patiently transcribing the long deeds and wills contained in the text and appendices. Then there are the myriad of librarians and record agents in England and America who listened to my requests and patiently helped me through their files and stacks. Even though I seldom learned their names,these anonymous people invariably dropped whatever they were doing to suggest, find, and copy the bits and pieces of reference material that led to the present story. I am constantly reminded of Blanche DuBois' last line in *A Streetcar Named Desire*: "I have always depended on the kindness of strangers." And I can state without equivocation, there are no kinder strangers than the world's librarians and archivists.

Finally, I would like to thank my wife, Mary Hall Fitch, for her generous help in this project. She accompanied me on field trips, sorted through the boxes of old family letters and papers, and read patiently through each draft of this book.

Finally, a few words about this second edition. No one could have been more surprised and pleased than the author when the first edition sold out. (Genealogical publishing is not noted for best-sellers!) There were, of course, a number of typographical and other errors in the first printing that needed correcting. But, more importantly, the publication of the first edition had uncovered two additional sources of information and illustration.

One of the readers of that first book was Charles Fitch-Northen, another octagenarian, living in the west of England, who, like Dr. Marc Fitch, had also researched the Fitch line back in the 1920s. He had found several important records not cited in the book. In particular, he had a reference that cleared up the mystery of the Jane Fitch who sold Brazen Head farm in 1581. And he had evidence of several more holdings in the Lindsell area by Roger[C] Fitch, the great-grandfather of our immigrant ancestors.

The new illustrations all come from the Essex Record Office, two from the Marc Fitch collection, the third from the ERO's own archives. I wish to thank Ms. Janet Smith of the ERO for her help in obtaining copies of these documents.

John T. Fitch
Cambridge, Massachusetts, 1994

Table of Contents

1 Introduction   1
   The Fitch Surname   1
   Origin of the Name   2
   Montfitchet or Mountfitchet as a Source   5
   Other Sources   5
   Fitch as a Place-Name   7
   The First Fitch   8
   The Fitches of Steeple Bumpstead   10
   The Visitations of Essex   12
   The Copies and Printed Visitations   14
   The Private Pedigrees   17
   Fitch Castle in the North   19
   The Fitch Arms   23
   Ramification and Extinction   31
   England and America   31
   Supplementary Material   32
   Dates   33
2 William^{F} 35
   Essex   35
   Wicken Bonhunt   39
3 John^{E} 67
4 Thomas^{D} 73
   Algore   74
   Lindsell   76
   Brazen Head Farm   78
   The Children   89
   A Growing Estate   89
   Lindsell Church   92
   Disposition of the Estate   103

	Richard, William, and Thomas	104
	Brazen Head Revisited	109
5	Roger^C	119
	Panfield	119
	Bocking	120
	The Church of St. Mary, Bocking	123
	The Will	135
	The Children	142
6	George^B	147
	Braintree	149
	The 1600 Map	163
	Sudbury	169
	Remarriage	171
	The Will	173
	The Children	178
7	Thomas^A	181
	Wool Cloth Manufacture in Essex	181
	Reve (or Reeve)	191
	The Will	198
	Anne and the Children	203
8	Genealogy	205
9	Bibliography	213
10	Glossary	217
11	Appendix: George^B	227
	1600 Deed	227
	The Will	231
12	Appendix: Thomas^A	239
	Bargain and Sale	239
	Enfeoffment	245
	Bond	247
	Final Concord	248
	The Will	248
	About the Author	255

1

Introduction

The Fitch Surname

The surname, now usually spelled *Fitch*, was spelled as *Fecche, Ficche, Fycche, Fiche, Fyche, Fytche,* and *Fitche* during the lifetime of just one member of the family in the 15th century. William Fitche (to use the last version and the one closest to our own) of Wicken Bonhunt, the progenitor of the line we shall be following, had his name spelled in at least these seven ways between 1428, when his name first appeared on a record, and 1466, when he died. At times, his name was spelled two different ways at the same time, as aliases. The records in which his name appeared, however, were not written by William; they were written by clerks. The clerk put down what he heard, and it might have done little good to ask William how he spelled his name; he may or may not have known himself. Furthermore, spelling itself was a highly individual matter—not just for personal names, but for words in general. The letters *i* and *y* were used interchangeably, the final silent *e* was added indifferently, and the *t* in the middle, though useful for us to distinguish among a German *Fich*, a French *Fiche*, and an English *Fitch*, were probably unimportant, even unimagined, distinctions to the manorial scribe.

One way of spelling *Fitch* in print, however, is really not correct: that is as *ffitch*. Although the famous 16th century brass and window of Thomas and Agnes Fitch in Lindsell and the 17th century signature of Reverend James Fitch *appear* to be spelled *ffytche*, what understandably looks like a double lower-case *f* was, until well into the 18th century, simply the standard way of writing a single upper-case *F*. On the other hand, there are some members of the family who, for whatever reasons, have settled on a peculiar combination of upper and lower case *f*s by spelling their name *Ffytche* and variations thereof.

Origin of the Name

There is not much point in looking for *Fitch* (in any of its numerous spellings) as a hereditary surname until the thirteenth century. There were surnames before that, of course—perhaps even including *Fitch*—but they were primarily used to distinguish between two persons with the same Christian name. An amusing, but well documented, example from a much later period in Scotland, cited by George Redmonds,[1] is that of George Gunn, who died in 1464. His son was Robert Georgeson, i.e. he was the son of George. Robert's oldest son was Donald MacRob (where *Mac* means *son of*), and Donald MacRob's son, in turn, was David Donaldson. This last named lived as late as 1595. Thus, someone coming across these four names—Gunn, Georgeson, MacRob, Donaldson—apart from their generational context would have no idea that any one of them was related to any of the others. Richard McKinley,[2] describing the counties of Norfolk and Suffolk, neighbors to the north of Essex, points out that "during the 13th century hereditary surnames became much more widespread, and by about 1300 possibly as many as half the families in East Anglia may have had hereditary surnames." Redmonds believes it likely that "the first inheriting of a surname was closely tied to the inheriting of possessions, status, or occupation," and that "in some

1. George Redmonds, from class notes for *Genealogy and Family History*, (Ripon, England: 1987).
2. Richard McKinley, *Norfolk and Suffolk Surnames in the Middle Ages* (Leicester University Press), pp. 21,22

regions this was a process which accelerated after the plague of 1349-50 known as the Black Death."[1]

Jennifer Ward, writing about the medieval Essex community, says:

> Yet, although family names had become hereditary for many of the artistocracy and gentry, further down the social scale the use of surnames was very fluid, and it cannot be assumed that they were hereditary before the mid-fourteenth century; villagers could often appear in the records under more than one name in some cases under more than two.[2]

To make this concept more concrete, it may be helpful to look, for example, at a list of rectors for a typical small parish church (Figure 1). These are taken from a plaque in the church of St. Mary's in Bocking, county Essex.

Notice that until 1366, each of the rectors is identified only by a first name and a place-name, probably the village where he was born. Then, in the same year, one of them has both a surname and a place-name. Finally, after 1378 each of the rectors has only a surname. Thus, we should not be surprised if we cannot find *Fitch* as a surname until well into the 14th century.

In 1877, Dr. Asa Fitch suggested the earliest origin, i.e. that *Fitch* was a Saxon derivative, that it could have sprung from the same root as the modern German names of *Fichte*, *Ficht*, and *Fecht*.[3] He

1232	Peter de Wakering
1249	Robert de Staunford
1270	Richard de Stanes
1271	Richard de Clifford
1285	Adam de Ilegh
1289	Robert de Watlington
1307	Gilbert de Bruere
1315	Roger de Sheryng
1327	Edmund de Ramesbury
1353	Martin de Ixning
1333	John de Honesworth or Clent
1349	John de Wytheredlegh
1351	Richard de Wynewyk
1352	Thomas de Oteford
1354	Adam de Everingham
1366	John de Barton
1366	Edm.Monachus de Bury or Bokingham
1377	John Jolden or Stanefeld
1378	Thomas Grocer Nicholas Bourne
1398	David Bagatour

Figure 1 - Deans and Rectors of Bocking.

1. George Redmonds, "Surname Origins," *NEXUS*, Vol IV, No. 3 (Boston, MA: New England Historic Genealogical Society, 1987), p. 127.
2. Jennifer C. Ward, ed., *The Medieval Essex Community: The Lay Subsidy of 1327* (Essex Record Office Publication No. 88, 1983), p. v.
3. R. C. Fitch, *op. cit.*, p. 3.

offered no examples, however, of Anglo Saxons or anyone else with these names, nor how any of these became *Fitch*. In fact, there are only a handful of modern English names which can be said to be derived from earlier Anglo Saxon names, and Fitch is not among them.[1]

P. H. Reaney's *Dictionary of British Surnames*[2] has a rather lengthy discussion of the origin of the Fitch name and what he considers its most common variant, *Fitchet*. His earliest citation is, in fact, an 1176 reference to Hugh, Robert, and Walter *Fichet*. His earliest citation for *Fiche* from 1243 has now been preceded by a 1240 reference which we shall examine in more detail, later.

> The common derivation of Fitch and Fitchet from the polecat is untenable. This word is from Old French *fissell*, plural *fissiaulx*, later *fissau* with forms *fitchewes* 1394, *fycheux* 1418, *fechets* 1535, *fichat* 1653 (A New English Dictionary, Oxford 1888-1933, Bedfordshire). This late development of -*et* cannot account for the 12th century *Fichet*. We may compare the French *Fiche, Fichet, Fichot* which Dauzat derives from Old French *fiche* 'an iron point,' from *ficher* 'to fix, plant.' *Fitch* is thus 'an iron-pointed implement,' used by metonymy for *Fitcher*, the workman who uses this, and *Fitchen* and *Fitchet* are diminutives. As Hugh *Malet* is said to have abandoned for a time his nickname 'little hammer' in favour of *Fitchet, fiche* must have been used of a pointed weapon, a spear or lance, and *Fitch* and *Fitchett* of a spearman or a knight famous for his exploits with the lance. By the side of these, French has the Norman *Fiquet* whence the English *Fickett* ... *Fitch*, like *Fick* and *Fichet* may have been used as a personal name, cf. also *Fechel* de Fercalahn. This would account for the diminutives.

Thus, Reaney derives the name from Old French or Norman French.

---

1.   Sir Anthony Wagner, *English Genealogy* (London: Oxford University Press, 1972).
2.   P.H.Reaney,*A Dictionary of British Surnames* (London: Routledge and Kegan Paul).

Montfitchet or Mountfitchet as a Source

Others, besides Reaney, have wondered about a possible Norman antecedent for *Fitch*. And, since the proved line of descent begins in Wicken Bonhunt in the northwestern part of Essex (Figure 2), one is tempted to look in that neighborhood for the name. Only five miles south of Wicken Bonhunt is Stansted Mountfitchet. And, because of the possibility of association with one of the important Norman baronial families who lived there and gave the village its name, the temptation to consider *Mountfitchet* or the family name *Montfitchet* as a source is strong indeed. As a patronymic, however the quest leads to a dead end; the last of the family, Richard de Montfitchet II, died in 1258 without ever having married, and there is no evidence he had any children out of wedlock. As a place-name, however, it is not unreasonable to consider *Mountfitchet* as a source. Someone might easily have shortened the longer *Mountfitchet* place name for that purpose. All this speculation, however, ignores the fact that 18 years *before* Richard died, there was already a man named Fitch living in the next county. We shall meet him shortly.

Other Sources

David Hey[1] places surnames in six categories:

1. Those derived from personal names
2. Those derived from occupations
3. Topographical names, derived from features of the landscape
4. Locative names, derived from specific place-names or localities
5. Nicknames
6. Terms of relationship.

He then discusses the relative importance of these six sources:

1. David Hey, *Family History and Local History in England* (London: Longman Group UK Limited, 1987), p. 29.

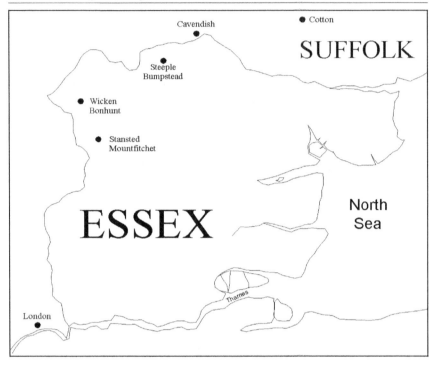

Figure 2 - The Essex-Suffolk Border

The locative names are particularly rewarding to study, for they are relatively easy to use when assessing mobility. They, more than any other type often have a simple origin. Perhaps the most interesting finding of all this recent work is the conclusion that a great number of our English surnames originate with single families.

It would seem that for *Fitch*, at least, we can rule out derivation from a topographical feature or a relationship. That leaves us with Reaney's suggestions of an occupation, i.e. a workman who uses an iron-pointed implement, or a nickname, as in the case of Hugh Malet, the "little hammer," who called himself *Fitchet*, or a personal name and its diminutives. Reaney's derivations seem unnecessarily indirect. Nature (and perhaps genealogy) prefers the simple answer. And it seems that the simplest source, as Hey suggests, is a locative or place-name.

Fitch as a Place-Name

In the case of *Fitch*, a likely place-name source, sug- 1168 gested by Dr. Marc Fitch,[1] who has spent more than 50 years researching *Fitch* family genealogy, appears to be a place named *Fiche*, in or near Cotton, county Suffolk (Figure 2). He points to a charter, or deed, in which Manasser de Dammartin gives to his nephew all the lands in Mendlesham, Wickham Skeith, or Cotton, in Suffolk, (three neighboring towns about 12 miles east of Bury St. Edmunds and about 20 miles from the Essex border) that he held on the day the duke of Saxony married King Henry's daughter. This puts the date at 1168 or soon thereafter. The charter includes the phrase "... *et terra Fiche deffendere pro iiij acris ad seruicium regis* ..." referring to four acres of *Fitch* land (a *j* was often used instead of a terminal *i* in Roman numerals).[2] But, how did this place-name *Fiche* itself originate?

The most plausible explanation, suggested by Marc Fitch, is that the place-name derived from the word *fitch* itself, which means vetch or fitch-grass. (The botanical name for the plant is *Vicia sativa*.) It appears in the 1382 Wyclif Bible in the Book of Isaiah, chapter 28, verse 25 in the phrase "Barly, and myle, and ficche in their coestes." In the 1388 version, the word becomes "fetchis." Other early forms of the word were *fecch(e), fechche, fetche, fetch,* and *veitch*. The 1611 Authorized or King James' version of the Bible has at least two uses of *fitch*. The same phrase from Isaiah becomes

> When he hath made plain the face thereof, doth he not cast abroad the fitches, and scatter the cummin, and cast in the principal wheat and the appointed barley and the rie in their place?

1. Wagner, *op.cit.*, pp. 192-196.
2. Sir Christopher Hatton, *Book of Seals*, 1950, p. 239.

And in the fourth chapter of Ezekiel, we find in the ninth verse:

> Take thou also unto thee wheat, and barley, and beans, and lentiles, and millet, and fitches, and put them in one vessel, and make thee bread thereof ...

The Oxford English Dictionary also provides a 1625 example of the use of the words *fitch* and *vetch* in the same sentence as synonyms from Hart's *Anatomy and Ur.* which stated that "Red Vetches or Fitches in the residence ... are recorded ... to signifie ... great inflamation of the Liuer" (where *Liuer* probably means *Liver*). Thus, a place called *Fitch* would most likely be a field where vetch was growing. And a person who worked such a field could become known by that name. To sum up, why look for a complicated derivation from French or German, when a perfectly good English word already exists?

The First Fitch

1240   The first actual *person* with the name *Fitch* that Marc Fitch has been able to identify was a William Fich of Cotton, whose name appears on an Assize Roll (a record of one of the courts) in 1240:

> 24 Hen. III
> Hundr' de Cleydon p'xij. De Willo fich de Cotton & soc' suis de fine p' t'nsg' iij.m. p' pl' hub'ti G'nagan. Willi de Cotton. Rici fil' Joce de ead. Hug' fil' Rici de ead. Ric' fil' Ascelin de ead & hamon le Neue de Thorneye. m. 57d.

This will be the only time we print a document in either Norman French or Latin, and we do it only as a reminder that these were the languages of the court. Fortunately, a researcher for Marc Fitch long ago transcribed and translated many of these court documents for which we shall hereafter use only the translation. In this case, the translated court record reads:

> 24 Hen. III [1240]
> The hundred of Cleydon [comes] by twelve [hundredors]. Of

William Fich of Cotton and his fellows for a fine of trespass, 3 marks. By sureties Hubert Gernagan, William of Cotton, Richard son of Joyce, of the same place. Hugh son of Richard of the same. Richard son of Ascelin of the same and Hamo le Neve of Thorney.[1]

It almost seems a shame that the earliest reference to our name turns out to be in the court record of one caught trespassing and being fined 3 marks therefor. Fortunately for our reputation, we won't have to reveal many of these. But we should not let the substance of this record obscure the more important fact that this William Fich, the first one of that name on record, just happens to live in the same village in which we have already found the first occurrence of the *place-name* Fiche.

Before leaving this record, and at the risk of getting bogged down in details, there are several unfamiliar terms which, if we define now, will prove useful throughout this book. First the date, which gives the year in terms of the regnancy of the king, in this case Henry III. He reigned from 28 October 1216 to 16 November 1272. Because the first year was from 28 October 1216 through 27 October 1217, the 24th year was from 28 October 1239 through 27 October 1240.[2] Thus, without a more specific time within the regnal year, the probability is that the court record is from some time in 1240. There is a further discussion of dates near the end of this chapter.

The term "Hundred of Cleydon" goes back to *Domesday*, when the counties were divided up for legal purposes into *Hundreds*, each of which was thought to contain roughly one hundred families. Then there is the amount of the fine, "3 marks." The mark was equal to two-thirds of a pound. Thus, 3 marks would be equivalent to 2 pounds. And note the mixture of names, some with

1. Great Britain, Public Record Office (hereafter P.R.O.), Suffolk Assize Rolls, J. I, 1, 818, m. 57d. as transcribed and translated by C. L. Ewen in the Marc Fitch Collection (hereafter, M.F.C.), held at the Essex Record Office, Temporary Accession 2366, Ewen Vol. A, f. 13.
2. C. R. Cheney, editor, *Handbook of Dates for Students of English History* (London: Offices of the Royal Historical Society, University College, 1978).

surnames, others identified by where they came from, and still others by their kinship.

1297   Charles Fitch-Northen, who has done extensive research on the Fitch family, has found three Suffolk Fitches—William, Richard, and Roger Fych—of Holbrook, mentioned in the Coram Rege Roll for Trinity Term, 25 Edward I, 1297.[1] It appears that the King himself was presiding over this particular Court session.

1327   Another William Fiche paid a subsidy tax (for the poor) at Cavendish, Suffolk, on the border of Essex (Figure 2), in 1327.[2]

The Fitches of Steeple Bumpstead

1381   The earliest Essex county reference is to a John Fych, labourer, who paid a 4 pence poll tax in 1381 in Steeple Bumpstead, Essex, about eight miles from Cavendish (Figure 2). Canon John A. Fitch,[3] has collected a number of early references to the name in that village. In 1404, a Thomas Fycche appeared on a deed concerning the Manor of Lacheleyes.

1407   In 1407, Walter Fyche, John Fyche, and Richard Fyche were all fined for various trespass offenses, specifically for letting their animals feed in the manor Lord's pasture. Wagner notes that these references are all "in records of lawsuits and taxation returns, and the bearers of the name appear to be yeomen, husbandmen or cotters,"[4] i.e. of various ranks among the farm workers in the feudal system.

1494   The first Steeple Bumpstead Fitch from whom we can draw a connected pedigree (from the French *pied de gru* or crane's foot, because of the radiating lines portraying the various generations) was Richard Fyche whose will was dated 27 October 1494. Wagner continues:

1. *Placita Coram Rege de Term. Trin., 1297*, P.R.O. No. 151.
2. Wagner, *op. cit.*, p. 227.
3. Canon John A. Fitch, "The Antecedent Family" in a manuscript history of Fitch, 1989, quoting from notes by B. W. Glover.
4. Wagner, *op.cit.*, p. 227.

His descendants in time became far more numerous than those of the other [Lindsell] line and it is probable that most bearers of the name in England today descend from him. Marriage with heiresses did little for his progeny, most of whom in the sixteenth and seventeenth centuries seem to have been either small freeholders or tenants of modest holdings. Many wrote themselves yeoman in their wills and until the days of the Industrial Revolution the land claimed almost all, though here and there a younger son entered the Church or became an attorney. None of this branch was entered at the Heralds' Visitations ... [1]

Although it seems likely that these two families—the Steeple Bumpstead and Lindsell Fitches—separated as they were by less than 25 miles, were related, there has been no formal connection made. One cannot help but be struck, however, by the occurrence of the same names in both families. With the exception of Walter, all the Bumpstead names mentioned here—John, Thomas, Richard—occur frequently in the so-called Lindsell line. Unfortunately, every Tom, Dick, and Harry in those days was named John, Thomas, or Richard. George Redmonds says that 68% of the 14th century Christian names were either John, Henry, Richard, Thomas, or William. But, Marc Fitch points out that "Movement in early days from one established family centre frequently means no more than lack of patrimony for a younger son; this should be borne in mind as with the sudden appearance of a man in Widdington when previously in Essex only Steeple Bumpstead had produced examples of the name."[2] Wagner states that kinship to the Lindsell branch was accepted by both lines and by the heralds in the seventeenth century. This later statement is true, but it is likely that the claim was based on a falsified pedigree and the acquiescence of a Lindsell-derived Fitch.

---

1. *ibid.*, p. 228.
2. Marc Fitch, personal communication, 11 September 1989.

The Visitations of Essex

1538   Because of the number of abuses in claims of pedigrees and displays of arms, Henry VIII in 1538/9 initiated a series of "Visitations" to the counties to be performed periodically by the Heralds of the College of Arms in London.

1558   Beginning during his daughter Elizabeth's reign in 1558, they visited Essex and the other counties, demanding that "all persons that do or pretend to bear arms, or are styled 'esquires or gentlemen,' produce and shew forth by what authority they do challenge and claim the same."[1] Ultimately, however, they had to rely on what they were told or could observe by talking with those who were living at the time of the visitation. As G. D. Squibb, Norfolk Herald Extraordinary, has written:

> The sources of the genealogical information in a visitation pedigree are three, namely, the personal knowledge of the head of the family, family tradition handed down to him, and finally information derived from records ... What the man says of his parents, his brothers and sisters and his children and grandchildren is the authentic core of the pedigree ... This first-hand information would sometimes extend to grandparents, but rarely beyond. A pedigree which sets out earlier ancestors calls for careful scrutiny ... for they are not only liable to contain errors made bona fide, but also to be falsified by a desire to show a descent from some illustrious or well-known family of the same name.[2]

Thus, the records of the Heralds were subject to human memory and error. The people at the top of the Herald's manuscripts lived a hundred years and more before the visitations! This point is absolutely critical to understanding why the actual pedigree for Fitch which we shall present here differs in its early generations from the pedigrees that we examine in this *Introduc-*

1.   R. C. Fitch, *op.cit.*, p. 24.
2.   G. D. Squibb, *Visitations Pedigrees and the Genealogist* (London: Pinhorns, 1978), pp. 3,4.

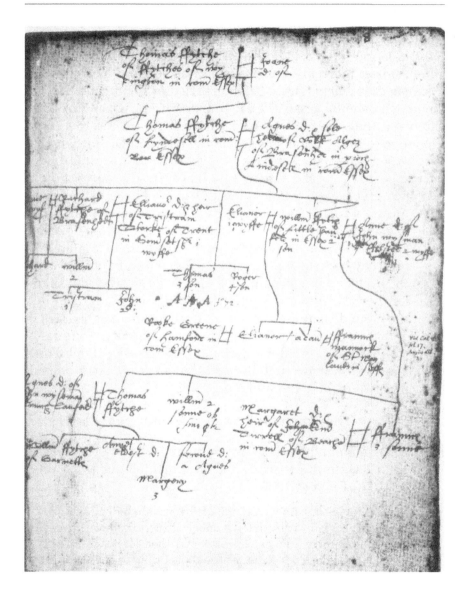

Figure 3 - 1614 Visitation of Essex
(College of Arms Book C.15, Pt. 3.8, from *History of the Fitch Family* by R. C. Fitch)

tion and that many of us have seen in manuscript or print. We shall rely, instead—particularly for these early generations—on *contemporary* records, the Court Rolls that carefully recorded, often in post mortem inquiries, who was son and heir of whom, because these facts had to be determined *at the time* in order to know who should inherit what property from whom. We shall often see that the names and relationships are recorded more than once—first perhaps to report the death of the father, then later when the son comes back to court to claim his inheritance.

1614 To return to the visitations, however, the earliest Fitch pedigree (Figure 3) on file at the College of Arms was recorded in 1614 by John Raven, Richmond Herald, acting as deputy for William Camden, Clarenceux King of Arms.[1] (There were earlier visitations to Essex, in 1558 and 1570, but they do not seem to have included any Fitches.[2]) When the College was asked in 1929 to provide a certified pedigree for the *Fitch* history being written by Roscoe Conkling Fitch, they found that, even in this official document, the Heralds of 300 years earlier had got the first generation wrong. As we shall see in greater detail, Court Rolls prove that the first generation, shown in Figure 3 as Thomas and Joane, should have been John and Juliana.

The Copies and Printed Visitations

But, compounding these errors many fold, were the *copies* of the visitations that were made and later printed. As A. T. Butler, wrote to R. C. Fitch in 1929:

> Several copies must have been made by private individuals of most of the Visitations and a number of these, after drifting about the country from one library to another, landed eventually in the British Museum. These copies were never official records in any way and were subject to additions and altera-

1. Anthony Richard Wagner, *The Records and Collections of the College of Arms* (London: Burkes Peerage Ltd., 1952), p. 70. See Book C.15, Pt. 3.
2. *ibid.*, pp. 69, 70.

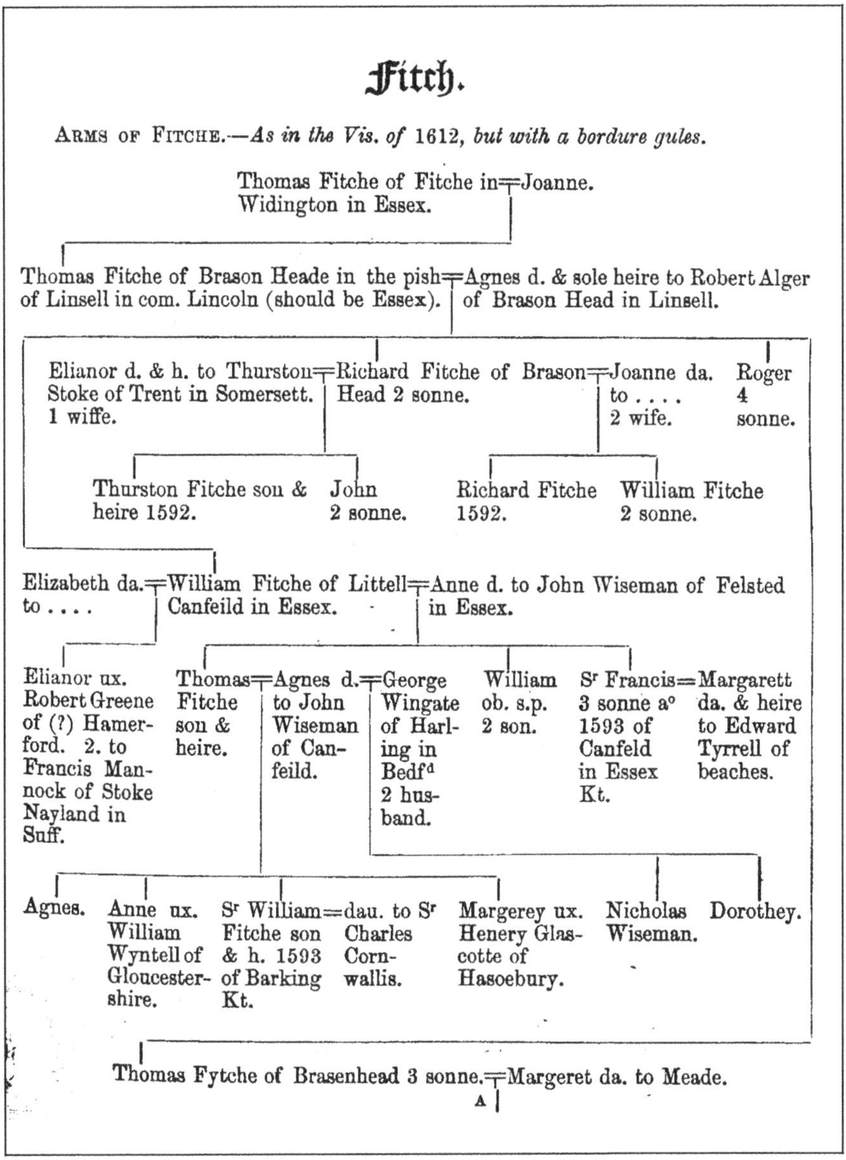

𝔉𝔦𝔱𝔠𝔥.

ARMS OF FITCHE.—*As in the Vis. of* 1612, *but with a bordure gules.*

Thomas Fitche of Fitche in⊤Joanne.
Widington in Essex.

Thomas Fitche of Brason Heade in the pish⊤Agnes d. & sole heire to Robert Alger
of Linsell in com. Lincoln (should be Essex). | of Brason Head in Linsell.

Elianor d. & h. to Thurston⊤Richard Fitche of Brason⊤Joanne da.   Roger
Stoke of Trent in Somersett. | Head 2 sonne. | to   4
1 wiffe. | 2 wife.   sonne.

Thurston Fitche son &   John   Richard Fitche   William Fitche
heire 1592.   2 sonne.   1592.   2 sonne.

Elizabeth da.⊤William Fitche of Littell⊤Anne d. to John Wiseman of Felsted
to . . . . | Canfeild in Essex.   · | in Essex.

| Elianor ux. Robert Greene of (?) Hamerford. 2. to Francis Mannock of Stoke Nayland in Suff. | Thomas Fitche son & heire. | ⊤Agnes d. to John Wiseman of Canfeild. | ⊤George Wingate of Harling in Bedfᵈ 2 husband. | William ob. s.p. 2 son. | Sʳ Francis 3 sonne aᵒ 1593 of Canfeld in Essex Kt. | ═Margarett da. & heire to Edward Tyrrell of beaches. |

Agnes.   Anne ux.   Sʳ William═dau. to Sʳ   Margerey ux.   Nicholas   Dorothey.
William   Fitche son   Charles   Henery Glas-   Wiseman.
Wyntell of   & h. 1593   Corn-   cotte of
Gloucester-   of Barking   wallis.   Hasoebury.
shire.   Kt.

Thomas Fytche of Brasenhead 3 sonne.⊤Margeret da. to Meade.
A |

Figure 4 - Printed Version of Visitation of Essex
(From *The Visitations of Essex* by W.C. Metcalfe, courtesy of The Harleian Society,
London)

tions at the caprice of their various owners, and it is from these copies that the printed so-called Visitations were made.[1]

Or as the Norfolk Herald, Squibb, put it:

Sometimes the text has been collated with the original in the College of Arms and is for historical, though not for legal, purposes almost a substitute for the original. Sometimes the text bears so little resemblance to any original visitation that it is only by an excess of courtesy that it can be called a visitation. Sometimes the text is not that of a visitation at all. For example, there was no visitation of Bedfordshire in 1582 and what is printed under that title in Harl. Soc. vol. 19 is only a collection of Bedfordshire pedigrees by an unknown compiler.[2]

As Butler has indicated, the British Museum has a number of copies of the visitations.[3] An interesting and informative example of the kind of error (or chicanery) that has resulted can be found in the printed copies of the visitations, edited by Walter C. Metcalfe and published by the Harleian Society.[4] In the printed version of the visitation of 1558 (Figure 4), Richard Fitche, son of Thomas and Agnes, has been reduced to the role of second son (2 sonne), and his younger brother, William, has been promoted to first born! Figure 3 (the College of Arms original)—although hard to read—plainly shows on the third level down from the top that William was the second son. We also know from Court Rolls that Richard was the eldest. As Squibb writes:

... the alleged visitations of Essex by Clarenceaux Hawley in 1552 and by Hervey in 1558, printed in Harleian Society, vol.

1. R. C. Fitch, *op. cit.*, pp. 22,23.
2. Squibb, *op.cit.*, p. 7.
3. See Essex Visitations, Harley MSS 887-1398, Harley 1484, ff. 52-58, Harley 1137, Harley 6065, Suffolk Pedigrees Add. MS 5824 ff. 189-190-191.
4. Walter C. Metcalfe ed., *The Visitations of Essex by Hawley, 1552; Hervey, 1558; Cooke, 1570; Raven, 1612; and Owen and Lilly, 1634*, vol. xiii (1878) (London: The Harleian Society, 1878). The Fitch pedigrees are printed on pp. 8 (1552), 51 (1558), 197 (1612), and 397 (1634).

13, ... are of doubtful authenticity ... the edition of Essex, 1612, produced by W. C. Metcalfe contains material from the 1570 visitation together with later non-visitation material and cannot be regarded as anything more than a collection of Essex pedigrees of unknown authenticity.[1]

The Private Pedigrees

1636 Even more fanciful were vellum pedigrees commissioned by individual Fitches in the 17th century. One of these, owned now by Dr. Marc Fitch, is 12 feet 6 inches long(!); another (the top of which is shown in Figure 6), at the Essex Record Office in Chelmsford, is a more modest 9 feet 6 inches.[2] Both of these recite descent from a John Fitch of "Fitch Castle in the North" (Figure 5), one claiming he lived in 1297, the other in 1354. The latter even carries an annotation stating that the castle is in Durham (Figure 8). The fact that no such castle or ruins of a castle or even foundations for a castle have ever been discovered in Durham, or elsewhere in

Figure 5 - John Fitch of Fitch Castle in the North
(From the booklet *Heraldry in Essex*.)

1. Squibb, *op.cit.*, pp. 12,15.
2. Great Britain, County Council of Essex, *Heraldry in Essex*, Essex Record Office (hereafter E.R.O.) Publication 19, 1953, pp. 29,30. The pedigree itself is ERO D/DDS-F2, Parchment.

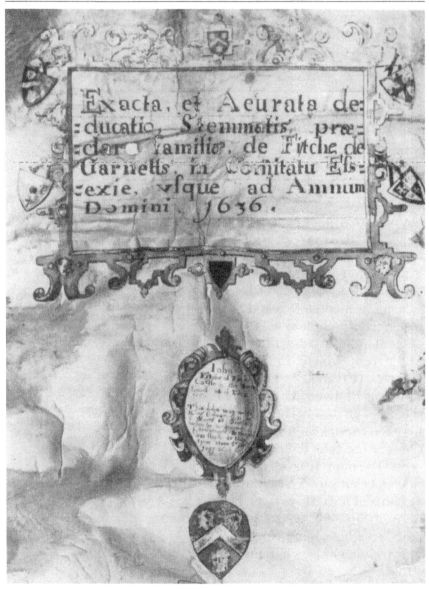

Figure 6 - 1636 Pedigree of Fitch
(Cat. No. D/DDS-F2, reproduced by courtesy of the Essex Record Office)

the north of England, or even in the northern part of Essex, has done little to assuage the apparently insatiable American appetite for an ancestral castle and a coat of arms. The coat of arms exists, and we shall discuss it shortly; the castle is almost certainly a myth.

Fitch Castle in the North

In 1710, the Reverend William Holman wrote a history 1710 of Essex, which, as far as we know, exists only in manuscript form. In it, he writes:

> The original of the Fytches is from the North of England and upon examination I find in ye parish of Hamsterly a house now called Fytches at present a Farm House but has formerly been a very large and ancient Manor House as by the Foundations of great extent dugg up from time to time & by the Report of the Neighbours and other Evidences The parish of Hamsterly is a chappell of Ease to South Church neer Aukland Castle in the Bishoprick of Durham.[1]

Fifty years ago, Dr. Marc Fitch looked into this "castle in the north" and also found that there had evidently been a manor house named "Fitches" in the parish of Hamsterley in county Durham (see Figure 9), but that "The owners of the manor are, in fact, reasonably well attested and there are certainly no Fitches among them."[2] The site is now called "Fitch Grange" (Figure 7). It is more likely, he feels, that the name of the

Figure 7 - Fitch Grange, Witton-le-Wear, Durham
(Photo courtesy of Peter Buell-Fay, London.)

1. M.F.C., *op.cit.*, F/B/1 h.
2. Letter from Dr. Marc Fitch to "a fellow-Fitch" (1957), abstracted by Joyce P. Fitch.

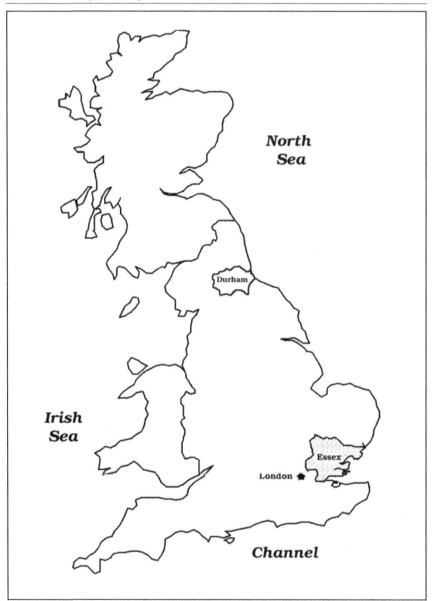

Figure 8 - Durham County ``in the North''

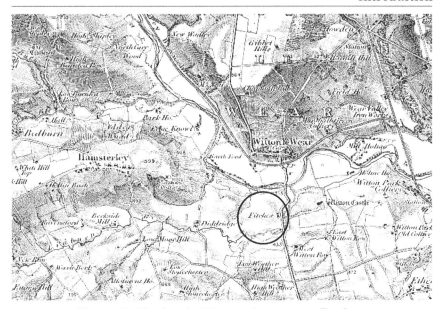

Figure 9 - Fytches in Hamsterley, county Durham
(From 1-inch Ordnance Survey of England and Wales: Durham, Sheet 9, courtesy of David & Charles (Publishers) Ltd.)

Hamsterley manor and the site in Cotton to which we have already referred both denote a place or field where vetches are found abundantly. In Mower's *Place Names of Durham*,[1] there is an entry for the farm called *Fitches* in an area called Witton-le-Wear.

> FITCHES (Witton-le-Wear) 1382 Fychewacke - Bishop Hatfield's Survey. 1392 Fyccheworth - 35th Report of the Deputy Keeper. A difficult name, Possibly M.E. [Middle English] fiche-worth = vetch enclosure. The modern form would then be a shortening ... where the first element of a name is used by itself in the possessive case.

As to how this manor may have become a "castle" in the pedigrees, Hutchinson's *Histories of Durham* states that the

---

1. A. Mower, *Place Names of Durham*, 1920, p. 87, as quoted by C. L. Ewen in M.F.C., Ewen, Vol. B, f. 214.

"Eures held Hamsterley 'for centuries' and no castle is mentioned there. But in the forest there were some ancient British ramparts popularly called the Castles."[1] As to who actually incorporated the concept of a "Fitch castle in the north" into the pedigrees, Dr. Fitch writes:

> In the first quarter of the 17th century, one Edward Jekyll of Barking ... married a Fitch. ... Having found an erstwhile manor in the parish of Hamsterley in Durham—conveniently distant from Essex—called Fitches, he adopted it without more ado ... The Heralds Sigar and Pinson who drew up my vellum pedigree about 1625 were more discretely imprecise, and while elevating the manor into a castle merely located it as "in ye North," thus effectively throwing most would-be enquirers off the track ... At that time, officials were often not above composing long and frequently spurious pedigrees, their length being governed by the depth of their patron's pocket ... With this vague description, typical of pedigrees of the period, the whole thing was printed ... by the Harleian Society and thus it is that the belief in castles and a noble descent is wide spread amongst bearers of our name.[2]

Or, as Wagner puts it:

> The making of false pedigrees is an immemorial vice, practised in antiquity, the Middle Ages, and modern times alike, but the age of Elizabeth I has a specially bad name for such activities. The rise of so many new families to wealth and station in a society where the prestige of ancient blood was great combined with a growing but as yet ill educated zeal for the study of English antiquities to produce a market for deplorable concoctions as well as for genuine research.[3]

J. Horace Round, a turn-of-the-century critic divided the bulk of spurious pedigrees into four classes:

1. *ibid.*, quoting from Hutchinson, pp. iii and 309.
2. Dr. Marc Fitch letter, *op.cit.*
3. Wagner, *op.cit.*, p. 358.

… those that rested on garbled versions of perfectly genuine documents, … those which rested on alleged transcripts of wholly imaginary documents, those which rested on actual forgeries expressly concocted for the purpose, and lastly those which rested on nothing but sheer fantastic fiction.[1]

But, finally, in defense of his fellow heralds, Squibb writes:

It is somewhat remarkable that in an age when the officers of arms were prepared to provide their private clients with pedigrees of inordinate length and incredible splendor, they should have displayed such rectitude when engaged in their official duties on behalf of the Crown.[2]

The caveat to be drawn from all this is that if the pedigree is not an official document at the College of Arms, it is not to be trusted. And, even in the case of the official Fitch pedigree at the College, it is flawed at the start!

The Fitch Arms

Another of the puzzles we need to examine is the matter of the Fitch Arms: When and how did the Fitches acquire them? To make matters more complicated, there are two different coats of arms, usually referred to as the *Ancient* arms of Fitch and the *16th century* arms. They are completely different.

The *Ancient* arms are described by Sir Bernard Burke as:

Or, a pellet between three cross crosslets fitchée sable.[3]

Fitche
(Ancient)
Arms—Gold a roundle between three crosslets fitched sable.

Figure 10 - Ancient Arms of Fitch

---

1. J. Horace Round, as quoted in Wagner, *op.cit.*, p. 358.
2. Squibb, *op.cit.*, p. 4.
3. Sir Bernard Burke, *The General Armory*, (London: Burke's Peerage Ltd., 1884) p. 349.

Figure 11 - 1358 Charter sealed by John of Cavendish
(Cat. No. Add Ch 15747, courtesy of The British Library)

The word "or" in this context means *gold*. A "pellet" (also described as a *roundle*) is a solid disc in the center of the shield. Cross crosslets are simply Christian crosses with the tops and cross-bars also crossed. They are "fitchée" or *fitched*, meaning they are pointed so that they can be planted in the ground. (Can the similarity of the word "fitchée" and the family name be only a coincidence? Reaney, who derives the name from *fiche* would probably say no.) The word "sable" means that the background color or *tincture* is *black*. Figure 10 shows these arms.

But the question is: Did anyone named Fitch ever use these arms? Burke ascribes them to a Fytche (which he spells *Ffytche*) of Thorpe Hall, Elkington, county Lincoln. But, since he also has this Fytche "descended from a branch of Fytche of Lindsell, Danbury Park, and Woodham Walter in the County of Essex,"[1] the matter is highly suspect; the last male of that line died in 1777, and there are no recorded predecessors who moved to county Lincoln. Dr. Marc Fitch is of the opinion that no one named Fitch ever used the so-called Ancient arms.

1. *ibid.*

Nevertheless, there *is* an interesting record at the College of Arms of someone who *did* use these arms, and the coincidences are tantalizing. In 1358 a man named John of Cavendish (the same Suffolk border village where William Fich paid the subsidy tax 31 years earlier), but living at Walsham manor in Suffolk, affixed his seal to a charter or deed (Figure 11).[1]

Although there is no reference here to Fitch, the seal, shown in detail in Figure 12 from a slightly later document,[2] may be significant. It is described as:

Figure 12 - Seal of John of Cavendish
(Cat. No. Doubleday Cast F46, courtesy of The British Library)

> A shield of arms: three crosses crosslet, in fess point a roundle.

Around the edge is the legend "S' IOHANNIS: DE CAVENDYSH" where the *S'* is an abbreviation for *Sigillum* or seal. From a heraldry viewpoint, the description of the three crosses around a "roundle" is virtually identical to the shield of arms, which at some point became known, correctly or incorrectly, as the *Ancient* arms of Fitch. One can only wonder whether the John of Cavendish who used these arms was the progenitor of a Fitch family line.

---

1. W. de G. Birch, *Catalogue of Seals in the Department of Manuscripts in the British Museum*, Vol. II (London: Printed by Order of the Trustees, 1892), No. 8422, p. 617. The manuscript itself is Additional Charter 15747.
2. *ibid.*, No. 8423, Harleian charter 76E.45, and No. 8424, Sulph. cast from No. 8423, D.C., F. 426.

Figure 13 - 16th Century Arms
(From *History of the Fitch Family* by R. C. Fitch)

The second set of Fitch arms is called the *16th century* arms (or *Fitch modern)* perhaps because that is when they were formally applied for at the College of Arms (Figure 13). These are usually described as:

> Vert a chevron between three leopard's faces or.[1]

In this version, prepared by the College of Arms in 1929 and used by R. C. Fitch as the frontispiece for the first volume of his history (Figure 13), the background of the shield is green ("vert"), and the chevron and leopard faces are gold ("or"). When a crest is shown above the arms, it is described as:

> A leopard's face gold, in his mouth a sword proper, the hilt gules.

The word "gules" means *red*. It is impossible to say when the Fitches first started to use these arms. Sir Anthony Wagner, formerly Garter King of Arms, speculates that:

> He [Thomas] appears to have used arms based perhaps on those of his neighbours the Wentworths, who had acquired the manor of Lindsell and others near it by marriage in 1423. A shield of arms formerly on Thomas Fitch's brass in Lindsell church had vanished by 1699.[2] 1699

As far as we can determine, there is no evidence of a shield of arms ever having been part of the Thomas Fitch brass. The date 1699, however, was when a Sir Comport Fitch of county Kent was trying to establish his relationship to the Essex Fitches and, thereby, the right to use the Fitch arms. A herald named Robert Dale, who was evidently working for Sir Comport, went to look at the brass in Lindsell church and noted "but the arms torn away,"[3] though what he saw that gave rise to his conclusion is a mystery. Sir Comport was granted the right to use the arms, "with the

1. Burke, *op.cit.*, p. 349.
2. Wagner, *op.cit.*, p. 227.
3. Index card at the College of Arms.

Difference of three Cross Croslets Fitché Gules upon the Chevron."[1] It seems unlikely the College would have specified this "Difference" as a random modification; they chose, instead, what must have already been known as another form of the Arms of Fitch.

Later, several Fitches in the nineteenth century used arms which combined the ancient and sixteenth century versions (Figure 14).[2] Here we have both the crosses *and* the leopard's heads, given equal weight.

Figure 14 - 19th Century Arms
(From *Armorial Families* by A. C. Fox- Davis, courtesy Charles E. Tuttle Co., Inc.)

The earliest actual use of either Fitch arms that we have been able to find is on the brass of Thomas' second son, William Fitch, in All Saints Church, Little Canfield (Figure 15). William died in 1578. Thus, it is not surprising that the leopard head arms are known as the *sixteenth century* arms. In his will, he asked his executors to prepare "a convenient and fair marble stone engraved with my arms and the pictures of myself, my wife and children..."[3] (The portraits of his two wives survive, but his own effigy has been obliterated.) It also seems much more logical that he, rather than his father, would have been the one to "borrow"

1. R. C. Fitch, *op.cit.*, facing p. 27.
2. Arthur Charles Fox-Davis, *Armorial Families, A Directory of Gentlemen of Coat-Armour*, Vol. 1 (Rutland, VT: Charles E. Tuttle Co.: Publishers, 1970), pp. 675,6.
3. F. G. Emmison, *Elizabethan Life: Wills of Essex Gentry & Merchants* (Chelmsford, England: Essex County Council, 1978), pp. 81-83.

Figure 15 - All Saints Church, Little Canfield

the Wentworth arms, because he had bought Lindsell Hall and Camoys Hall from Thomas Lord Wentworth in 1529. The Wentworth arms (Figure 16), which, according to Thomas Woodcock of the College of Arms, date to at least as early as 1450, are described as:

Sable a chevron between three leopard's faces gold.

They differ then only in the color of the background. William's arms include a crescent moon, facing upward, at the apex of the chevron (Figure 17) to indicate that he was the second son. (The third son would have a ring, the fourth a star.)[1] A. T. Butler of the College of Arms wrote in 1929 that:

1. Michael Olmert, "Hail to Heraldry" in *Smithsonian*..

29

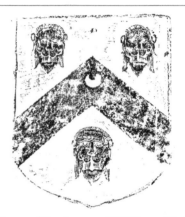

Figure 16 - Wentworth Arms
(From *A Roll of Arms* by G. A. Moriarty,
courtesy of New England Historic
Genealogical Society)

Figure 17 - Arms of William Fitch
(Rubbing made from one corner of the
brass of William Fitch, All Saints Church,
Little Canfield)

The Fitch Arms (bearing the leopard faces) were confirmed by the grant of a Patent of Arms in 1588 to Sir William Fitch of Garnetts in High Easter, Essex.[1]

1588 This Sir William was the grandson of the William who apparently first used the arms. From 1588 on then, the leopard faces and chevron have been the "official" arms of the Fitches of Essex. If this all sounds like an incredible theft of patrimony, read what G. Andrews Moriarty, Jr., writing on Arms for the New England Historic Genealogical Society, has to say on the subject:

> The social revolution of the first half of the sixteenth century produced a great number of new families, whose unauthorized use of coats led to the establishment of the so-called "Visitations," which extended from Elizabeth's time to the reign of Charles II. These Visitations did something towards keeping the use of coat armor within the proper limits. Unfortunately the Elizabethan heralds left much to be desired, and, provided the necessary fees were forthcoming, would assent to almost anything. By the time of Charles II [1660-1685]

1. R. C. Fitch, *op.cit.*, p. 9.

the appropriation of arms had become so common that the heralds admitted that they were unable to cope with the situation; and ever since that time, both in England and America, especially during the eighteenth and nineteenth centuries, the appropriation of arms by persons with no right to them has gone on practically unchecked and furnishes a striking example of the silly snobbery of mankind.[1]

Nevertheless, for what it's worth, both the College of Arms and the New England Historic Genealogical Society acknowledge that descendants of Thomas Fitch of Bocking are entitled to apply for a Patent of the Arms and crest bearing the leopard's heads.

Ramification and Extinction

What is interesting to note—and again we are indebted to Marc Fitch for bringing this out—is that virtually all the *Fitches* in England today are descendants of Richard Fyche of Steeple Bumpstead. The English descendants of William Fiche of Wicken Bonhunt have all died out—with the exception of those that emigrated to America. Actually, this is a not uncommon phenomenon. Redmonds[2] points out that some family surnames in the Middle Ages—in York, for example—became extinct in that area, but may be found elsewhere. Others, which may have started in small villages, ramified. In particular, a surname that may have become extinct in England, may be widespread in the United States. In the case of the *Fitches* of Wicken Bonhunt, that is exactly what happened; all the parallel branches—some of them prosperous, knighted, well-connected—simply died out in the 18th and 19th centuries. Our one narrow line survived and multiplied, not in England, but in the new land of America.

1. G. Andrews Moriarty, Jr., "Introduction," *A Roll of Arms, registered by the Committee on Heraldry of the New England Historic Genealogical Society* (Boston: 1928, reprinted 1950), p. 5.
2. Redmonds, *op.cit.*

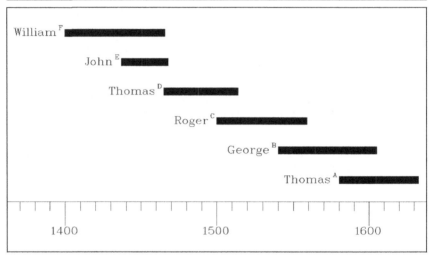

Figure 18 - Timeline for A Fitch Family History, Part 1

England and America

This book, then, ends at the shoreline. It deals with the six generations we know about in England. Figure 18 is a "time line" for the six people we will be following. The generation numbering system is the so-called Register Plan of the New England Historic Genealogical Society, which calls for superscripted numbers for Americans and upper case letters for their old-country ancestors. The system counts up from the father of the immigrant ancestor, Thomas of Bocking, going back in time. Thus, Thomas is identified generationally as Thomas^A, and we go back to William of Wicken Bonhunt who is William^F. This permits a continuation of the system further back in time should additional generations be identified. For the same reason, the Register Plan counts up from the immigrant as we go forward in time. Thus, we start on this side of the ocean with James[1]. This allows a continuation into the future for generations unborn. To avoid confusion between generation numbers and footnote numbers in the text, we have chosen to add square brackets around the generation numbers for the Americans. Thus: James[1] rather than James[1], which might well send the reader looking for footnote 1.

Supplementary Material

Following the narrative family history, there are several appendices. The first is a straightforward *Genealogy*. In Register Plan, backup data are provided in parentheses; hence, footnotes are not required. As a result, the genealogy is provided in the standard Register Plan. As for sources and references, a complete citation is provided at the first reference to an information source. Standard terminology is used for additional references. Those sources which provide more than incidental information are also to be found in the *Bibliography*. Similarly, most archaic or unusual terms are defined when first used, but when the definition is not given (or if it has been forgotten), it can usually be found again in the *Glossary*. Finally, some interesting material was considered too long to be included word-for-word in the body of the narrative. In such cases, the full text is carried in an *Appendix* with a name corresponding to the generation being described.

Dates

A final note about dates: A number of dates in the text are given in double-dated form, e.g. "Fraunces, m. Bocking, 5 Feb. 1606/7, James Stracey." The reason for this is that prior to the year 1752 and the adoption in England and the American colonies of the Gregorian or New Style Calendar of 1582, each new year under the Julian or Old Style Calendar began on Lady day, 25 March, rather than 1 January. Thus, since 5 February in the example comes before 25 March, the year under the old system would have been 1606, whereas under the new system, the year would have been 1607. To avoid confusion, then, the year, when known, is given as 1606/7. If, however, the date is given only as 5 Feb. 1606, you cannot assume that it is really 1606/7; it only means that we know that 1606 is the year given in the reference. If the reference is an original source document, it may be that the year really is 1606/7, and you would be safe in writing it that way. But if the reference is from a secondary source, you cannot tell whether or not the researcher has already updated a Julian 1605 to a Gregorian 1606. If you were now to write it as 1606/7, you could easily be off by a year.[1]

Reference was made in the previous paragraph to "Lady day," 25 March. We shall encounter other references to Saints' Days and will, therefore, now provide a partial list:

> Feast day of the Blessed Virgin Mary: 25 March.
> Feast day of Sts. Philip & James: 1 May (first day of the Easter Quarter Sessions).
> Feast of St. John the Baptist: 24 June.
> Michaelmas day: 25 September.
> Birth day of our lord Christ: 25 December.[2]

And so, we turn to Part 1 of our story: the documented line of descent from William[F] Fitche (ca. 1400-1466) of Wicken Bonhunt, county Essex, England.

1. Leo H. Garman, C.G., "Genealogists and the Gregorian Calendar," in *NEXUS*, Vol. VI, No. 2, April 1989 (Boston: New England Historic Genealogical Society), pp. 61,2.
2. Eve McLaughlin, *Simple Latin for Family Historians*, 2nd. ed., (Birmingham, England: Federation of Family History Societies, 1986), p. 9.

2

William[F]

I n 1400, when our story begins, Europe was emerging from the Middle Ages. The great plagues that had decimated the populations of the second half of the 14th century were over; the feudal system that bound serfs to their lord and land was breaking down; and in England, Henry IV had just become king. We say Henry was king of England, but that's not saying very much. The total population was only about two million souls, down because of the plague from about two and a half million. These few people were scattered over the southeastern part of the island, the area facing the Channel and the North Sea.[1] The heart of this area is the county of Essex.

Essex

Edwards in his *History of Essex*[2] (and almost all of what we say here comes from that book), quotes an observer as stating that Essex is flat and uninteresting, to which a local wag's response is purported to have been, "No, it isn't; Essex is slightly *undulating* and uninteresting!" To the genealogist or family historian, however, Essex is gently rolling and historically fascinating. The county (Figure 19) faces the sea, off the southeast coast of England, its borders defined on the north, south, and west by rivers.

1. John A. Garraty and Peter Gay, editors, *The Columbia History of the World* (New York: Harper & Row, Publishers, 1984), p. 384.
2. A. C. Edwards, *A History of Essex* (London, England: Philamore & Co. Ltd., 1985).

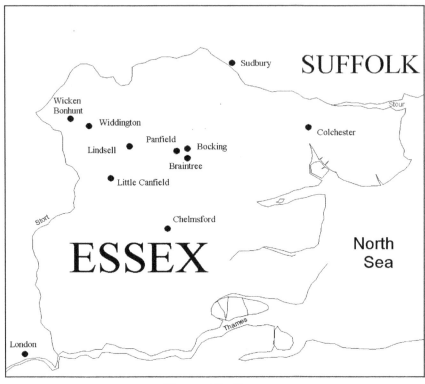

Figure 19 - Essex

The northern border is defined by the River Stour, which separates Essex from Suffolk; the southern border by the River Thames, which divides it from Kent; and on the west by the River Stort, which separates Essex from Hertfordshire. In general the land is higher in the west and "undulates" its way to the East and the sea. Essex used to be heavily forested to the southwest — much like the Black Forest of southwest Germany. The expansion of London, however, which sits just outside the southwestern corner of Essex, has swallowed up Waltham Forest and a number of Essex towns as well. Epping Forest, however, still remains as part of Essex.

It is important for us to keep in mind that Essex is actually a very small area, no more than 50 miles from north to south and 60 from east to west. The villages in which our forbears lived are only five or ten miles apart, and one can easily visit all of them in a day's drive.

The Romans built at least three important roads ca. 50 through the county; their routes are now the principal highways of the area: the A12 which stretches from London (Londinium) in the southwest through Chelmsford (Caesaromagus) in the center to Colchester (Colonia)—a retirement community for Roman soldiers—in the northeast; the A120 which runs across the county through towns in which we will be interested—Little Canfield, Braintree—to Colchester in the east; and, finally, the M11 which runs from London up the western border of the county. The Romans left more than roads, of course; there are buildings, walls, and burial mounds throughout the county.

After the Roman Empire collapsed, it was the Saxons 600 who invaded from the continent. In fact, it was the *East* Saxon kings who gave Essex its name. They ruled for about four centuries, roughly from 600 to 1000 A.D. This period also saw the spread of Christianity, after the missions of St. Augustine in 597 and St. Cedd in 653. Cedd's church of St. Peter's-on-the-Wall, built on the wall of a ruined fortress, stands today and may be seen at Bradwell-on-Sea where the River Blackwater empties into the sea.

The Danes and Saxons fought over the area during the 1000 ninth and tenth centuries, and, in fact, all England was ruled by the Danes briefly from 1016 to 1042. The Saxon line was restored just as briefly with Edward the Confessor and King Harold before the Norman invasion, the Battle of Hastings (during which, as one guide put it, "King 'arold bought it"), and the accession of William the Conqueror in 1066.

It was in 1085, nearly twenty years later, that King 1085 William ordered his survey of England. Actually, Essex is

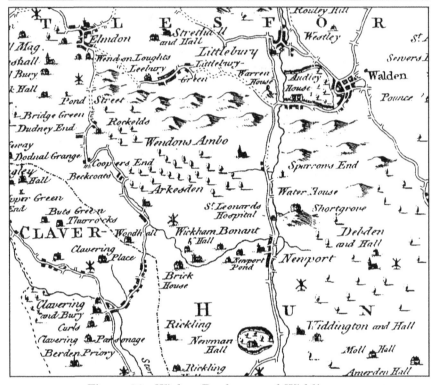

Figure 20 - Wicken Bonhunt and Widdington
(From *History and Antiquities of Essex* by Philip Morant, courtesy of Essex County Library)

covered in the smaller of the two-volume *Domesday* books, usually referred to as the *Little Domesday*. This survey found 440 separate places of settlement in Essex and a total population of about 70,000. The higher land to the north and west of the road from London to Colchester was the most densely populated. Edwards theorizes that this may be because "the boulder clay of the north was more fertile and less difficult to work than London clay, and partly because the coastal marshlands were extensive and continued for centuries to be unhealthy, ague-ridden areas."

Figure 21 - Wicken Hall

Wicken Bonhunt

From various court records which we shall examine in greater detail later, we learn that William was a *husbandman*, a tenant farmer, who raised grain as well as cows and sheep in Wicken Bonhunt in the northwest part of Essex (Figure 20) Like much of the rest of Essex, the landscape comprises fields of grain cut by meandering streams and winding lanes. Groves of tall trees give away the presence of the streams; impenetrable hedgerows define the wandering roads. As a tenant farmer, he must have leased what land he had from one or the other (or both) of the local manors: the Manor of Wicken (Figure 21) and the Manor of Bonhunt. Wicken Hall, owned in William's time by the Barlee (or Barley) family, is northwest of St. Margaret's church (Figure 22); Bonhunt Hall is about a mile northeast of the church. Figure 23 shows the (now ruined) private chapel for the manor of Bonhunt, endowed in 1340 by John Flambard. (A search of the manor court

Figure 22 - St. Margaret's Church, Wicken Bonhunt

rolls for Bonhunt between 1416 and 1527 reveals no references to William or any other Fitch having leased land there;[1] the only Wicken court rolls are of a much later date.[2])

Bonhunt may have been the older of the two villages which later merged to form the single village of Wicken Bonhunt. (William was identified as being first from Bonhunt and later from Wicken.) Eilert Ekwall[3] tells us that Bonhunt was a very old village. It was *Bonhunta* in *Domesday*. It meant either "Bana's huntsmen" or, from Old English, *(ge) bann-hunten,* meaning "huntsmen liable to be summoned." Wicken was *Wikes* in a 1203 Feet of Fines. The word seems to be derived from *Wic,* which

1. Court Rolls, Manor of Bonhunt, E.R.O. D/DU 335/11-13
2. Court Rolls, Manor of Wicken, E.R.O. D/DU 335/15-29.
3. Eilert Ekwall, *The Concise Oxford Dictionary of English Place-Names,* 4th ed. (Oxford: Oxford University Press, 1985).

Figure 23 - Ruined Chapel of St. Elene, Bonhunt

means "dairy farm." By 1238, there were references to the combined name as *Wykes Bonhunte* and in 1412 to *Bonhunt in Wykyn*. Reverend Philip Morant[1] says that the reason for adding *Bonhunt* to *Wicken* (which he spelled *Wickham*) was to distinguish it from two other parishes in the county, namely, *Wickham St. Paul* and *Wickham Bishop's*.

We estimate 1400 as about the time of William's birth. 1400 Richard II had just been forced to abdicate, and the Duke of Hereford had been crowned as Henry IV, establishing the Lancastrian dynasty. Henry spent most of his thirteen years as king suppressing rebellions, by Richard's followers, by the Scots, by the Welsh, and by Sir Henry Percy.

On the death of Henry IV, his son, the Prince of Wales 1413 (the "Prince Hal" in Shakespeare), became Henry V. The rebellions continued, and he re-opened the Hundred Years

1. Rev. Philip Morant, *The History and Antiquities of the County of Essex*, Vol. II (London: 1763-1768, Republished by EP Publishing Limited with the Essex County Library, 1978), p. 587.

War against France as well. At Agincourt, he defeated the French and had himself named successor to King Charles VI of France. He died in 1422 with England further in debt than under his father.

1422 Henry VI became king when he was less than nine months old. Under the protectorate of two uncles, England was defeated at Orleans by Joan of Arc. Henry's rule was dominated by struggle, culminating in the battle between his own family, the Lancasters, and the family of the Duke of York, the Wars of the Roses.

1428 In 1428, William's name appears for the first time on a document, on the records of the Exchequer of Pleas.[1] The record reads:

> Mich. 7 Hen. VI Essex. William Fecche puts himself against John Parker of Rykeling, husbandman. Breach of service contract at Wykyn.[2]

This court appearance took place at the Michaelmas session in 7 Henry VI. It is the first of many such suits filed by William, whose name here is spelled *Fecche*. It is also the first of many spellings of his name. The case is evidently some sort of breach of contract grievance against a John Parker, another husbandman, from Rickling (Figure 20), just to the south of Wicken Bonhunt. Before going any further, we should include a word about the Exchequer of Pleas.

> The jurisdiction of the Exchequer as a court of common law was originally confined to matters directly concerning the King's revenue. But this definition was loose enough to secure to the officers of the Exchequer and their dependants the privilege of pleading and being impleaded in their own Court and to enable any accountant at the Exchequer or anybody indebted to the Crown to sue in this Court upon a suggestion of *quominus*, that is, of his being 'the less' able to satisfy the Crown by reason of the cause of action he had against the defendant. By a fiction

---

1. Exchequer of Pleas, 6-7 Henry VI, P.R.O. E13/134.
2. M.F.C., Ewen Vol. B., f. 160, Com. Pl. (De B.) Rl's. CP 40; 671, pt 3.m.360.

similar to that which ultimately opened the King's Bench to all kinds of personal actions, the application of the writ of *quominus* was eventually so far extended that practically everyone might institute in the Exchequer proceedings in any personal action and in ejectment.[1]

The records of these proceedings were also called Plea Rolls (because this was a court of Common Pleas) and De Banco Rolls (De Banco meaning "from the Bench"). Court generally met four times a year for terms of varying duration. These were Hilary on 13 January; Easter, which of course varied from year to year but was in March or April; Trinity, eight weeks after Easter; and Michaelmas, which began a few days after that feast in September. In this particular case, the court appearance took place during the Michaelmas term. Michaelmas itself is on 29 September, but the court invariably started its term on the octave, the eighth day after that, or 6 October. The term usually ran until the quindene of St. Martin, i.e. fifteen days after 10 November or, in other words, 25 November. So the closest we can date this record is between 6 October and 25 November 1428.

In the next record, William (*Ficche* this time) is repre- sented by an attorney. 1435

> Mich. 14 Hen. VI
> William Ficche, by his attorney, puts himself the fourth day against Thomas Wheler of Claueryng, laborer, in a plea that he render to him 24 sheep worth 40s. which he unjustly detains. And he came not. And the Sheriff was ordered that he summon him, etc. And the Sheriff now returns that he has nothing, etc. Therefore be he taken to be here in 15 days of St Hilary. C.P. Rolls.[2]

In this case, William is suing Thomas Wheler of Clavering (Figure 20), another village just to the west of Wicken Bonhunt.

---

1. *Guide to the Contents of the Public Record Office*, Volume 1 Legal Records, Etc. Revised to 1960 from the Guide by the late M. S. Giuseppi, F.S.A., (London: Her Majesty's Stationery Office, 1963), p. 92.
2. M.F.C., *op.cit.*, f. 502.

Evidently Wheler is holding 24 sheep worth 40 shillings that
William claims belong to him. It's not clear why Wheler *has*
William's sheep; it may be that they wandered onto his property
(we shall encounter other cases where people pastured their stock
on other people's land) and he decided to keep them. Note that
that this is not William's first attempt to get the sheep; it's his
fourth. We shall encounter this "fourth day" phrase over and over
again; it means that this was the fourth time the defendant had
been summoned to appear. It was evidently only on the fourth
appearance by the plaintiff that he could demand action be taken
to get the defendant into court. In fact, the sheriff had already
been ordered to summon Wheler to court, but evidently couldn't
find him. Now he is told to take him bodily and have him at court
15 days after St. Hilary, 13 January. Incidentally, the "etc." used
here and there in the record is not necessarily the shorthand of
the transcriber; the word was sometimes used by the original
scribe to avoid repeating endless "boiler plate," which he would
otherwise have been obliged to write out by hand.

As will become redundantly apparent, William was a liti-
gious soul; he seemed bent on suing everyone in the county—and
if he ran out of defendants in Essex, then in the neighboring
counties as well. Furthermore, either the defendants were very
skilled in hiding themselves, or the sheriff was incredibly inept
at finding them; in either case, they were never to be found, and
one wonders if William was ever able to collect a farthing from
any of them.

1436 The next year, during the Easter term, he was back in court
trying to collect more debts.

> East. 14 Hen. VI Essex. William Fycche of Bonhunt put
> himself the fourth day against Thomas Punte of Neuport,
> husbandman, in a plea that he render to him 10 marks ; and
> against John Herlyng of Neuport, husbandman, 40s. And
> they do not come, etc.[1]

1. *ibid.*, f. 502.

Here we have the first indication that William (now *Fycche*) lives in Bonhunt (though the earlier breach of contract suit was for services in Wicken). The record doesn't indicate why Punte and Herlyng of Newport just to the east (Figure 20) owe the money, but these are fairly substantial sums.

He obviously didn't collect the money, because a year 1437 later, we learn:

> East. 15 Hen. VI Essex. John Herlyng of Neuport in the said county, husbondman was summoned to answer William Fycche of Bonhunt in the said county in a plea that he render to him 40s which he owes to him and unjustly detains, etc. And whereof the said William by Thomas Adams, his attorney, says that whereas he on Monday next before the feast of the Nativity of St John the Baptist, 13 Hen. VI at Wykyll demised to the said John 1½ ac. of meadow, etc. in Wykyll to hold to him and his assigns from the said feast until the end of the term of two years then next following, etc. paying yearly 9s, etc. Neither rent nor purchase money having been paid William has damage to the value of £10 etc. John by Nicholas Sleyworth comes and defends the force and wrong, and says that William ought not to have his action, etc. They severally put themselves upon the country. A jury is summoned for the quinzaine of Trinity. The Sheriff returns that the writ *adeo tarde*. Further summonses are for the octave of Michaelmas and the octave of Hilary.[1]

The plot thickens. William brings his attorney, Thomas Adams, to face John Herlyng and his attorney, Nicholas Sleyworth. We now learn that Herlyng owes the 40 shillings in back rent, according to William, for an acre and a half of land in "Wykyll" (presumably Wicken) he "demised" (leased) to Herlyng two years ago. Herlyng was supposed to pay 9 shillings a year; William says he hasn't received anything and that he has suffered 10 pounds worth of "damage." Herlyng says he doesn't owe the money, and the lawyers for the two sides decide to "put them-

---

1. *ibid.*, f. 503.

selves upon the country," meaning they will let a jury decide. The jury was to be summoned for fifteen days after Trinity, in other words about a month and a half later. But the sheriff reports *"quod breve adeo tarde venit quod exequi non potuit,"* i.e. that he got the writ too late to be executed by the return day.[1] So the court issues the summonses again for eight days after Michaelmas, 6 October, and eight days after Hilary, the following January.

At the same session we learn that the other defendant, Thomas Punte, didn't show up.

> Essex. William Fycche of Bonhunt v. Thomas Punte of Neuport, husbondman, 10 marks unjustly detained. He comes not. Distraint ordered. *Nihil* returned. Order to take, etc.[2]

Because he "comes not," Punte was ordered *distrained*, meaning he was to be forced to come to court, effected, usually, by seizing some of his property. Evidently that didn't work, because the sheriff has returned "nihil," meaning "nothing," an abbreviated form of *nihil est*, which means "there is nothing." This return to the court order simply means he has been unable to serve the writ.[3] As a result, Punte is now ordered arrested. Another record, incidentally, unrelated to William, reveals that Punte was a king's bailiff and was also wanted in connection with a missing bag of documents.

That was at the Easter session. Later that same year,

> Mich. 16 Hen. VI William Fiche by his attorney proffers himself the fourth day against William Martyn of Little Walden in the county aforesaid, labourer, in a plea that he render to him 40s which he owes to him and unjustly detains, &c. And he came not. And the sheriff was commanded that he summon him, &c. And the sheriff now returns that he has

---

1. John Bouvier, *Bouvier's Law Dictionary* (St. Paul, Minnesota: West Publishing Co., 1914), p. 3219.
2. M.F.C., *op.cit.*, f. 503.
3. Henry Campbell Black, *Black's Law Dictionary* (St. Paul, Minnesota: West Publishing Co., 1979), p. 942.

nothing, etc. Therefore be he taken that he may be here on the Octave of St Hilary, &c.[1]

William is now William *Fiche*. Little Walden, where his opponent comes from, is north and a bit east of Wicken Bonhunt. Incidentally, 1437 is also the year we estimate that William's son John was born.

The next year, William, still not having collected from Martyn, has his attorney, Thomas Adams, try again. 1438

> Trin. 16 Hen. VI Essex. William Fyche by Thomas Adams, his attorney, puts himself the fourth day against William Martyn of Little Walden, laborer, in a plea that he render to him 40s which he owes and unjustly detains, etc. As many times be he taken, etc.[2]

Here we have William's name spelled *Fyche*, the fifth variant thus far.

At the Easter session in 1439 he brings suit against three men. 1439

> East. 17 Hen. VI Essex. William Fyche by his attorney, puts himself the fourth day against John Bristowe of Totenham, Midx. yoman in a plea that he render to him £21 and against John Colman of Buntyngford, herts., cordewaner in a plea that he render to him, 43s. And against William Taillour of St. Neots Hunts, taillour in a plea that he render to him 40s. which they owe and unjustly detain, etc. And they come not. And the Sheriff was ordered that he summon them, and he now returns that they have nothing, etc. Therefore be they taken that they may be here from Holy Trinity in 15 days, etc.[3]

The suits are even more far-ranging now. John Bristowe, who William claims owes him the princely sum of £21, is from Tottenham, county Middlesex, just outside Waltham Forest and the southwest corner of Essex. He is a *yeoman*, a man of respectable standing, who farmed his own freehold land and was quali-

---

1. M.F.C.,*op.cit.*, f. 180.
2. *ibid.*, f. 504.
3. *ibid.*, f. 504.

fied to serve on a jury. John Colman is from Hertfordshire, the neighboring county to the west. He is a *cordwainer*, a shoemaker. And William Taillour is from still another county, Huntingdonshire (now Cambridgeshire). St. Neots is to the west of Cambridge. And, as his name tells us, Mr. Taillour is a tailor. As usual, William has been unsuccessful in collecting from these three and they are ordered to be taken.

1440 We have to wait until the following year to find out why at least one of these men owes William money.

> East. 18 Hen. VI John Colman of Buntyngford in the county of Hertford, cordwaner, was summoned to answer William Fyche in a plea that he render to him 43s which he owes to him and unjustly detains, etc. And whereof the said William by Nicholas Sleyworth, his attorney, says that whereas the said John on Monday next after the feast of the Pentecost, 14 Henry VI at Neuport had bought from the said William seven quarters of malt for 43s to be paid to the said William on the feast of St Michael then next following nevertheless the said John, although often required, the aforesaid 43s. to the said William has not yet paid but to pay the same to him hitherto has denied and still denies, whereof he says that he is the worse and has damage to the value of 100s. And whereupon he brings suit, etc. And the said John by John Horn, his attorney, comes and defends the force and wrong, when etc. And he says that he does not owe to the said William the aforesaid 43s. nor any sum therein as he against him above had declared. And this he is prepared to defend against him and his suit as the court may consider. Therefore it is considered that he wage his law to him therein twelve-handed. Pledges for waging the law: John More & Robert Coton. And to come with his law here on the octave of Holy Trinity, etc. And it is said to the attorney of the said John that then he must have here the said John, his master, in his own person to offer to wage his law therein aforesaid etc.[1]

---

1. *ibid.*, ff. 181,2.

So, now we learn that back in 1436, William sold John Colman, the shoemaker, "seven quarters of malt" for 43 shillings. A *quarter* when used as a measure of grain was a quarter of a ton or 8 bushels. *Malt* usually refers to barley which has been steeped in water, allowed to germinate, and then dried; it is, of course, still used primarily for brewing beer and ale. Notice that William is now represented by Nicholas Sleyworth, the same attorney who opposed him three years earlier! Also note that William claims to have been damaged to the tune of 100 shillings, more than double the amount owed. The difference may have been to cover his costs in bringing Colman to court. The fact that this alleged transaction took place at Newport would seem to indicate that William may have sold produce from his farm at a market there. Colman's lawyer, John Horn, denies that Colman owes William anything and is prepared to defend him "as the court may consider." The court decides that Colman is to "wage his law ... twelve-handed." This form of defense, according to *Blackstone's Commentaries,*[1] is an outgrowth of the older form of defense, the *wager of battle,* in which the defendant gave a pledge to win his cause by doing battle, the belief being that God would protect the person in the right. This (milder!) form of battle, waging law, could only be employed in matters of debts or simple contracts. As for the additional qualifier that Colman would wage his law "twelve-handed," Blackstone says:

> He that has waged, or given security, to make his law, brings with him into court eleven of his neighbours: a custom, which we find particularly described so early as in the league between Aldred and Guthrun the Dane; for by the old Saxon constitution every man's credit in courts of law depended upon the opinion which his neighbours had of his veracity. The defendant then standing at the end of the bar, is admonished by the judges of the nature and danger of a false oath. And if he still persists, he is to repeat this or the like oath:

1. Lord Blackstone, *Blackstone's Commentaries*, Book 3, Chapter 22, VI (Portland: Thomas B. Wait, & Co., 1807), pp. 341-348.

'hear this, ye justices, that I do not owe unto Richard Jones the sum of ten pounds, nor any penny thereof, in manner and form as the said Richard hath declared against me. So help me God.' And thereupon his eleven neighbours or compurgators shall avow upon their oaths, that they believe in their consciences that he saith the truth ...

Richardson[1] says the defendant needed *twelve* compurgators, the value of whose oaths depended on their worth, which, in turn, depended on their rank in society. But, eleven or twelve, it does put one in mind of a jury, and what is a jury after all but a group of people who decide whether or not the defendant "saith the truth." So, in this case, Colman provided sureties, through John More and Robert Coton, who are named "pledges for waging the law," that he would be back eight days after Trinity with his eleven neighbors, who have only to swear that they believe him to be a truthful man. For, as Blackstone adds, "the wager of law was never permitted, but where the defendant bore a fair and unreproachable character ..." Finally, Colman probably wasn't at this particular hearing because his attorney is told to make sure he does show up for the trial.

Having settled on a trial for his suit against Colman, William turns to Mr. Taillour the tailor.

Essex. William Taillour of St Neots, Hunts. tailor, was summoned to answer William Fyche in a plea that he render to him 40s. which he owes to him and unjustly detains, etc. And whereof the said William Fyche by Nicholas Sleyworth, his attorney, says that whereas the said William Taillour on Thursday next after the feast of Easter, 12 Henry VI at Neuport had bought from the said William Fyche four cows for the said 40s. to be paid the said William Fyche on the feast of the Nativity of St John the Baptist then next following, nevertheless the said William Taillour, although often required, the aforesaid 40s. to the said William Fyche has not yet paid, but to pay the same to him hitherto has denied

1. Richardson, *op.cit.*, p. 51.

and still does deny, whereof he says that he is the worse and has damage to the value of 10 marks. And thereupon he brings suit, etc. And the said William Taillour by Thomas Gilmyn, his attorney, comes and defends the force and wrong, etc. And he says that he does not owe to the said William Fyche the said 40s. nor any sum therein as the said William Fyche against him above has declared. And touching this he puts himself upon the country And the said William Fyche likewise.[1]

So, William not only sells grain at Newport, he also has cows for sale. And he's been trying to collect 40 shillings from the tailor for four cows for the past six years! Again, Taillour denies the debt and the two parties agree to a trial. This record is followed by several orders relating to summoning the jury. In this case, it may be that the dispute never came to trial, because we also read that year:

Essex. William Fyche by Nicholas Sleyworth, his attorney, proffers himself the fourth day against William Taillour of St. Neots in the county of Huntingdon, Taillour in a plea that he render to him 40s. which he owes to him and unjustly detains, etc. And he came not. And as often times the Sheriff was commanded that he should take him, etc. And safely, etc. So that he should have his body here at this day, namely in 15 days of Easter Day etc. And the Sheriff has now returned that he is not to be found, etc. Therefore the Sheriff was ordered that he cause him to be called from county to county until, etc. he be outlawed if not, etc. And if, etc. then that he should take him. And safely, etc. So that he may have his body here on the morrow of St Martin. And wherein, etc.[2]

Well now Mr. Taillour is in deep trouble. The sheriff says he can't find him, so the court orders that he be "called from county to county," i.e. by other courts, and if he can't be found then he is to be "outlawed," which meant that anyone could arrest him—

1. M.F.C., *op.cit.*, f. 183.
2. *ibid.*, f. 184.

Figure 24 - Priors Hall, Widdington

even kill him—on sight. But, it appears that if the sheriff found him first, he was to take him "safely" and bring him to court.

1440/1 In January 1440/1, William appears to have acquired a piece of manorial land in Widdington, a few miles to the southeast of Wicken Bonhunt (Figure 20). Widdington cannot have looked much different 900 years ago when, as *Widintuna*, it appeared in *Domesday*. Actually, the name is even older than *Domesday*; in Old English, it was *Wipig-tun*, a *tun* among the willows, where *tun*, in turn meant a fence or enclosure. Later the term *tun* came to mean a homestead or village, so we might think of it—whether as *Withitone*, *Wyditon*, or the more modern *Widdington*—as a village among the willows.[1]

William the Conqueror gave some of the parishes in the area as a thank offer to the priory of St. Valery-sur-Somme in France. It was their ownership for 300 years that gave Priors Hall farm

---

1. Ekwall, *op.cit.*

Figure 25 - Priors Hall Barn, Widdington

(Figure 24) its name. He gave the rest of Widdington to his forester, Robert Gernon (or Greno as he is called in *Domesday*). Gernon, the Duke of Boulogne, who may have been a relative of the Conqueror, received many grants of land, but built his castle at what is now Stansted, a few miles south of Widdington. It was Robert Gernon's son William who dropped the surname Gernon and took the name Montfitchet (presumably for Montfiquet in Normandy). And it was an 8th generation descendant, Sir John Gernon, who took the name, John of Cavendish (see page 11).

During the Hundred Years War with France, which began in 1337, King Edward III seized the English possessions of St. Valery-sur-Somme. He gave Priors Hall farm to Bishop William of Wykeham who, in turn, gave it as an endowment to New College Oxford, which he founded. Among the treasures of the countryside today is a barn (Figure 25) built in the 14th century by New College and used right up to 1976 when it was given to the Department of the Environment.[1] Richard II succeeded Edward III in 1377, and, the Montfitchets having long since died out, he gave Widdington—or *Wodeton*—to John Duke, Junior. Duke had no sons, so when his daughter Agnes married John Greene Esq.,[2] Greene became lord of the manor of Widdington.[3] Four generations later, his descendant, Rooke Greene, married one of William's fourth generation descendants, Eleanor Fitch.

The lord of the manor would regularly have conducted two types of court: a court leet and a court baron. The former dealt with petty offenses and usually met twice a year. The latter dealt with, among other things, the transfer of land from one tenant to another. The court records were written on *membranes*, sheets of vellum, which were then attached one to another to form a *roll*. The Widdington Court Roll for 18 January 1440/1 shows:

> Fine 2s 18 January 19 Henry VI
> To this court came William Michell and surrendered into the lord's hand half an acre of land to the use of William Fiche, to which same William the lord granted seisin thereof. To hold to the same William and his heirs of the lord, at the will (of the lord) by all of ancient services. And he gave the lord of fine as appears. And did fealty to the lord.[4]

There are a number of things that can be said about this brief entry in the court record. And for the unfamiliar terms, we are indebted to John Richardson's *Encyclopedia*.[5] First, the "fine" of two shillings. The word *fine* in this context refers to a money payment made by a tenant to his lord on the transfer of property to him. A compilation of such transactions is a *feet of fines*. But,

---

1. D. Sherlock, *Priors Hall Barn Widdington* (Great Britain: Department of the Environment, Crown Copyright 1983).
2. Morant, *op.cit.*, p. 566.
3. Amended List of Rectors and Patrons, St. Mary the Virgin, Widdington.
4. Court Rolls, Manor of Widdington, New College, Oxford. Note: Court Roll quotations herein are taken from R. C. Fitch, *op.cit.*
5. John Richardson, *The Local Historian's Encyclopedia* (New Barnet, Herts, England: Historical Publications Ltd., 1974).

how much was two shillings worth in the Middle Ages? We can gain some idea of its value by noting that William valued his sheep at a little more than a shilling apiece and his cows at 10 shillings.

We have already explained regnal dates, so we can turn next to the transaction itself. We learn that William Michell has come to court and surrendered half an acre of land. Why would he do that? As Edwards explains it:

> The lord's arable lands on the open fields were no longer worked by unfree labourers, but were leased out to tenants who were free to cultivate them in any way they wished. Moreover, if any lands reverted to the lord through lack of heirs or any other good reason, the lord did not re-grant them to others on the old basis, but leased them out for a money rent.[1]

Even if William bought the lease from Michell, the land would still have to be *surrendered* at court, so that the lord could collect a fee *en passant*. In this case, the lord of the manor turned over the land that Michell had held to William Fiche. Notice that the "lord granted seisin thereof." Seisin was a term meaning possession rather than ownership. A grant of land was only valid when the tenant had given the lord *livery of seisin*—usually a symbolic gift; a tenant was then *seised in deed*. Thus, William and his heirs were to have possession of the land, but such possession was at the will of the lord. It's important to note that the lord of the manor didn't actually own the land he was leasing to William; nobody but the king *owned* land. All others had possession of land by grant of the king—usually for some *quid pro quo*. As we have seen, the land in Widdington had originally been granted to Robert Gernon. In the Middle Ages, he would have been obligated to serve the crown, probably by agreeing to provide troops and horses in time of war. He, in turn, would have parceled out his lands to farmers. They would have owed him service, perhaps as foot soldiers in time of war, but certainly as workmen for a certain

---

1. Edwards, *op.cit.*, p. 37.

number of days a year on land that he kept for his own use. These *ancient services* were all spelled out in *Domesday*.

As the feudal system broke down, however, more and more often, the *quid pro quo* for a piece of land—at all levels of the transaction—would have been money. In other words, if Fiche didn't continue to provide the ancient services (now probably no more than money payments), the lord could revoke his right to the land. And for this, Fiche paid the two shilling fine "and did fealty to the lord," i.e. acknowledged the lord of the manor—very *pro forma—as his lord and master*. Within a few days of leasing the land at Widdington, William was back in the Common Pleas court to sue five different men for various amounts.

> Hil. 19 Hen. VI Essex. William Fiche, by his attorney, proffers himself the fourth day against John Kirkelond of Little Hadham, Herts, carpenter, in a plea that he render to him 44s. And against Thomas Chamberlayn of Neuport, cotiler John Benwyck of Walden, cordewaner, William Pesy, miller, William Clanford of Wenden, husbandman, in a plea that each of them renders to him 40s. which they owe to him and unjustly detain, etc. And they came not. And the Sheriff was ordered that he summon them, etc. And the Sheriff now returns that they have nothing, etc. Therefore be they taken so that they may be here from Easter Day in three weeks.[1]

These are fairly straightforward, except for the new term "cotiler" (*cotiller*), which referred to one who worked cooperatively on a farm. In this case, we don't know the basis of the claims or whether William ever collected on them. It is likely that William himself wasn't at the Essex court that day (he was represented by his attorney) because he was busy over in the Middlesex court in another suit.

> Middx. William Fycche of Wykyn, Essex, and Walter Grene, armiger, in their own persons proffer themselves the fourth day against William Bradford, vicar of the church of Tottenham, in a plea that he render to them 5 marks which he owes

1. M.F.C., *op.cit.*, Ewen f. 517.

to them and unjustly detains. And he came not. And the Sheriff was ordered that he summon him, etc. And the Sheriff now returns that he has nothing, etc. Therefore be he taken so that he may be here from Easter Day in 15 days.[1]

At about this time, William may have moved his domicile from Bonhunt to Wicken, because from this record on he is said to be "of Wykyn." His co-plaintiff, Walter Grene is identified as an "armiger." Originally, an *armiger* was one who attended a knight to bear his shield. By this time, however, it simply meant someone who had the right to a coat of arms. Charles Fitch-Northen identifies this Walter Grene (Greene) as the father of John Greene, the lord of Widdington manor. And he wonders if, perhaps, William might have been an agent for the manor in these various lawsuits—particularly since his own little plots couldn't possibly have produced "the quantities of grain, malt, sheep, cows, etc. for which he persistently sued for payment."[2]

In September William's attorney (now Simon Elryng- 1441 ton) tried again to collect from the five that still owed him money. The court roll in this case is damaged, but the gist of it is that the sheriff can't find them either.[3]

Three years after trying to collect 43 shillings from 1442 John Colman of Buntyngford, William tries again.

> Trinity 20 Hen. VI Hertford (sic) William Fycche, by his attorney, proffers himself the fourth day against John Colman of Buntyngford, herts., cordewaner in a plea that he render to him 43s. And against John Hiccheman of Neuport in the said county bocher in a plea that he render to him 40s. etc. They have not come and the Sheriff is ordered to take them, and returning a *non est inventus* is again ordered etc.[4]

He has added another defendant here, John Hiccheman, whose occupation is probably butcher. In the Attorneys' Roll

1. *ibid.*, f. 517.
2. Personal correspondence of 9 and 11 Mar. 1991.
3. *ibid.*, f. 518.
4. *ibid.*, f. 185.

William Fycche's attorney is identified as J. Wilcokkes. The phrase *"non est inventus"* is the sheriff's return to a process requiring him to arrest the body of the defendant, when the latter is not found within his jurisdiction.[1] This same John Wilcokkes represented William Fycche and Walter Grene in Middlesex court twice that year to follow up on the suits against John Bristowe and vicar William Bradford. The vicar is to be outlawed if not found.[2]

That same year, William was himself sued.

> John Garlound of Walden, the elder, merchant, and William Hawekyn of Neuport by his attorney, proffers himself the fourth day against William Fyche of Wykyn, Essex, husbondman and Thomas Punt of Neuport, Essex, husbondman in a plea that each of them render to him 40 marks and 10 pence which they owe to him and unjustly detain, etc. And they came not. And the Sheriff was commanded that he summon them. And the Sheriff now returns that they have nothing, etc. Therefore be they taken, etc. At which day the Sheriff had not sent the writ. Therefore as at first be they taken that they may be here on the octave of Michaelmas, etc.[3]

It's little wonder "they have nothing;" poor William doesn't seem to have been able to collect from anyone else. Undeterred, however, he is back on the attack.

> William Fycche alias William Fytche, by his attorney, proffers himself the fourth day against John Ponde of Neweport, Essex, whelewryght in a plea that he render to him 14 marks. And against Geoffrey William of Totenham in Middlesex, husbondman in a plea that he render to him 46s.8d And against John Colman of Buntyngford, Herts., hostiler and William Clanford of Wenden, husbondman in a plea that each of them render to him 40s. which they owe to him and unjustly detain. And they came not, etc. Usual order to take, etc.[4]

---

1. Black, *op.cit.*, p. 950.
2. M.F.C., *op.cit.*, f. 185.
3. *ibid.*, f. 520.
4. *ibid.*, ff. 520,1.

It's interesting to note that William's name is deliberately spelled two different ways; *Fycche* we have seen before, but *Fytche* is now the sixth variant. It does not appear to be a question of the clerk not knowing how to spell his name; it looks as if William himself spelled it differently at different times. The "alias" will crop up again in succeeding records. As for the defendants, John Ponde is a *wheelwright*, one who makes and repairs wheels. John Colman, whom we have met before, and who was a shoemaker, now seems to be a *hostler*, one who takes care of horses at an inn. 1443 At the Easter session in 1443, William brought suit against another Newport man.

> East. 21 Hen. VI Essex. John Fraunceys of Neweport in the said county, chapman was summoned to answer William Fycche alias Fitche in a plea that he render to him 14 marks which he owes to him and unjustly detains, etc. And whereupon the said William by John Wilkokkes, his attorney, says that whereas the said John on the feast of St Leonard, 21 Hen. VI at Wyken by his certain writing obligatory did acknowledge himself to be bound to the said William in the said 14 marks to be paid to the said William on Christmas day then next following nevertheless John although often requested the said 14 marks to the said William has not yet rendered but to render the same unto him has hitherto denied and still does deny, wherefore he says he is the worse and is damaged to the value of 20 marks. And thereupon he brings suit, etc. And produced here into court the writing, etc. The said John by Nicholas Sleyworth, his attorney, comes and defends the force and wrong, etc.[1]

Now we have a seventh spelling, *Fitche*. In the case at hand, the defendant, John Fraunceys, is a Newport merchant, a *chapman*, one whose business is buying and selling. It appears that Fraunceys actually signed a promissory note for the 14 marks.

1. *ibid.*

But Nicholas Slayworth, the attorney, now working for the other side again, denies the debt.

1443/4 In January, another man sued Fyche and Thomas Punt.

> Hilary 22 Hen. VI Essex. John Harlyng the elder of Neweport, Essex, by his attorney, puts himself the fourth day against William Fyche of Wykyn, husbondman and Thomas Punt of Neweport, husbondman in a plea that each of them render him 20 marks which they owe to him and unjustly detain...[1]

And at the same session,

> William Ficche by John Wilcokkes, his attorney, puts himself the fourth day against John Pope of Lammersshe, Essex, maltman and William Clanford of Little Wenden, husbondman in a plea that each of them renders 40s. which they owe and unjustly detain, etc. And they came not. Usual *non est inventus*, etc. To be here the octave of St. Michael.[2]

Pope, the maltman (presumably someone who made malt from grain) was from Lamarsh, clear across the county on the Suffolk border. Little Wenden no longer exists, but we can probably assume it to be the same as, or very near to, what is now Wendens Ambo, just above Wicken Bonhunt (Figure 20). There was also to be a jury trial for the case between William and John Fr;aunceys, but it was respited or postponed "because none of jury came."[!][3]

1445 The next Plea Roll record is from the Easter session of 1445.

> Easter 23 Hen. VI Essex. William Fycche by his attorney puts himself the fourth day against: John Kynge of Wydeton, Ess., husbondman, Debt 8 marks John Elys of Neuport, Ess. taillour, Debt 40s John Kirkelond of Little Hadham, Herts., carpenter. Debt 5 marks Defendants have not come and the Sheriff commanded to summon them returns a *nihil* and is further commanded to take them.[4]

1. *ibid.*, f. 521.
2. *ibid.*, f. 521.
3. *ibid*, f. 521.
4. *ibid.*, f. 186.

The first of these, John Kynge, is from "Wydeton," one of 1446
the numerous early spellings of Widdington. Four years have
passed since John Garlound and William Hawkyn sued William for 40 marks and 10 pence. Since then, Hawkyn has died.

> Easter 24 Hen. VI Essex. William Fyche of Wykyn, husbond-
> man, was summoned to answer John Garlound of Walden,
> the elder, merchaunt in a plea that he render to him 40 marks
> and 10d, which he owes to him and unjustly detains, etc. And
> whereupon the said John by John Broun, his attorney, says
> that whereas the said William on 6 August 19 Hen. VI [1441]
> at Walden, by his certain writing obligatory did acknowledge
> himself to be held and firmly bound to the said John and to
> a certain William Hawkyn of Neuport now dead, in the said
> 40 marks and 10 pence to be paid to the said John and
> William Hawkyn on the feast of the Purification of the B.V.M.
> [Blessed Virgin Mary] then next following, nevertheless the
> said William Fyche although often requested has not ren-
> dered the said 40 marks and 10d to the said John and William
> in the lifetime of the said William Hawkyn and to the said
> John after the death of the said William Hawkyn but to
> render the same to them has denied, and to render the same
> to the said John has denied, wherefore he says that he is the
> worse and is dampnified to the value of £20. And therefore
> he brings suit, etc. And brings into court the said writing, etc.
> And William Fyche by Richard Skylfull, his attorney, comes
> and defends the force and wrong, etc. And prays licence to
> imparl until the octave of Trinity, and has it, etc.[1]

What a wonderful name for a lawyer: Richard Skylfull!
Dickens could have done no better. The word "dampnified," or as
it is now spelled *damnified*, means to have caused damage or
injurious loss to someone.[2] The lawyer's request to "imparl" (an
abbreviation of *imparlance*) means that he wanted more time to
answer the pleadings of the other party.[3]

1. *ibid.*, ff. 522,3.
2. Black, *op.cit.*, p. 354.
3. *ibid.*, p. 677.

1448 In January of 1448, William tried again to collect from Hycheman and Harlying of Newport.

> Hilary 26 Hen. VI Essex. William Fyche of the parish of Wyken, by his attorney, proffers himself the fourth day against John Hycheman of Neuport, Essex, bochier in a plea that he render to him 46s. and against John Harlyng of Neuport husbondman, John Fycche of Stanbourne, Essex, husbondman, and William Sache of Neuport, glover in a plea that each of them renders to him 40s which they owe to him and unjustly detain, etc. And they came not. And the Sheriff was commanded to summon them, etc. And the Sheriff now returns that they have nothing. Therefore be they taken that they may be here in three weeks of Easter, etc.[1]

The interesting item here is the appearance of a John Fycche from "Stanbourne," which is undoubtedly *Stambourne,* just to the east of Steeple Bumpstead. So, even if the two branches of the family were not directly related, at least they had contact, if only in court!

Later that year, at the Michaelmas session, William brought suit against Thomas Hoker of Newport, a husbandman, and against Robert Hermyte, laborer, and William Pesy, husbandman, both of Latton, Essex. In each case, it's 40 shillings he's after.[2] The only *Latton* we can find is in Wiltshire, far to the west, so if there was such a village in Essex, it seems to have disappeared.

1449 In April or May, William, represented by his attorney files yet another suit.

> Trinity 27 Hen. VI Essex. William Fycche, by his attorney, proffers himself the fourth day against Richard Dommyng of Walden, wolman John Harlyng of Neuport, the younger, bocher, and William Neus of Hadham, Herts, husbondman in a plea that each of them render to him 40s. etc. They have

1. M.F.C., *op.cit.,* f. 523.
2. *ibid.,* f. 524.

not come and the Sheriff commanded to summon them returned a *nihil*, etc.[1]

These suits have been going on so long that William has not only sued John Harlyng, senior, the husbandman, but now his son the butcher as well. Richard Dommyng evidently deals in wool, and William Neus is from just across the border in Hertfordshire.

In 1450, we learn that William has moved up in the 1450 social framework of the time.

> Easter, 28 Hen. VI Essex. William Fyche of Wykyn, yoman by his attorney proffers himself the fourth day v. John Hycheman of Neuport, bochere in a plea that he render to him 6 marks. And against John Harlyng of Neuport, the elder, husbondman in a plea that he renders to him 40s which they owe to him and unjustly detain. *Non est inventus*, and command to take, etc.[2]

For William to be known as a *yeoman* he must have acquired a reasonably sized estate of freehold land. In other words, he was no longer just a tenant farmer; he had accumulated enough wealth to buy property outright. That put him in a social class just below that of *gentleman*.

Eighteen years after leasing his first piece of land from 1458 Widdington manor, William Fyche was back at the manor court to pick up the rights to another acre. The lord of the manor was probably still John Greene, Esq. who "presented to the living" of the parish, i.e. appointed the priest, (rector or vicar as the case may be) as late as 1466.[3]

> Fine 20d 16 January 37 Henry VI
> Fealty
> To this court came Richard Petworth and surrendered into the hand of the lord one acre of land lying in Marshfield next the way called Tyrelleswey, whereof one head abuts upon the lord's land called Chestonshott, to the use of William Fyche

1. *ibid.*, f. 187.
2. *ibid.*, f. 524.
3. Morant, *op.cit.*, p. 566.

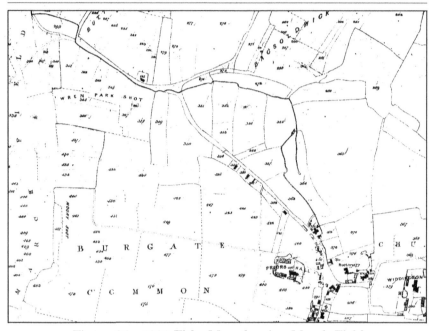

Figure 26 - 1839 Tithe Map showing March Field
(Cat. No. D/CT 398, reproduced by courtesy of the Essex Record Office)

and his heirs, to whom the lord granted seisin thereof, to hold to him and his heirs, at the will of the lord, according to the custom of the manor by the ancient rent and services. And he made fine and fealty as appears at the head.[1]

This transaction is similar to the earlier one, except that the land this time is being surrendered by a Richard Petworth. More importantly, the land is named this time, and we can find it on a map. Figure 26 is an 1839 *tithe* map, drawn up to determine taxes. Priors Hall and Widdington Hall are at the lower right. And, despite the fact that this map was made 400 years after William's time, we can still find "Marshfield" (now *March Field*) lettered vertically along the river at the west. It was probably originally named *Marshfield* because it was near the marshy area at the

1. Court Rolls, Manor of Widdington, New College, Oxford.

William^F

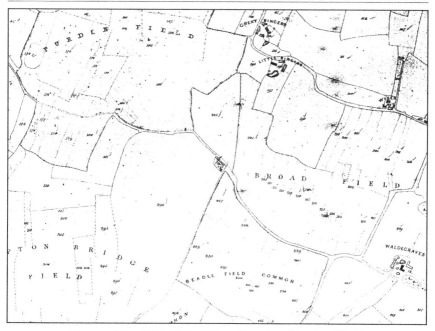

Figure 27 - 1839 Tithe Map showing Purden Field
(Cat. No. D/CT 398, reproduced by courtesy of the Essex Record Office)

river's edge (and renamed to make it more saleable!). So, William's one-acre piece was probably one of the little strips we see marked out on the chart.

Edward IV, son of the Duke of York, defeated the Lancastrians and was proclaimed king, replacing Henry VI. We have one last Plea Roll entry for William in June of 1465.

1461

> Trin. 5 Edw. IV Essex. William Fycche, by his attorney, proffers himself the fourth day against Richard Joye of Great Donmowe in the county aforesaid, yoman, in a plea that he render to him 40s. that he owes to him and unjustly detains, etc. And he came not, and so as at first the Sheriff was commanded that he distrain him. And the Sheriff now returns that *adeo tarde*, etc.[1]

1. M.F.C., *op.cit.*, f. 204.

Great Dunmow is a few miles to the east of Widdington.

1466 Our final piece of information about William is that he is dead at the age of about 66. He probably died early in 1466, because his death was reported at the court of the manor in April of that year:

Thursday after St. George Martyr, 6 Edward IV
And that William Fytche died since the last Court. And that he held of the lord, the day he died, in his demesne, as of fee, at the will of the lord according to the custom of the manor, two acres of land, whereof one lies at Tyrelles Way and the other lies in Pardenfeld. And that John Fytche is son and next heir of the same William, etc. And because the same John does not now come to claim the said lands from the lord's hand, therefore the bailiff is ordered to answer to the lord of the issues, until etc.[1]

And so, William has died possessed of two acres of land in the lord's "demesne." Normally, this was land retained by the lord of the manor for his own use and upon which tenants gave free services. In this case, however, it is clear that William was renting the land, even though it was part of the main farm of the manor. One of these acres, the piece at Tyrelles Wey is obviously the land he got from Richard Petworth. The other piece—the one in "Pardenfeld"—may be the land he got from William Michell. If so, it has grown from a half acre to a full acre. We can also find *Purden Field* on the map (upper left of Figure 27) near Newport.

More importantly, we learn that his son and heir is John Fytche. For some unstated reason, John didn't show up at court to make his claim at this session, but the bailiff has been ordered to sort out the issues and report to the lord. As we shall see in the next chapter, John will come to court in a year to put in his claim.

1. *ibid.*

3

John^E

W e can estimate the birth year for John^E, son of   1437
William^F, as no later than 1437, because a manor
court roll, which we shall review below, reported his age in
1467 at "30 years and more." Like his father, he lived in
Wicken (now Wicken Bonhunt) in westernmost Essex.

The earliest mention of John is on a Court Plea of 1458:   1458

Trinity 36 Hen. VI
Essex. John Fych of Wykyn in the county aforesaid husbandman was attached to answer Geoffrey Clerk in a plea why
with force and arms the close of the said Geoffrey at Wykyn
he did break and his corn and grass to the value of 100s there
lately growing he did feed, tread down and consume. And
other harms to him did he to the grievous damage of the said
Geoffrey. And against the peace of the Lord our King, etc.
And whereupon the said Geoffrey by Thomas Jakelyn, his
attorney, complains that the aforesaid John on 20 June 35
Hen VI [1457] with force and arms, namely swords, bows and
arrows the close of the said Geoffrey at Wykyn did break and
the corn, namely corn, pease, oats and grass the value, etc.
there lately growing with certain beasts namely horses, oxen,
cows and sheep did feed, tread down, and consume, the said
trespass as to the feeding, treading down and consuming of
the grass aforesaid continuing from the aforesaid 20 June
until the feast of St Michael [29 September] then next following, divers days and places. And other harms etc. to the

grievous damage, etc. And against the peace, etc. whereupon he says that he is the worse and has damage to the value of 40 marks. And thereupon he brings suit, &c. And the aforesaid John in his own person comes. And defends the force and wrong when, etc. And says that he is not guilty of the trespass aforesaid as the aforesaid Geoffrey above against him complains. And of this he puts himself on the country. And the aforesaid Geoffrey does likewise. Therefore the Sheriff is commanded that he cause to come here in 15 days from Michaelmas Day, 12 etc. by whom, etc. And who neither, etc. to recognize, etc. Because as well, etc. And upon this the aforesaid John puts in his place John Goiyk against the aforesaid Geoffrey in the aforesaid plea, etc.[1]

First, we learn that John Fych (an *eighth* way of spelling the name) is still living in Wicken and is a husbandman or tenant farmer. He is charged with breaking into the "close" of Geoffrey Clerk the year before with "force and arms" and letting his animals feed there. A "close," in this context, is an enclosed field. The phrase "force and arms" was used in common law pleadings in declarations of trespass to denote that the act complained of was done with violence.[2] Clerk charges, in fact, that John used "swords, bows and arrows" to break in (although it isn't clear why he would need weapons to break through a fence). The complaint says John let his horses, oxen, cows, and sheep feed on the "corn" (a term which in England could mean any kind of grain), and that the "corn" consisted of "corn" (this time it probably refers specifically to wheat), peas, oats, and grass. And he evidently kept this up for the whole summer (although there is no explanation of why Mr. Clerk didn't ask him to stop!). At any rate, all this "feeding, treading down and consuming" has damaged Clerk in the amount of 40 marks, a sizable sum of money. John denies he is guilty of trespass and "puts himself on the country," meaning he wants a jury trial. Having come in person to answer the charge, he now

1. M.F.C., *op.cit*, Ewen Vol. B, ff. 189,190
2. Black, *op.cit.*, p. 580.

says that John Goiyk will speak for him at the trial. Unfortunately, we do not know the results of the trial.

Edward, son of the Duke of York (who had been named 1461 successor to Henry VI before York was killed), became king as Edward IV.

Assuming he married before his son Thomas was born, John must have taken a wife during or before 1464. He married a woman named Juliana. We do not know her last name.

John's father, William^F died. 1466

After his father's death, John waited a little more than 1467 a year before coming to the manor court at Widdington to lay claim to William's land.

> 14 May 7 Edward IV
> And that William Fycche died since the last Court and died siesed in his demesne, as of fee, according to the custom &c., of and in one acre of land lying in Mersshfeld by Turelswey, one head whereof abutting upon Chestonshott; and another acre of land lying in Purdonfeld. And that John is his son and next heir and is aged 30 years and more and he comes here in Court and begs to be admitted to his heritage aforesaid and is admitted. To hold to him and his heirs of the lord, by the verge, at the will of the lord, according to the custom of the manor by the ancient rent and services. And he made fine and fealty.[1]

Thus, John is "admitted" to his father's land—again, as long as he pays his rent and serves the lord of the manor. (The record, in this case, doesn't give the "fine.") At that same session of the court, John picked up almost three more acres, through the surrender of land by others.

> And that Thomas Martyn ... surrendered into the lord's hand three roods of land and one acre of meadow lying in the field

---

1. Court Rolls, Manor of Widdington, New College, Oxford.

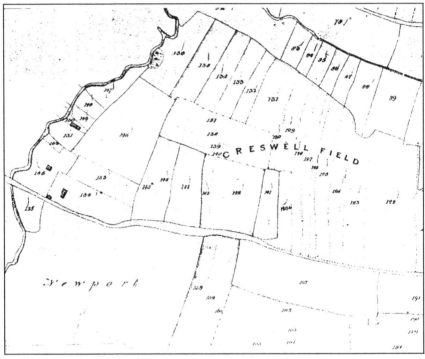

Figure 28 - 1839 Tithe Map showing Creswell Field
(Cat. No. D/CT 398, reproduced by courtesy of the Essex Record Office)

and meadow called Cresselfeld and Creswelmede ... to the use of John Fycche ...

To this court came John Revell and surrendered into the lord's hand one acre and a half of meadow lying in Creswelhole to the use of John Fycche ... [1]

These three pieces, *Cresselfeld*, *Creswelmede*, and *Creswelhole* are almost surely parts of *Creswell Field* on the 1839 tithe map of Figure 28.

1468 So, at the age of 30 plus, John held nearly five acres of arable land and meadow. Unfortunately, he held it only a year, for

1. *ibid.*

he died the following year at about the age of 33, when his son Thomas[D] was only three years old.

9 April, 8 Edward IV
That John Fytche died after the last court and that he held of the lord, the day he died, in his demesne, as of fee, according to the custom of the manor, &c., one acre and a half of meadow, lying in Creswelfeld late John Revell's and 2 acres of land, whereof one acre lies in Purdonfeld late William Fytche's, his father's. And that Thomas is his son and next heir and aged 3 years etc. And because of his youth, the custody of the said land and meadow committed to his mother, Julian, to hold and occupy the same to the use of the said heir, until &c. paying &c.

And that the said John Fytche, lying in extremis, surrendered into the lord's hand 3 roods of land and one acre of meadow lying in a field called Creswelfeld and Creswelmede … to the use of Julian, his wife.[1]

If ever there was a "smoking gun" in Fitch family history, this record is it. For by firmly establishing the generational chain from William to John to Thomas, it destroys the credibility of all the "Visitations," which have a Thomas and Joanne as the parents of Thomas of Lindsell. And lest there be any doubt that the Thomas in this court record is the Thomas who married Agnes Algore, the one commemorated in the brass and glass of Lindsell church, etc., further court records in 1487 and 1505 (which we shall examine in the next chapter) make it even more certain that the name of Thomas' father was John, not Thomas. And if the visitation records are wrong on that point—even those of the College of Arms—how can we possibly put any faith in the purported generations before that?

Getting back to the substance of the court record, however, what John has apparently done on his death bed has been to leave most of his land to his son, but because Thomas is only three years old, Juliana is to live there and act as guardian for it until he's

1. *ibid.*

old enough to take care of it himself. And then, to be sure Juliana herself is taken care of, he sets aside a little more than an acre for her use. As we shall see in the next chapter, Thomas was to wait a long time before he could take possession of this latter piece, long even after his mother died.

As a postscript, Juliana remarried after John's death. Her second husband was Richard Westeley. On the basis of a court record in 1505 which indicates that at that time she had been dead for 30 years, it seems likely that she died about 1475.

4

Thomas^D

Thomas Fitch, son of John^E, must have been born about
1465, because, as we saw in the previous chapter, the
court rolls mention that he was three years old when his
father died in 1468.

Edward IV, who had been king all during John's lifetime, died in 1483. He was followed, briefly, by his son,
Edward V, a boy of thirteen. The boy's uncle, the Duke of
Gloucester, had the young king and his even younger brother
confined to the Tower and took the throne himself as Richard
III. The two boys were murdered, possibly at their uncle's
direction.

Richard, the last of the Yorkist dynasty, was king for
only two years. Henry, son of Margaret Beaufort, with a
remote and tenuous claim to the throne, invaded England
from France and defeated Richard's forces in the battle at
Bosworth Field, a battle in which Richard was killed. As
Henry VII, he married Edward IV's daughter, and thus
united the houses of York and Lancaster, founding the Tudor
dynasty. He would be king during most of Thomas' adult life.

When he was twenty-one or twenty-two, Thomas was
admitted to his inheritance at the Widdington manor court.
The date was Thursday after St. Leonard the abbot, 3 Henry
VII which was 9 November 1487. The clerk quoted from the

record of 9 April 1468 (see previous chapter) noting the death of John Fytche.[1]

1490   It must have been about 1490 that Thomas married Agnes Algore and apparently moved to her parish of Lindsell (Figure 19). At that time he would have been about 25 years old. We can be certain they were married before the end of 1490, because a court record in December that year refers to them as married. At any rate, it was with this marriage that the Fitch fortunes took a significant turn for the better. Agnes was an heiress who brought to their marriage considerable property in Lindsell.

Algore

1409   The Algore family goes back in the records about as far as the Fitches. They lived in the nearby parish of Lindsell. The first record of an Algore is that of John Algor who was a "capital pledge," meaning he was one of the leading villagers, on 30 November 1409.[2]

1413   In 1413, he re-appeared and "under pain of 10s" was given permission and time to re-build a small house on land called Bynwodes. Here, "pain" has the same connotation as "fine," i.e. it is simply a fee. There doesn't appear to be a clear series of connections between generations among the Algores, but John may have been followed by a William and then another William. From this second William on, the record is connected.

1468   3 March 7 Edward IV
>That William Algore ... (torn) ... a tenement and 14 acres of land with the appurtenances, called Hubbardes, to the use of Robert Algore, son ... granted thereof seisin.[3]

The term "tenement" here has a quite different connotation from its meaning today; it is a legal term (from the Latin *tenere*,

---

1.   Court Rolls, Manor of Widdington, New College, Oxford.
2.   Court Rolls, Manor of Priors Hall, Lindsell, New College, Oxford.
3.   *ibid.*

to hold) which refers to any kind of real property, including lands, houses, rents, even a franchise. The term "appurtenances" refers to a minor property, right, or privilege that goes along with the main property being transferred.

Robert Algore married a woman named Margaret Cow- 1468
ley, who was an heiress in her own right. In 1485 or 1486, she inherited Bynwodes (the same land on which, in 1413, John Algor had built a small house), Brodefeld, Bredgefeld, and Breggemede, all from her mother.[1] So for now the Algores had at least four properties from the Cowleys, 14 acres of land called Hubbardes, and a "tenement" or house and its "appurtenances" or outbuildings—kitchen, stable, etc. In a few years, it would all belong to Thomas and Agnes.

In what may have been a wedding present, Robert and 1490
Margaret Algore apparently turned over Bynwodes to Thomas and Agnes on 22 December 1490.

Tuesday in St. Thomas Apostle, 6 Henry VII
To this court came Robert Algore & Margaret, his wife, (as in the right of the said Margaret, examined apart by the steward) and surrendered into the hands of the lord a tenement called Bynwodes...and the lord re-granted the same to the said Margaret and her daughter, Agnes, wife of Thomas Fytche.[2]

This record is interesting because the house is given to Margaret and her daughter. One might speculate, therefore, that Agnes was less than 21 years old when she married and that her mother acted temporarily as custodian for her.

The next year, Robert Algore was dead, and the Decem- 1493
ber session of the manor court dealt with his property.

Saturday in St. Thomas Apostle, 9 Henry VII
And that Robert Algor died since the last court and that he

1. *ibid.*, fol. 64.
2. *ibid.*

held of the lord the day he died, at the will of the lord ... a tenement & 3 acres of land with the appurtenances, called Loves & one toft called Madges and one other called Dottes, as well as one other tenement and 14 acres of land called Hoberdes ... and that Agnes, wife of Thomas Fitche is his daughter and next heir ... admitted tenant thereof.[1]

So, we learn that Agnes was to be the heir. She may have been an only child, although the Algore name flourished in Lindsell until the middle of the 19th century. (Stephen Alger, a church-warden from about 1840 to 1860, died in 1874, and was evidently the last of the line.[2]) She takes control of *Hubbardes* (or "Hoberdes" as it is spelled here) with its 14 acres of land and buildings. And she also gets three more acres, also with some buildings called *Loves*, and a couple of "tofts" (which can be houses and outbuildings or the sites for same) called *Madges* and *Dottes*. All of these are in the parish of Lindsell.

Lindsell

Lindsell is a small rural parish about ten miles southeast of Wicken Bonhunt (see Figure 19). At its peak in the mid 19th century, it had a population of 400; now it is less than half that. In Old English, Lindsell was *lind-gesella*, where *lind* meant *lime* in the sense of lime trees and *gesell* seems to have meant a shelter for animals or a herdsman's hut. *Gesella* is the plural form, so *lind-gesella* is thought to have meant *huts among lime-trees*. By the time of Domesday, it was spelled *Lindesela* and *Lindeseles*, and by 1130, it was *Lindsel*.[3]

Although Lindsell was small, it did have at least three manors — "at least." because of a very confusing list provided by one of the earliest Essex historians, the Reverend William Holman. (Credit for an even earlier history goes to Thomas Jekyll

1. *ibid.*
2. Peter Swinbank, *Lindsell*, a pamphlet printed by the church.
3. Ekwall, *op.cit.*

Figure 29 - Lindsell Hall

who died in 1653; his manuscript, however, comprises only notes and was never completed.) In 1710, Holman wrote:

There are 3 manors ...

1   The manor of Linsell
2   The manor of Brazenhead
3   The manor of Lachlees
4   The manor of Pryors new college in Oxford[1]

This is a strange list, isn't it? He says there are three manors and then lists four! No other successor historian gives "Brazenhead" manor status, and it does sound as though Holman wasn't sure! All agree, however, that the main ones were Lindsell Hall, Lachley Hall, and Priors Hall—all of them in existence before William the Conqueror. The first two, Lindsell Hall and Lachley

---

1.   Holman MSS, E.R.O. T/P 195/15, Dunmow Hundred, History of Lindsell No. 7), p. 2.

Hall, were part of the much larger Honor of Clare, owned by the Earl of Clare. Priors Hall, which had originally been given by the Conqueror to the Monastery of St. Valery in Picardy had been seized by Henry V and given to New College, Oxford.[1] According to Rev. Arthur F. Osborne, Vicar of Lindsell, writing in 1944, Lindsell Hall (Figure 29) comprised a small home farm, ten acres of pasture, and probably about four hundred acres of woodland. After it was given to one of the Conqueror's followers, it passed through a succession of families; at the time of Thomas and Agnes, it was owned by Sir Roger Wentworth. After Thomas' death, the manor was bought from Baron Wentworth, in 1529, by Thomas' second son, William and remained in the Fitch family for two generations, after which it was sold to Sir Francis North, first Baron Guilford (died 1685).[2] His grandson was the first Earl of Guilford. and *his* son was the Prime Minister and later second Earl, who managed to lose America for England!

Brazen Head Farm

Most accounts of the family indicate that Agnes also received a farm called Brazen Head in the northeast part of the parish of Lindsell (Figure 30) and that she and Thomas lived there. Philip Morant, one of the early (1768) Essex historians, wrote of "Robert Alger, owner of a capital messuage in this parish called Brason-Head."[3] A *messuage*, according to the Oxford English Dictionary, has, as its probable origin, a graphic corruption of *mesnage* (from the French *menage*). A *capital* messuage is that occupied by the owner of a property containing more than one messuage.

Miller Christy, who lived at Lindsell Hall as a boy in the 1870s, wrote frequently at the turn of the century about the farm and the famous leonine door knocker—the "Brazen Head"—that gave the farm its name and which is now exhibited in the British

---

1. Morant, *op. cit.*, p. 445.
2. Arthur F. Osborne, *Lindsell, A Record of its People, Parish and Church* (Lindsell: 1944), p. 5
3. Morant, *op.cit.*, p. 445.

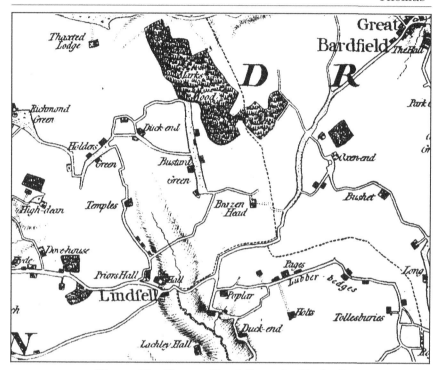

Figure 30 - Brazen Head Farm in Lindsell
(1777 Chapman & André Map, reproduced by courtesy of the Essex Record Office)

Museum (Figure 31). Christy appears to have first written about the farm in an 1892 article in Volume 1 of *The Essex Review.*[1] He wrote a longer set of notes in 1909 for the Society of Antiquaries of London at the time the door knocker was presented to the British Museum.[2] We shall quote extensively from this latter history. But, between these two papers, Christy, writing in the 1898 *Essex Review*, says that:

1. Miller Christy, "The 'Brazen Head' at Lindsell," *The Essex Review*, Vol. 1, 1892, pp. 104-106.
2. Miller Christy, "On Some Early Bronze Knockers and Sanctuary Rings Existing in England," *Proceedings of the Society of Antiquaries*, vol. xxii, Feb. 11, 1909, pp. 380-384.

Thomas Fitche's wife was Agnes, daughter and sole heiress of Robert Alger, of Brazen Head, in Lindsell, and she brought him Brazen Head, where the family continued to reside for several centuries, occupying evidently a good position in the county, as several members of the family were knighted, while others intermarried with the Wisemans and other families of good standing.[1]

The printed version of the first Visitation of Essex refers to Thomas as "of Brason Heade in the p'ish [parish] of Linsell," but that label was changed in later versions to read simply "of Lindsell." Since Brazen Head is not mentioned in the Lindsell court records when the Algors died nor when Thomas later died, it's probable that they held the farm "freehold," i.e. not as a rental from one of the Lindsell manors.

Quoting now from the proceedings of the Antiquaries at their meeting in 1909:

> Miller Christy, Esq. read the following notes on an early medieval latten[2] door knocker from Lindsell, co. Essex, exhibited by Henry Oppenheimer, Esq. who will present it to the British Museum:

> The large ancient brazen knocker which I exhibit was, for several centuries and until the last ten years or so, affixed to the front door of the small farmhouse at the Brazen-head Farm, in the parish of Lindsell, near Great Dunmow, in Essex. The house in question stands about a quarter of a mile to the west of the road from Dunmow to Great Bardfield, and is about four miles from the former.

> I have been familiar with the knocker for over thirty years, having lived when a boy at Lindsell Hall, within a mile of Brazen-head. At that time, I made inquiries of several old inhabitants to ascertain whether anything was known locally as to the history of the knocker; but I was unable to

1. Miller Christy, "On Some Interesting Essex Brasses," *The Essex Review*, vol. vii, 1898, p. 41.
2. From the Old French, a brasslike alloy, commonly made in thin sheets, formerly much used for church utensils.

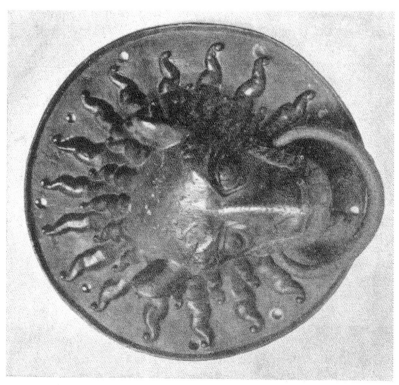

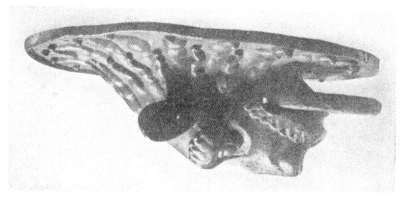

Figure 31 - The Brazen Head Knocker

obtain any information beyond the fact that some of the old people believed it to commemorate "the last wild animal killed on the farm"! I was told, however, of an old woman, Judy Boyett by name, now long dead, who regarded it with superstitious veneration and came, of her own accord, at certain intervals to polish it.

The knocker itself is shown in the accompanying illustration [reproduced here as Figure 31]. It is not solid, but is a thick heavy casting in bronze, weighing at a rough estimate, between fifteen and twenty pounds. It consists, as will be seen, of a circular disc, 14½ inches in diameter and approximately a quarter of an inch in thickness, with a narrow thickened rim. Nearly in the centre, but not quite, and standing out in very bold relief to a distance of about five inches, is the head of a lion or leopard, which is exceedingly well and effectively executed. It is surrounded by tapering rolls or curls of hair belonging to the mane. These rolls or curls, which all radiate outwards from the head, are of two different lengths, a small and short roll alternating with a larger and longer one. The smaller rolls overlie the longer, and each is about 3¼ inches in length. The longer rolls have their bases covered by the smaller rolls which overlie them, the portion which shows being 4 inches long. The lion's eyebrows and moustache are represented, very boldly and effectively, by smaller curled rolls of hair. The eyes are not pierced, though the nostrils are. In the mouth is a comparatively modern rough iron ring, which knocks on the narrow rim of the disc. The original ring was, no doubt of bronze, more ornamental and much larger that the present one. If it were intended for actual use as a door-knocker (which is doubtful), it probably knocked on a sounder placed three or four inches below the lower edge of the disc. Round the edge of the disc, just within the rim, and between the tips of some of the longer rolls of hair, are nine holes, originally filled by the bolts or nails which secured the knocker to the door. Four of these holes are obviously modern. The remaining five holes, which are clearly original, have not been drilled, but have first been cut through from the back by some kind of sharp narrow graving-tool, held at an angle of about forty-five degrees, the hole thus made being afterwards rounded and its edges smoothed.

As to the age of the knocker it is not easy to speak with precision, but I suggest that it belongs to either the eleventh or the twelfth century. No one, I think will regard it as later than the beginning of the thirteenth century.

Of the history of the knocker practically nothing is known. One can, therefore, do little more than speculate as to how it may have come into the position in which it recently was.
It is impossible to suppose that so fine and costly a knocker can ever have been made expressly for the door of any farmhouse, however considerable. In the present day, the house at Brazen-head is small and of modern red brick, having been built no more than forty years or so ago. An earlier house, which stood on the same site, was ancient, moated, and of some size. It became ruinous and was pulled down before the present house was built, the knocker being transferred from the door of the old to that of the new. A curious old pigeon-house, of timber and plaster, which belonged to the earlier house, and is perhaps Tudor, still stands.

Yet the farm of Brazen-head seems to have been known by its present name at least four centuries ago, and it is difficult to suppose that it can have come by that name otherwise than because of the presence of this knocker on its door. The available evidence goes to show, though not very conclusively, that the knocker was at the farm (or, at any rate, that the farm was called Brazen-head) *before the year 1500....*

The earliest to notice the knocker is the Rev. William Holman, whose manuscript history of Essex, written about 1710, and now preserved at Colchester Castle,[1] says "Brazen Head has, on the outward gate, the effigies of a head in brass or copper [A footnote by Christy says that the words 'either of a deer or hind' have been erased.]—a wolf's head, as Mr. Fitch

1. The Holman Manuscript is now preserved at the Essex Record Office, Document No. T/P 195/15.

tells me—very large and well cast." The later historians (Salmon, 1740; Morant, 1768; A Gentleman, 1769-72; Wright, 1832-34, and others) all seem to have derived their information about the knocker from Holman's manuscript, and tell us nothing more than he does.

But, if there is nothing to show how the knocker came to be at Lindsell, we may at least be sure that it was made originally to serve as the knocker or sanctuary-ring of some large abbey or cathedral church. In these circumstances, it is natural to suggest that it may be monastic spoil; but this idea seems to be negatived by the fact, shown above, that Brazen-head was so called (doubtless from the knocker on its gate) at least thirty years before the Dissolution of the monastic houses, and perhaps long before. There were, within ten miles or so of Lindsell, at least five religious houses, from any one of which the knocker may have come, whether before or after the Dissolution, namely Walden, Tilty, Little Dunmow, Hatfield Broad-Oak, and Panfield. If it came from one or other of these (of which, however, there is no evidence) it seems most likely to have come from Walden; for the church of Lindsell was appropriated to the Abbey of Walden in the early part of the fourteenth century and so remained till the Dissolution. The arms of the abbey still remain, indeed, in the glass of the east window of the church.

In the absence of any adequate explanation of the appearance of this fine knocker at the Brazen-head farm, it may even be worth while to point out that the arms of Fitch of Lindsell are *vert a chevron between three leopards' heads gold* (crest, *a leopard's head gold, in his mouth a sword proper, hilted gules*) and to suggest that, by some means unknown, some member of the Fitch family may have obtained possession of the knocker, and have had it affixed to the door of this house, because it reminded him of the armorial bearings of his family.

The knocker remained on the front door of the house until about ten years ago, when during some alterations, the owner of the farm had it removed to his residence in Great Dunmow, where it remained until recently. Now, I am glad to be able to announce, it has been placed beyond risk of loss or exportation to America [Ed. note: Heaven forbid!]. Having been acquired, by the liberality of Mr. Henry Oppenheimer, it has been presented, through the National Art Collections Fund, to the British Museum.

There was some discussion of Mr. Christy's presentation at the meeting of the Antiquaries. Everyone seemed convinced that the knocker dates from the 12th century. Furthermore, because it is so similar to the one on the nave door at Durham cathedral (Figure 32), it was almost surely made for some religious structure, not for a farm house. As Mr. Christy pointed out later in his presentation, it probably wasn't a *knocker* at all; it was more likely a ring used to pull a door shut, often referred to as a "sanctuary ring." After describing seven of these, he said:

> ...not a single one shows any sign of ever having been provided with a metal boss or sounder for the knocker-ring to knock upon; while in no case is the ring thickened, or provided with a knob or boss at the bottom, as all of them surely would have been had they even been intended to knock on a metal sounder.[1]

If, therefore, the Brazen Head knocker was really a sanctuary ring, it is difficult to imagine how it could have come into private hands prior to the dissolution of the monasteries in 1538. And, if the name of the farm derived from the knocker, then there could have been no "Brazen Head" farm earlier than 1538, i.e. not when Robert Alger held it, nor when Thomas and Agnes lived there. The earliest sure proof we have of the farm actually having that name comes from a deed to the farm in December 1581.[2] Christy (in a portion of the proceedings not quoted) cites the Visitations of Essex as evidence that the farm was known as

1. Miller Christy, *Bronze Knockers, op.cit.*, p. 389.
2. Deeds of Lindsell, Little Bardfield, and Hatfield Peverel, 1581-1656. Essex Record Office, D/DU 52/1.

Figure 32 - Sanctuary Ring, Durham Cathedral
(From *Proceedings* for 1909, courtesy of Society of Antiquaries of London)

Brazen Head "before the year 1500." And the *printed* version of the 1558 Visitation clearly says that as early as 1490, i.e. when Thomas married Agnes, she was of "Brason Head"? But the answer to this riddle, it seems to me is best provided by a Mr. Paley Baildon who, in commenting on Christy's presentation, pointed out that the farm may well have been called Brazen Head at the time of the 1558 visitation, but that the name "might have been transferred to the earlier date without warrant. Hence, this was no proof that the knocker was not monastic loot."[1]

The sequence of events, then, might have been as follows. When Thomas and Agnes were married, about 1490, the farm was called something else. The 1581 deed refers to "messuages and lands called *Bullingtons* or *Brazen hedd* and *Potters*." In other words, the farm may well originally have been called *Bullingtons* or *Potters*. This is given added weight by a later (1605) court proceeding which refers to "Brasenhed alias Bullingtons place."[2]

Some time after the Dissolution in 1538, but before 1581, the sanctuary ring was obtained and the farm—or perhaps just the farm *house*—was named after it as Brazen Head. A 1618 deed refers to a "Messuage called Brasen heade,"[3] indicating it may originally only have been the house that bore the Brazen Head name. This might even have happened as late as 1558 when William Fitch of Garnetts was granted the coat of arms with the leopards. One of the Fitch owners of the farm may have noted the superficial similarity between the leopard's head and what is surely a lion's head on the sanctuary ring and simply decided to buy it and mount it as a door "knocker" on the farm house. And with that done, he decided to call the farm and/or its capital messuage, *Brazen Head*. But, this is just speculation.

As mentioned in the Society of Antiquaries proceedings, the door knocker was removed to the British Museum in about 1909.

---

1. *Proceedings, op.cit.*, p. 391.
2. Deeds, *op.cit.*, 52/5.
3. *ibid.*, 52/7.

When last seen by the author, it was mounted on the wall in Room 42 of the Museum. Its label read:

> Bronze lion's head door-knocker, English, about 1200. From Brazen Head Farm, Lindsell, Essex. The knocker from which the farm evidently took its name, was first recorded about 1710, although the place-name Brasen Heade is found in a local document of 1552.[1]

The reference to 1710, a curator said, is to the Holman manuscript. He also believed it was Holman who said the name could be "found in a local document of 1552." If so, we have no information as to what that document might have been; it long precedes any deed now existing.

After Thomas' death, the farm passed to his eldest son, Richard. There is, at the Essex Record Office, a fragile bundle of deeds detailing later transactions affecting the ownership of the farm, and we shall have more to say about these later in this chapter.

1491 In the last chapter, we learned that when Thomas' father died, his mother, Juliana, was given the land in Widdington manor to hold until he was older. She undoubtedly was also given whatever freehold land John[E] had in Wicken Bonhunt. We also learned that she remarried—a man named Richard Westley. Now, some years after her death, Thomas sued his step-father.

> East. 6 Hen. VII
> Essex. Thomas Fytche, by his attorney, proffers himself the fourth day against Richard Westley of Hempsted in the country aforesaid, yoman, in a plea why with force and arms the close and house of the said Thomas at Newporte he did break and enter. And other enormities, etc. to the grievous damage, etc. And against the peace of the present lord our King, etc. And he came not. And the Sheriff was commanded that he attach him, etc. And the Sheriff now returns that he has nothing, etc. Therefore be he taken that he may be here on the Octave of Holy Trinity, etc.[2]

1. Department of Medieval and Later Antiquities, 1909, 6-5.1.

Hempstead is only a few miles northeast of Newport, and Newport is very near Wicken Bonhunt. Thus, the dispute appears to be over land that Westley is occupying but which Thomas feels belongs to him. We shall return to Thomas' further problems with Westley fourteen years later.

The Children

Richard, their eldest son was born about 1492, the year 1492 that is etched in every American school child's memory as the year that Columbus discovered America. We shall return to Richard (and each of the other sons) after Thomas' death.

Margaret, the first of three daughters was born at about 1494 this time (we learn later that she was about 11 years old in 1505). She was apparently named for her grandmother, Margaret Algore. And, we may as well announce the births of two more girls, Katherine and Joan, because we do not know when they were born.

William, the second son was born about 1496 (a brass 1496 in the church at Little Canfield says he was 82 when he died in 1578). And, as with the girls, there are two more sons whose birth years we do not know: Thomas, the third son, and Roger[C], the fourth. Thus, we can account for seven children, four boys and three girls, by name. But Thomas' brass in the church at Lindsell (Figure 36) indicates that he and Agnes had a total of eleven children: six boys and five girls. It seems unlikely any of the others survived, though they are shown as children, not babies, in the brass.

A Growing Estate

Now, it is Thomas' turn to add to the estate. On 21 1497 December 1497, he nearly doubled the land at Hubbardes by taking over 12 adjoining acres.

Thursday in St. Thomas Apostle, 13 Henry VII
Thomas Fytche took from hands of the lord 12 acres of land

4.   M.F.C., *op.cit.*, Ewen Vol. B, f. 209.

in field called Baresley next tenement called Hubberdes, etc.
in tenure of said Thomas Fytche, etc.[1]

1505 In November of 1505, Thomas finally took possession of the Creswell Field land (Figure 28) that his father, John, had left for his widowed mother, Juliana.

> Thursday after St. Leonard abbot, 21 Henry VII
> Thomas Fitch, as son and heir of Juliana Fitch, admitted to three roods of land and one acre of meadow in field called Cressewelfeld and Cresswelmedowe etc. formerly belonging to Juliana wife of John Fitch who was after wife of Richard Westely, which Richard Westeley after the death (a long time before this court) of Juliana, for 30 years held said land and occupied without licence and authority of this court.[2]

Evidently, Westeley (the scalawag!) had kept the property for 30 years after Juliana died, before the manor court finally took it away from him and gave it to Thomas, to whom it rightly belonged after his mother's death.

The next month, Agnes' mother, Margaret Algore, died, and the death was reported at Lindsell court on December 21st.

> Sunday in St. Thomas Apostle, 21 Henry VII
> Margaret, formerly wife of Robert Algore died since last court; "languens in extremis" surrendered certain lands for use of Margaret senior daughter of Thomas Fytche and her heirs; if she die without any, to Katherine another daughter of Thomas Fitch and her heirs; if she dies without any to Joan another daughter of Thomas Fitch and her heirs; if she die without any, to right heirs of said Margaret formerly wife of Robert Algore and said Margaret being under age, 11 and more, she to be in custody of Thomas Fitche, and Katherine and Joan likewise.[3]

With this record, we learn that grandmother Margaret is taking care of her namesake with a special gift of land. Only if

1. Court Rolls, Manor of Priors Hall, Lindsell, New College, Oxford.
2. Court Rolls, Manor of Widdington, New College, Oxford.
3. Court Rolls, Manor of Priors Hall, Lindsell, New College, Oxford.

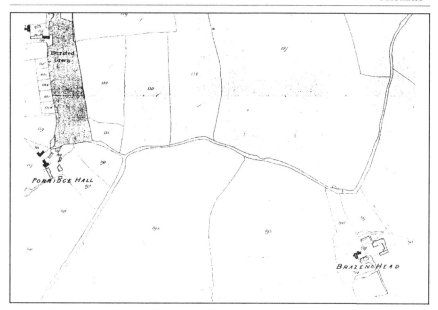

Figure 33 - Black Acre, Field 130, near Brazen Head (1846)
(Cat. No. D/CT 222.5, reproduced courtesy of the Essex Record Office)

granddaughter Margaret dies without heirs is the land to go to the other two girls in succession. And only if all three fail to produce children will the land go to Margaret's own heirs—presumably Agnes, herself, or a nephew or niece in the Algore family. As mentioned earlier, the Algore family—or Alger as it was later spelled—continued to live in Lindsell until the last member of the family, Stephen Alger who was church-warden at St. Mary's, died in 1874.[1]

Henry VII who had consolidated English rule in Ireland 1509 and made peace with Scotland died in 1509. He was succeeded by his son, Henry VIII.

There is one final real estate transaction to note. The 1511 date is 21 December 1511.

1. Christy, *Brazen Head*, p. 107.

Sunday in St. Thomas Apostle, 3 Henry VIII
Thomas Fytche and Agnes his wife exchange for one acre of
land called Blakacre lately in tenure of Margaret Yorde,
widow and Robert her son, one acre of land called Ryklottes-
acre lately in tenure of Robert Algore.[1]

This small exchange evidently trades an acre of the Algore
estate for an equal size piece called Blakacre. A lot named Black
Acre can be found as field 130 in the 1846 map of Figure 33.[2]

1514 Thomas Fitch died on 24 April 1514, at the age of 49, and
was buried in the parish church at Lindsell.

Lindsell Church

The parish church of
Lindsell is called St. Mary
the Virgin (Figure 34), and
at the time of Thomas'
death, its priest was "presented" or appointed by
Walden Abbey. This Bene-
dictine abbey (and convent)
at nearby Saffron Walden
also provided an annual sti-
pend for the support of the
priest. The abbey shield can
still be seen as part of a
stained glass window in the
present church.[3] We shall
have more to say about the
glass later.

A brass, commemorat-
ing Thomas (and Agnes),
still in remarkably good con-

*Figure 34 - St. Mary the Virgin
Church, Lindsell*
(Photo by Ian Rose, 1999)

1. Court Rolls, Manor of Lindsell Hall, New College, Oxford.
2. E.R.O., D/CT 222.5
3. Swinbank, *op. cit.*, p. 11.

dition, is set in the floor before the chancel arch (Figure 35). A good description of the brass (Figure 36) is provided by Christy:

> The male figure (16½ inches in height) has a half-turn to the left; is bare-headed, his long hair falling upon his shoulders; and his upraised hands, instead of being placed together as usual, are held apart. He is attired in the long gown of a civilian, beneath which his broad round-toed shoes are just apparent. It is open and turned back at the neck and down the front, showing the lining of the fur, which is also apparent at the wrists, where the extremely wide, open sleeves are turned back into cuffs.

Figure 35 - Brass in front of Chancel, Lindsell

The female figure (16¼ inches in height) has a half-turn to the right, and the hands are placed together. Her long gown, cut low at the neck, fur-trimmed at the bottom, and having tight sleeves, turned back at the wrists into broad cuffs, which are fur covered, is loosely confined at the waist by a girdle, of which the ornamentally embroidered end falls nearly to the ground. She wears the pedimental head-dress.

The six sons (about 4¾ inches in height) are placed beneath their father, while the five daughters (about 4½ inches in height) are placed beneath their mother. The former have a

Figure 36 - Brass of Thomas and Agnes Fytche
(Cat. No. MS 32490 M M 43, courtesy of The British Library)

half-turn to the left: the latter, to the right. Both wear costumes almost exactly similar to those of their parents, except that the gowns of the sons lack fur trimming, while the costumes of the daughters lack both fur trimming and the ceinture, and their head-dresses, having no backs, allow their long hair to fall down their backs to far below the level of the waist.

The inscription (on a plate 17 by 2½ inches) immediately below the principal figures reads:

Hic iacet Thomas ffytche & Agnes uxor ei' qui q'dem Thomas / obijt xxi° die Aprilis A° dni~ M° V° xiiij° quoru~ aiabus de' propiciet'.

Translated:

Here lies Thomas Fytche and Agnes his wife, which same Thomas died the twenty-first day of April, in the year of our Lord 1514; on whose souls may God have mercy.[1]

There is also a set of stained-glass portraits in the east window over the altar (Figure 37). Portrayed in separate panels are two couples at prayer. Closer examination reveals that the man in Figure 38—on the right in the window—is considerably older than the man in Figure 39, which is on the left, although the two women appear to be about the same age. Reverend Holman, writing in his 1710 history of Essex, described the windows as follows:

> In the first light towards the bottom of a window on the west side of the parish church of Lyndsell in Essex are painted in glass the figures of a man and his wife behind him kneeling both at desks with books thereon, and lifting up their hands in a praying posture the man in a crimson loose gowne with a white surplice underneath, and the woman in a long close vest of the same crimson colour, for Will. Fytch and Elizabeth And in the 3ᵈ light of the same window two like figures of a

1. Christy, *Essex Brasses*, pp. 39,40.

Figure 37 - East Window, Lindsell
(William & Elizabeth at left, Thomas and Agnes at right)

man and a woman kneeling in the same manner and habited as the other for Tho Fytche and Agnes Alger ...[1]

Beneath the portraits are legends, difficult for the non-specialist to read: they are in Latin, lettered with 16th century orthography, and employ numerous abbreviations. A pamphlet (available at the door), most recently edited by vicar Peter Swinbank, points out that, "At one time they formed part of the north window." (Note that Holman says the window was on the *west*. At any rate, wherever they were originally, the window in which they are now set, being over the altar, is, as is traditional, the east window.) The pamphlet continues, "The inscriptions are mutilated..."[2] But, as best one can make them out, the one on the left (Figure 39) reads:

1. M.F.C., *op.cit.*, F/B/1 h.
2. Swinbank, *op.cit.*

Figure 38 - Thomas and Agnes Fytche

Figure 39 - William and Elizabeth Fytche
(Photos courtesy of Peter Buell-Fay, London)

Dni Wyle/ate p aiabz/ate /pprosperitate,

and the one on the right, Figure 38 reads:

Thom? Fytche/?fuit s/dus filius/Dumowe/ algrz,

where the *"/"* represents the leading between pieces of glass. No attempt has been made to reproduce the tildes or squiggles over some of the letters (indicating abbreviations), the crossed stem of the lone *p* (for a missing *ro*), and have had, rather lamely, to substitute a *z* for the character indicating an *es* or *us* word-ending and a *"?"* for a character or symbol not recognized. The above transcription differs in minor detail from that given in the pamphlet, but, as will become apparent, it really doesn't matter. The important feature of the legends has always been the name of our venerated ancestor, Thomas Fitch—clear for even the non-specialist to read. But, what caught our attention on the most recent visit, and determined us to look further into the matter, was the conclusion in the vicar's pamphlet stating, "The persons represented are presumably William Fytch and his wife Elizabeth, and their son Thomas and his wife Agnes. The latter pair are also commemorated by the brass before the Chancel Arch."[1]

The inscription does seem to include the letters *Wyle/* in the first line, which might be the start of *Wylelmi,* i.e. *William.* And the second line seems to say something about Thomas Fitch being the son (*filius*) of someone. One archivist who was shown the printed transcription opined (correctly, it turns out) that the *s/dus* just before *filius* was an abbreviated *secundus.* Thus, the inscription makes it appear that Thomas was the second son— perhaps of William. The only problem with this interpretation is that it conflicts with the Fitch pedigree by the College of Arms. Thus, we can be quite sure that Thomas' father was not named William (or even Thomas, as reported in the various Visitations of Essex).[2] His name was John. Furthermore, Thomas was his *only* son. On the other hand, *Thomas* had a son named William;

1. *ibid.*
2. Metcalfe, *op. cit.,* pp. 8, 51, 197, 397.

not only that, but this William was his *second* son. And, William's first wife was *Elizabeth*.

So then the question became: Could these two couples be Thomas and Agnes Fitch and their *son* William and his first wife, Elizabeth? And, if so, why were the inscriptions so confusing? At the Essex Record Office in Chelmsford, we found the answers: the probable source of the error regarding the relationship between the persons portrayed and an explanation for the strange inscriptions.

The first answer was on the 9½ foot pedigree, compiled in 1636 for this William's grandson, Sir William Fitch of Garnetts, with later annotations and additions, mentioned in the *Introduction*. One of the annotations next to the first William's name gives the text of the *original* inscription under the portraits when they were still mounted in the north window. This note, though hard to read, is very close to a similar transcription included in the so-called *Holman MSS* quoted by Bernard Rackham.[1] Rackham gives the date for the manuscript as 1720, although, as we have seen above, Christy puts it at 1710. At any rate, what Holman copied from the window was the following:

> *Orate p˜ a˜iabz Willi Fytche et Elizabet [ux] quondam (manent) in Rectoria de Dunmowe [qz] fuit secundus filius Thome Fytche et Agn[e]t heres Robt Alge[z]*

where, again we have not been able to reproduce the orthography precisely, and have indicated some of the differences between the pedigree version and the Rackham version with square brackets.

Now the relationship seems to sort itself out, for the *complete* inscription reads (approximately):

> Pray for the souls of William Fytch and Elizabeth his wife, formerly of the parish of Dunmow who was the second son of Thomas Fytch and Agnes heiress of Robert Alger.

1. Bernard Rackham, "The Ancient Stained Glass at Lindsell Church," *Transactions of the Essex Archaeological Society*, XX New Series 1933 (Colchester: 1933), p. 76.

So, the puzzle seems half solved, anyway. The inscription is about Thomas and his son, not Thomas and his father. Yet, right after quoting the above, Rackham inexplicably adds, "The persons represented are presumably William Fytche and his wife, Elizabeth, *and their son* [emphasis added], Thomas Fytche and his wife Agnes." But, whether this 1933 article was the source of the error in the church pamphlet or simply repeated an earlier mistake, we do not know. Digging back still further, we now think that Miller Christy, the author of the 1898 article in *The Essex Review* about the brass, may have been the original culprit. In it, he states:

> According to the Heralds' Visitations of Essex of 1558, 1612, and 1634, [and a footnote cites *The Publications of the Harleian Society*, vol. xiii (1873) pp. 51, 197, and 397 as *his* source] this Thomas Fitche was a son of William Fitche, of Fitche's, in Widdington ... Thomas Fitche and his father William are also commemorated by a fragmentary inscription in the great east window of the church, the glass of which they not improbably had inserted.[1]

But, that isn't what the Visitations say, at all! In both the original manuscripts of the visitations and in the printed versions referred to above (Figures 3 and 4 in the *Introduction*), Thomas' father is listed as another *Thomas*! And that, too, as we have already seen, is wrong, as the more reliable Court Rolls prove. This is sheer speculation, but Christy may simply have picked the wrong Thomas and Agnes off the Visitation. Note in Figure 3 that William *did* have a son Thomas—not by Elizabeth but by his second wife—and that that Thomas also married an Agnes. But *that* Agnes was a Wiseman, not an Algor. At any rate, it appears that the source of the William-as-father-of-Thomas notion must have been the 1898 *Essex Review* article.

In a final footnote, Christy's article says that "Speaking chiefly from memory, I believe that Salmon (Hist. of Essex, p. 197)

---

1. Christy, *Essex Brasses, op.cit.*, p. 41.

has wrongly given the fragments of this inscription." Since he says that Salmon, who wrote *his* book in 1740, was wrong, it seems an unlikely source for his own interpretation. Actually, Salmon was only quoting from the Holman manuscript and says not a word about the relationship! He writes:

> In the North Window of the Church the Effigies of a Man and Woman praying, and

> *Orate pro aiabus Willi Fytche & Elizabet quondam—*

> Again Effigies of a Man and Woman praying;

> *—Thomae Fytche & Agnetis—*

> In another;

> *Orate p prosperitate Dni Wylelmi Cooke—*

The last Vicar presented by the Convent was of that Name.[1] Still, it doesn't completely solve the puzzle of the present legends. There are words under the portraits in Figures 38 and 39 that don't appear in the original text: *prosperitate*, for example. Where did that come from? The answer is in that third inscription that Holman noted and that we have just quoted. For the original north window had still *another* panel, depicting a shrine, with that last inscription, which asks us to pray for prosperity and ends with the name of still *another* William: namely, William Cooke, vicar of St. Mary's from 1501 until 1550. (The *Dni* for *Domini* means *Lord*, but could, before 1600, be used to indicate a clergyman.) This inscription, then, accounts for the completely irrelevant *Dni Wyle/* and the *p prosperitate* in the present window.

But, note that we aren't being asked to pray for the soul of William Cooke; in fact, it sounds as though he's the one doing the praying. If so, the north window may have been made and installed before 1550. Perhaps, as Christy suggested in his *Review* article, father and son paid for the window themselves—and threw in a panel for the vicar as well. It seems unlikely, however,

1. Nathaniel Salmon, *History and Antiquities of Essex*, 1740, p. 197.

Figure 40 - Alienation of Lindsell Church to William Fitch
(Courtesy of the Marc Fitch Collection)

that Thomas Fitch would have commissioned a window which included only one of his sons, and that one not even his eldest. Furthermore, the supplication for prayer is for William and Elizabeth, not Thomas and Agnes. An 18th century historian, who signed his name only as "A Gentleman," provides us with some enlightening information: when Henry VIII dissolved the abbeys, he granted Lindsell, in 1538, to Thomas, Lord Audley, and in 1543, Lord Audley "alienated," i.e. transferred title to, the church to William Fitch, Esq.[1] The document, formalizing the alienation, signed by Henry VIII, with his great seal affixed, is shown in Figure 40.

---

1. A Gentleman, (pseudonym for Peter Muilman of Great Yeldham), *History of Essex*, Vol. 3, 1741 (or 1771?), pp 216-8.

Thus, the most likely person to have commissioned the windows was William, who had bought Lindsell Hall in 1529 and then got title to the church in 1543. Since the concept of prayer for the departed would have been discouraged after the dissolution of the chantries in 1547 (about which we shall have more to say in the chapter on Roger[C]), we might even speculate that the windows were installed in the narrow time frame from 1543 to 1547. At that time, William's first wife Elizabeth was probably still living. He didn't remarry until about 1557, which would explain why his second wife, Anne, isn't in the picture.

Disposition of the Estate

Because Thomas had held land in the manors of both 1514 Widdington and Lindsell, both courts were responsible for apportioning the inheritance. At Widdington that year, Agnes and her eldest son, Richard, came to make their claim.

> Thursday after St. Leonard Abbot, 6 Henry VIII
> And that Thomas Fycche who held of the lord, the day of his death, at will, 3 roods of land one acre of meadow lying the field called Cressewelfeld and Cressewelmedowe ... And that Richard Fycche is his son and next heir of the said Thomas and of full age, who is present in court and comes and begs to be admitted tenant of all the aforesaid ... and is admitted ...Whereupon in the same court came the said Richard Fycche and surrendered into the lord's hands the aforesaid land and meadows with their appurtenances to the use of Agnes, his mother, late the wife of the said Thomas ... And as well the said Richard as the said Agnes made fine and fealty to the lord as appears at the head.[1]

Later that year, on December 23rd, Agnes, William, and Roger appeared in the Lindsell court to claim their property from the lord of that manor.

> Friday in St. Thomas Apostle, 6 Henry VIII
> Thomas Fytche died since last court, who held 12 acres of land

1. Court Rolls, Manor of Widdington, New College, Oxford.

in field called Barsley, etc. and who 'languens in extremis' surrendered same to use of Agnes his wife for her life, with remainder to William Fytche, son of same Thomas and Agnes.

Also one field called Herteshede, etc., to use of said Agnes, for her life, with remainder to Roger, son of said Thomas and Agnes.

And said Agnes surrenders into hands of the lord one tenement and 14 acres of land called Hobbardes, and the lord re-grants same to said Agnes, and William Fytche, son of said Thomas and Agnes.

And said Agnes is admitted to one toft and 3 crofts on land called Gobyes, which she and Thomas Fycche her late husband held jointly.[1]

Before moving on to Roger, the son from whom we are descended, it is worth spending some time explaining what happened to the older brothers and what happened to Brazen Head farm.

Richard, William, and Thomas

Richard, (Figure 41) the eldest son, born about 1492, married twice and probably had at least five children. His first wife, Ellianor, the daughter and heir of Tristram Storke of Trent in county Somerset, bore two sons, Tristram and John. Tristram, acknowledged as son and heir in Chancery Proceedings, married but apparently had no children. John also apparently died without issue. After Ellianor died in about 1533, Richard married Jane (maiden name unknown). They had at least three sons: Richard, William, and George. The College of Arms has this second wife as Joane Ashe, daughter of Richard Ashe, but Charles Fitch-Northen has shown that this is incorrect. Joane was the wife of Richard, *Junior*. In a Priors Hall, Lindsell, court entry regarding their holding of Palmer's Grove, it says:

1. Court Rolls, Manor of Priors Hall, Lindsell, New College, Oxford.

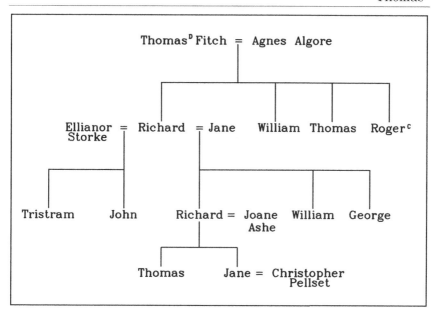

Figure 41 - Family of Richard, son of Thomas and Agnes

...intention that the lord should regrant the premises to the aforesaid Richard Fitch for the term of his life to remain thereafter after his decease to Richard Fitch his son and to Joan wife of the said Richard the son and their assigns for the extent of the lifetime of Jane wife of the aforesaid Richard Senior. and after the death of the said Jane to remain there after to the Desposition and fulfilment of his last will.[1]

Richard died and was buried in Lindsell in 1579. We shall return to his widow Jane and her disposition of Brazen Head Farm later in this chapter.

William, the second son (Figure 42), was born in 1496. He seems to have been a shrewd investor, eventually amassing a sizable estate. In 1529, as we have seen, he bought Lindsell Hall from Thomas Lord Wentworth,[2] and, in 1557, also bought Camoys Hall in Topesfield from the same Lord Wentworth.[2] Then, in

1. Court Rolls, Manor of Priors Hall, Lindsell, New College Oxford.
2. Morant, *op.cit.*, Vol. II, pp. 445, 361, 462, 457, 415

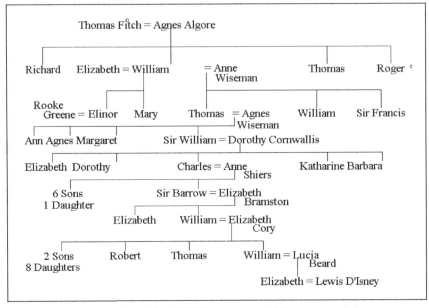

Figure 42 - Family of William, son of Thomas and Agnes

rather quick succession, he bought Great Canfield in 1561,[1]
Garnetts and Meeks in 1563,[1] Little Canfield (where he lived),
Albyns in Stapleford Abbott and Navestock, after 1569 from
George Wiseman,[2] and Priors Hall at Parsonage Farm, Stebbing,
in 1575.[2] To give some scale to his holdings, consider the size of
just one of them: Albyns Manor. It comprised "5 messuages, 240
acres of arable, 40 acres of meadow, 140 acres of pasture, 50 acres
of wood"—some 470 acres of land with 5 buildings.[3] William also
married twice, first Elizabeth (maiden name unknown) and then
Anne Wiseman, daughter of John and Joan Wiseman of Felsted.
He had two daughters by his first marriage and four sons by his
second. William died in 1578 at the age of 82, and there is a

1. Morant, *op.cit.*, Vol. II, pp. 445, 361, 462, 457, 415.
2. R. C. Fitch, *op.cit.*, p. 47.
3. R. B. Pugh, ed., *A History of the County of Essex*, vol. 4 (London: Oxford University Press, 1956), p. 225.

commemorative brass in the church in Little Canfield (Figure 15). The brass originally showed William between his two wives, but the man's figure is now completely gone. The Fitch arms (Figure 17) are displayed above the figures and in each of the four corners of the brass.

As an aside, there is one gossipy bit about William, from court records of 1570:

> One spinster, on 21 October 1570, between 12 and 1 a.m. at the house of William Fytche gentleman, her master, at Little Canfield (Hall) gave birth to a dead infant in the backhouse and threw it into his horse pond; no verdict given.[1]

William's oldest son, Thomas, married Agnes Wiseman (a confluence of names that, as discussed earlier, may have clouded the interpretation of the stained glass in the church at Lindsell). The second son, William, became a monk, known as Brother Benedict of Canfield. The remaining son (the fourth does not seem to have survived) was Sir Francis Fitch, who married but had no children.

The male line, then, descended from Thomas through his single son, Sir William Fitch of Garnetts. Four generations later, that line ended in 1777 with the death of Thomas Fitch, brother of William Fitch, Governor of Bengal.[2] William's daughter married Lewis D'Isney, and because she was an heiress twice over (having also inherited the estate of her well-to-do uncle, Thomas of Danbury Place), D'Isney added her name and arms to his, becoming—long before the women's movement made hyphenated names fashionable in America—Lewis Fytche-D'Isney.

Thomas, the third son of Thomas and Agnes (Figure 43), was, like his oldest brother, Richard, known as "of Brasonhead," an attribution we shall discuss in detail in the next section. We do know that in 1527, Richard had to surrender some of his land to Thomas.

1. F. G. Emmison, *Elizabethan Life: Disorder*, (Chelmsford, England: Essex County Council, 1970, p. 157).
2. Wagner, *op.cit.*, p. 227.

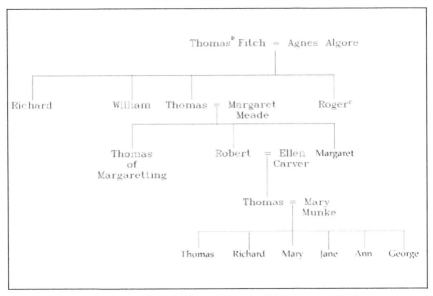

Figure 43 - Family of Thomas, son of Thomas and Agnes

3 May Henry VIII (1527)
(As by Court Thursday after St. Leonard abbot, 6 Henry VIII
[see the earlier entry for that date, 9 November 1514], on
death of Thomas Fitch, Richard being his son and heir,
certain lands were surrendered by said Richard to Agnes his
mother, wife of said Thomas, after her death to remain
according to the last will of said Thomas, to use of Thomas
Fitch son of said Thomas Fitch, said lands now surrendered
to said Thomas son of Thomas Fitch).[1]

This seems to indicate that Agnes died some time before
3 May 1527 and that some of the estate that Richard had received
from his father and had turned over to his mother for the rest of
her life now went to his brother Thomas.

Thomas married Margaret Meade and had three children,
two boys and a girl. His oldest son was known as Thomas of

---

1. Court Rolls, Manor of Widdington, New College, Oxford.

Margaretting. This same Thomas married Ann Bentley, but had no children. The second son was Robert, who married Ellen Carver and had three children. Robert's oldest was a Thomas who married Margaret Munke. They had three sons and three daughters. The oldest son was Thomas who may be the one (i.e. he was about the right age) who married Frances Wiseman.[1]

My understanding is that the Thomas Fitch line also died out. Except for Thomas' and Agnes' second son, William, who prospered and had three knighted descendants, the other children were somewhat less prosperous. According to Wagner,

> By the early seventeenth century they had included apothecaries, clothiers and clothmakers, staplers and leathersellers, several clergymen and a naval surgeon. By 1700, however, all trace of them in Essex is lost. A branch settled in Warwickshire has been traced a little later, but the only lines traced to the present day spring from settlers in New England.[2]

The "settlers in New England," of course, were the descendants of Roger[C], the fourth son of Thomas and Agnes, whom we shall follow in the next chapter.

Brazen Head Revisited

As already mentioned, there is, in the Essex Record Office, a bundle of deeds and other papers relating to the disposition of Brazen Head Farm. The earliest of these is dated 1581, sixty-seven years after Thomas died. So, we shall have to speculate about the history of the farm during this undocumented period. It seems likely that Richard (Figure 41), being the eldest son would have inherited the farm. And the College of Arms pedigree refers to him as Richard "of Brasonhead." However, the third son, Thomas, is *also* listed as "of Brasonhead, Lindsell, Essex" on the same pedigree.

1. Metcalfe, *op.cit.*, p. 527.
2. Wagner, *op.cit.*, pp. 227, 228.

Figure 44 - Entrance to Brazen Head Farm today

Morant says that Richard had four sons who *had no issue* and that, hence, Brazen Head went to his brother, Thomas.[1] The problem with this explanation is that Richard's son Richard (to whom we shall hereafter refer as "Richard, junior") apparently had at least two children—so that there doesn't seem to be any reason why Richard, senior, would have given away the farm to his younger brother. We can probably explain, though, why Brazen Head *didn't* go to Richard's eldest son, Tristram.

> Tristram Fitche of Hening (?) Essex, gentleman, complains reciting that one Richard Fitche of Lynsell, gentleman, father of your said Orator, was and is seised in his demesne as of fee of and in certain lands, etc. in Lynsell to him lineally descended from Thomas Fitche and Margaret his wife, his father and mother and was likewise seised in his demesne

1.   Morant, *op.cit.*, p.445.

as of fee of and in certain lands, etc., lying in Burton, Oxon., to the yearly value of £15 10s. by the year, and so being seised, about 30 years since he promised in return for a life tenancy of the tenements in Burton, to permit Orator to enjoy for ever lands in Lynsell. Richard entered into the lands of Burton, but has not kept to the agreement, alienating some parcels, etc. and by his will has devised away the residue of the premises, etc. ... Prays a writ of subpena.[1]

In the first place, Tristram has the wrong name for his own grandmother (Margaret instead of Agnes). But what Tristram is complaining about is that his father was reneging on a promise to give him the Lindsell land, after he had agreed to let his father spend the rest of his life on land in Burton. Here is the senior Richard's answer.

Elinor, late wife unto Defendant and natural mother unto Complainant had good title to the reversion of the lands in Burton. After her death the lands were injuriously witholden from Complainant the son and heir, he being then an infant. In recovering possession of the lands Richard the father having impoverished himself, his children assured to him the Burton lands for life. Complainant not only contempnyd Defendant, his poor father, but lived so prodigal a life that he consumed the estate of his wealthy wife and had to be relieved by his father.[2]

Now we learn that the Burton land belonged to Tristram's mother, Elianor, first wife of Richard, senior. It was to go to Tristram on her death, but somehow it was "injuriously" withheld from him. And now Richard, senior, says he "impoverished" himself getting it back. As a result the children told him he could live on the Burton land. But, instead of being grateful, Tristram was contemptuous of his father, spent all his wife's money, and

---

1. Chancery Proceedings, Series II, Fitche v. Fitche, in M.F.C., *op.cit.*, Ewen Vol. D, f. 488.
2. *ibid.*, ff. 488,9.

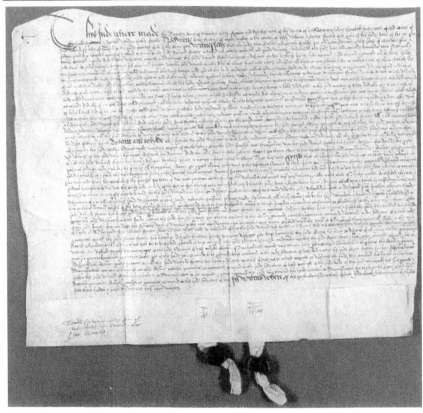

Figure 45 - Sale of Brazen Head, 20 December 1581
(Cat. No. D/DU 52/1, courtesy of the Essex Record Office)

had to be bailed out by Richard, senior. No wonder, the Lindsell land would go to Richard, junior!

1581   At any rate, the first document relating to the farm itself was, as we have indicated, drawn up just two-and-a-half years after the death of Richard, senior. Shown in Figure 45, it is dated 20 December 1581 and relates the bargain and sale, for £147, by Jane Fytche of Gt. Leighs, widow, and Geo. Fytche, gent. (son of said Jane) to Richard Fytche of Lindsell, gent. Her signature is the single letter "J;" his reads "by me George Fitch."

> Messuages and lands called Bullingtons or Brasen hedd and Potters (cont. 40a.) toft called Baldwynes (20a.) in Lindsell, crofts called Dykes Croft (4a.), Almans Croft (1½ a.), a meadow (1a.), tofts called Hurryes (24a.), Cocks Umfreys (13a.), and Catsalls (14a.) (the last three being copyhold of the manor of Lindsell Hall)

> Recites lease to John Cowland for two years from Mich. 1581 at annual rent of £30.[1]

George had married Ellen Browne, a lady of royal descent, the previous year and, after the birth of one child, moved to Great Leighs about eight miles southeast of Lindsell. Jane retired to Great Leighs also, presumably to live with her son, which may have been the reason for the sale of the farm. Jane died and was buried on 25 June 1593, George on 2 June 1610.[2] Because she had no will, George was granted administration of her estate.

Reverend Holman, writing in 1710, quotes a 1592 or 1593 document that sheds more light on Brazen Head:

> *In feodum militis Honoris de Clare*   1592/3
> 35 Eliz. Ricd Fitche gent pd his [Ingress?] Fine of a capitall mess. called Bollingtons als Brazon head in Lindsell held of the manor of Lindsell hall lately bought by him of Jane Fitch widow deceased late wife of Ricd Fitche Senior father of the sd Ricd.–the fine was 31ˢ[3]

This record is a *knight's fee*, i.e. a payment in lieu of service for the Honor of Clare, which as we learned earlier included the manor of Lindsell Hall. The reason we have not learned before that the land was copyhold of Lindsell Hall is that those manor records have not survived.

1. Deeds of Lindsell, Little Bardfield, and Hatfield Peverel, 1581-1656. Essex Record Office, D/DU 52/1.
2. Burial Register, Parish of St. Mary's Great Leighs.
3. Reverend William Holman, MSS for *History of Essex*, E.R.O. T/P 195/15.

Note that, in both the 1581 deed and the 1593 record, the land is called "Bullingtons" (or "Bollingtons") *or* "Brasen hedd and Potters'" *or* just "Brazon head" and that it comprised 40 acres. (Incidentally, the present day farm contains 500 acres.) It also appears that at least some of the land and/or buildings had been leased to a John Cowland. The term was for two years from "Mich. 1581," where "Mich." is an abbreviation for *Michaelmas*, September 29th. Thus the lease had taken place just three months before the 1581 document.

1602 The next significant document is twenty-one years later:

> 6 October 1602
> Articles of agreement. (Draft.)
> (i) Rich. Fytche, sen., of Lindsell, gent., and Rich. Fytche, jun. (s. and h. of said Rich. F) and (ii) Robt. Boyle of London, esq. (as friend and kinsman in trust for Dorothy Weston, widow of Robt. W. gent., of Feering.)
>
> Recites marriage bet. Thos. Fytche and said Dorothy Weston, and the transfer to said Thos. F. of messuage called Brasenhead and lands (140a.) in Lindsell and Lt. Bardfield [no details] in occ. of said Thos. F.
>
> To use of said Tho. F. and Dorothy W. for their lives and then to their heirs male; in default of such issue then to use of said Rich. F. and his heirs male. Thos. F. is to pay to Rich. F. an annuity of 20 marks out of the property.[1]

Now the son of Richard, junior, was a Thomas. He may well have married the widow, Dorothy Weston, and it appears that they were living on the farm. This agreement seems to reassure Dorothy's kinsman that she and Thomas will get to live on the farm for the rest of their lives and that it will then go to their male heirs, if any, *but* lacking same, the farm is to go back to other heirs of his father. In the meantime, Thomas is to pay rent to his father for the use of the property.

1. Deeds, *op.cit.*, 52/4.

A month after this draft agreement, Richard, junior, mortgaged the farm to his cousin, Sir Francis Fitch, son of his uncle William (Figure 42).

Mortgage. Indenture made 16 November 44 Elizabeth between Richard Fitch of Brasenhead in Lindesell, Essex, gentleman, of thone party And Francis Fitch of Ramsden Barringtons, Essex, esquire, on thother party. In consideration of £400 grants to Frauncis Fitch a farm called Brasenhead in Lyndesell, etc. Close of arable land called Barnefeild. Close of arable land called Longefeild. Close of arable land called Deadwomanfeild. Close of meadow ground called Longfeild Meade. Close of meadow ground called Deadwomansmeade. Close of arable land called Hempstall feild. Close of arable land called Longland. Close of arable land called Potters croft. Two crofts of arable land called Freelandes. One close of arable land called Redynge. Close of arable land called Bawdinges. Close of pasture called Potters leaves. Close of arable land called Dixcrofte. Close of arable land called Woodfeilde, etc.[1]

We can see, from this, that Brazen Head farm comprised a number of fields and meadows, each of which had its own distinctive name. And this transaction may simply have been a way for Richard, junior, (who has now risen to the station of a "gentleman") to raise money. It does not appear that he actually transferred the property to Sir Francis.

The next document indirectly provides evidence about 1605 the size of the main house on the farm:

27 June 1605
Mandate
Rich. bishop of London to Theophilus Aelmer, D. D., archdeacon of London and rector of Much Hadham (co. Herts.) and Ralph Ravens, D. D., vicar of Gt. Dunmow.
Recites proceedings of dispute between Rich. Fitche and s. Thos., and Wm. Man, all of Lindsell, about a pew in the church there, used as of right by the lord of the manor of

1. Close Roll, in M.F.C., *op.cit.*, Ewen Vol. B, f. 279.

> Brasenhed alias Bullingtons place (*domus sive mansio vel manerium quoddam vulgariter nuncupat Brasenhed al's Bullingtons place*).[1]

Since this was, ostensibly, a religious dispute, it was referred to an ecclesiastical court; the archdeacon's court was the lowest of these. In a supporting document, the pew in question is described as "Seat or pew under the Roode loft next to the chancel on the side of the church adjoining the chapel sometime belonging to Lachly Hall." This document includes several pages of "evidence" the Fitches (Richard, junior, and his son Thomas) offered to prove their case, but, unfortunately, not the decision. What it does show is that not everyone accepted Brazen Head as a manor. And so, we learn that even though Brazen Head is not among the three recognized manors of Lindsell, it must have been big enough for the owner to presume to regard himself as a "lord of the manor." This is apparently the reason for the dispute with a William Man about the use of a pew in the church, the Fitches claiming it as theirs by right.

1608   Sir Francis Fitch, who owned Thundersley,[2] died, leaving his manor at Ramsden-Barrington to his nephew, Sir William,[1] son of his brother Thomas. There was no mention of the mortgage he held on Brazen Head (perhaps it had been discharged), but he did make a bequest of £20 to his cousin Thomas, son of Richard, junior.[3]

1615   Seven years later, Thomas, now also referred to as "gent." mortgaged several fields in the Brazen Head farm for £100.

3 November 1615
Thos. Fitch of Gt. Dunmow, gent. to Gabriell Jellowes of Lindsell, yeoman.
Arable lands called Barnfield (cont. 16a.), Henstall field (7a.), Longland (9a.), Potter Croft (6a.) and a meadow called Dead-

---

1. Deeds, *op.cit.*, 52/5.
2. Morant, *op.cit.*, Vol. I, p. 265, 204.
3. Commissary Court of London, Essex & Herts.

*Figure 46 - Beams probably from Original House
in present day Outbuilding*

womans Meade (2a.), all in Lindsell and parcel of a farm called Brasenheade.[1]

Three years later, Thomas sold at least the messuage 1618 of Brazen Head together with various parcels of land to a group of four men:

1 April 1618
Feoffment for £433.
Thos. Fytche of Lyndisdale [Lindsell] gent., to Hen. Hinchley, jun., of Westminster, doctor of physic, Chris. Robinson of Ketton [Kedington, co. Suff.], gent., Rich. Jennyngs of Gt. Dunmow, esq., and Rich. Hinchley of Westminster, apothecary.
Messuage called Brasen heade, arable lands called Barnefield (cont. 16a.), Longfield (8a.), Hemstall field (7a.),

---

1. Deeds, *op.cit.*, 52/6.

Longland (9a.), Potters croft (6a.), Free lands (10a.), Reed-
ings (7a.), Bawdings (8a.), Dypeclose (2a.), pasture called
Potterslayes (12a.), all in Lt. Bardfield and Lindsell.[1]

This is the first time we have come across the term "feoffment." Earlier, it was the custom for the seller to hand over a piece
of turf from the property to the purchaser. Since this was done in
the presence of a witness, it was unnecessary to document the
transfer with a deed. By this time, however, such a conveyance
would usually be accompanied by a written *Feoffment* or *Deed of
Gift,* and after 1677, such a document was required.

There are several other transactions involving various members of the family over the next few years, but ultimately, Richard,
junior, quitclaimed the messuage at Brazen Head to one Dionis
Palmer in April of 1625,[2] and two years later, in April of 1627,
Thomas quitclaimed his interest to the same man.[3] Thus, by 1627,
the Fitch family no longer had an interest in Brazen Head farm.

1. *ibid.,* 52/7.
2. *ibid.,* 52/19.
3. *ibid.,* 52/21.

5

Roger^C

R oger Fitch, son of Thomas^D and Agnes, was born some 1500 time after 1496, when his brother William was born, and before 1514, when Thomas died. As the youngest of four sons, we could say he was born about 1500. And, as the youngest, he probably received the smallest share of his father's estate. His will says that he was a *yeoman*, like his grandfather, William^F. The *Oxford English Dictionary* defines a *yeoman* as "a man holding a small landed estate; a freeholder under the rank of gentleman; hence vaguely, a commoner or countryman of respectable standing, esp. one who cultivates his own land."

Panfield

From the same will, we also learn that he was "of Panfield" and asked to be buried in the churchyard there. Panfield (Figure 19) is a small village on the River Pant in central Essex, about six and a half miles east of Lindsell. Figure 47 is a photograph of St. Mary and St. Christopher Church, in the churchyard of which Roger asked to be buried. A former rector, describes it as "a small but intimate church, built largely of flint, and with a small bell-tower (3 bells) ... this (15th century) church stood where an old Saxon church undoubtedly stood ... The old Priory once stood not far from the church, but no trace remains. The present population of the village is about 1,200—farms, mainly arable, are around the village. In the village is Panfield Hall, part of which dates from Tudor times."[1] Figure 48 is taken from a 1777 map of the area, showing Panfield at the upper left. The church is depicted just under the "e" of "Panfield."

The name *Panfield* was *Penfelda* in *Domesday, Panfeld* in 1254 as listed in the Valuation of Norwich, and *Pantfeld* in a 1428 Feet of Fines. It derives from *feld on the Pant,* a *feld* being the Old English word for open country, free of wood, particularly common in old forest directories, and *Pant* the Welsh word for a valley.[2] So, *Panfield* is an open or rural area near the River Pant.

Figure 47 - St. Mary & St. Christopher Church, Panfield

Bocking

Across the river is the larger town of Bocking. And, although Roger was "of Panfield," his will speaks only of property he owned in Bocking. The name, in the form *Boccinge,* appears to date from as early as 995. It may derive from the personal name *Bocca,* a

1. Ronald W. Oswald, personal communication, September, 1989.
2. Ekwall, *op. cit.*

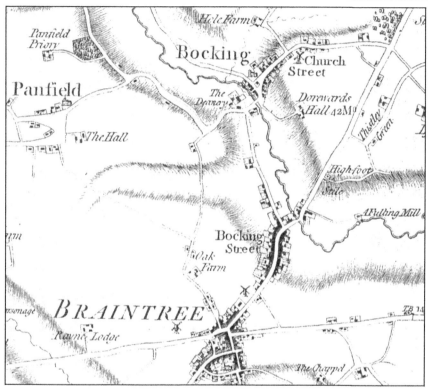

Figure 48 - 1777 Map of Panfield, Bocking, and Braintree
(1777 Chapman & André Map, reproduced by courtesy of the Essex Record Office)

side-form of *Bucca*, or it may have replaced the earlier *Beoccing*, derived from *Beocca*.[1]

Looking again at the map of Figure 48, it's clear that in 1777, the largest town in the area was Braintree to the South. But, in Roger's time, Bocking was the biggest of the three. In 1548, the population of Bocking was 800, whereas the population of Braintree was only 480.[2] And Panfield was no more than a rural village.

1. *ibid.*
2. W. F. Quin, *A History of Braintree and Bocking* (Lavenham, England: The Lavenham Press Limited, 1981), p.41.

It is interesting to compare the map of Figure 48 with a map of the area today (Figure 49). The streets of the early map can readily be found on the modern map. The "L" shaped Panfield Lane still connects the center of Braintree with what is now the Shalford Road that runs up the west side of the Pant River, past Panfield. Bocking End street starts from the same Braintree center that Panfield Lane does. It shortly becomes Bradford Street, where Roger had one of two houses he bequeathed in his will. A left at the fork onto Church Lane runs

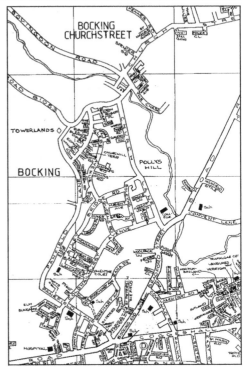

Figure 49 - Modern Map of Bocking
(Courtesy of N. J. C. Publicity (Southern) Ltd.)

out to the river where it leads to Church Street, site of St. Mary's Church. But, though the streets are the same, the names of the areas through which they pass have changed. The area along Bradford street that was called Bocking Street has been heavily developed and is now the area called Bocking. And what was Bocking, across the river and running along Church street is now called Bocking Churchstreet. Both are now really just suburbs of Braintree.

We shall have more to say about why Bocking was such an important center in the 16th and 17th centuries when we turn to Roger's grandson Thomas[A]. For now, however, we shall examine the other major bequest in Roger's will: "my house and free lands

Figure 50 - Bocking Hall
(Photo courtesy of Dorothy and Bob Pickford, Bocking Hall)

in Bocking sometime called St. Mary Chauntrie." In order to understand what this meant, we need to learn more about the church in Bocking.

The Manor of Bocking—the largest of several manors in and around the village—had been held by the Priory of Christ Church, Canterbury, as early as 995 when a Saxon nobleman, Aethe(l)ric, bequeathed the lands to the church.[1] And, even though William the Conqueror redistributed much of the Essex countryside and most of its manors to his friends, the church was able to hold onto Bocking. Figure 50 is a photograph of Bocking Hall today, which its present day owner describes as "the hub and workplace for the monks, the court being held in an upper room."[2]

The Church of St. Mary, Bocking

That also meant that the parish church in Bocking—St. Mary's—was under the control of Canterbury. But, since Bocking

1. *A Short Guide to The Deanery Church of St. Mary, Bocking*
2. Personal communication from Mrs. Dorothy Pickford, 1 January 1990.

Figure 51 - Church of St. Mary, Bocking
(Photo courtesy of David Mansell Photography, Braintree, www.esseximages.co.uk)

was outside the normal jurisdictional area of the Archbishop, the church was called a *Peculiar*, and the Rector of Bocking, as the commissary of the Archbishop, bore the title of Dean of the Peculiar.[1] The priory lost the manor at the time of the dissolution of the monasteries in 1538 (it went to Roger Wentworth), but the church remained under Canterbury control and is still called the Deanery Church of St. Mary, Bocking. The 1777 map of Figure 41 shows the rather large residence of the Dean — The Deanery—just across the river from the church, at the junction of the roads to Panfield and Braintree.

The church itself (Figure 51) goes back to about 1340, but was enlarged, altered, rebuilt, and modified right up through the 19th century. In 1362, an early benefactor of the church, William Doreward (see Doreward's Hall on the map of Figure 48), founded a chantry in one of the church chapels. A *chantry* (or *chauntrie* as

1. *ibid.*

it was spelled in Roger's time), from the French *chanter*, to sing, is "An endowment for the maintenance of one or more priests to sing daily mass for the souls of the founders or others specified by them. Also applied to the body of priests so endowed."[1] Later, in 1397, William Doreward's son John founded a second chantry in the north aisle chapel and—what is important to us—"purchased a small plot of land from the monks of Christ Church in order to endow this and the earlier chantries in perpetuity. ... On the land he purchased (now part of the churchyard), Doreward built a house for the chantry priest."[2] A record book for the period 1445 to 1450, kept by the "Travelling Warden" who checked on such matters for the Priory, indicates that the chantry priest, who also served as the village schoolmaster, received a salary of £7 a year. And as Quin tells us, he had "a house and garden in that part of the churchyard which lies on the far side of the Church."[3]

We cannot say exactly where the house stood, though the present owner of Bocking Hall conjectures that, "There is only one house that would be in the reckoning for a chantry, the one next to the old cottages now converted."[4]

About ten years after the monasteries were dissolved by Henry VIII, his successor, Edward VI, on becoming king in 1547, dissolved the chantries as well. On 4 November 1547, an Act of Parliament provided for the establishment of a commission to inventory the chantry properties—nearly 2400 of them. It seems likely the commission worked with the Court of Augmentation, which had been created in 1535 to administer the property of the dissolved religious houses. The next year, the commission reported on the chantries in Bocking, including St. Mary's:

> Saynt Marye Chauntrie there, founded to find a priest for ever by licence of Richard II; within the Parish Church there,

---

1. *Oxford English Dictionary*
2. Ann Hoffman, *Bocking Deanery, The Story of an Essex Peculiar*, (London, England: Phillimore & Co. Ltd., 1976), p. 25.
3. Quin, *op.cit.*, p. 24.
4. Pickford letter, *op.cit.*

worth £8.5s.4d. by the year whereof the 10th. to the king 14s,
& so remains clear £7.11s.3d.[1]

The reference to a license from Richard II, who reigned from
1377 to 1399, is because the founding of a chantry required not
only the approval of the church but the consent of the Crown as
well. The king also got a tenth of the income provided by the
property, in this case 14 shillings. Subtracting that from the gross
receipts left a little over £7, which as indicated above was the
salary of the chantry priest.

After this background information, the commission prepared a memorandum "as to the tenure of chantry lands, etc."

Chantry of the Blessed Mary in Bocking.

'Mr. Fytche hath the purchase'.

Shows rents of 15 small parcels, of which there are let to
Roger Wentworth Esq. a pasture called Saundermans, pasture called Pondemans and a piece of land called 'Saint
Maryes lande' and one tenement and garden are in the
tenure of Thomas Simon clerk late incumbent of the chantry,
as tenant at will paying 6s.8d. yearly.

'Thomas Symond clerk' signs a declaration 20 Nov. 2 Edw.
VI [1548], that the certificate shews all the rents belonging
to the chantry, and that Wentworth's lease dated August 37
Hen. VIII [1545] was made and delivered about 8 weeks
before the coming of the King's Commissioners and not
before.[2]

Now we learn that a "Mr. Fytche" has purchased St. Mary's
Chantry—probably from the commissioners—and that Thomas
Simon (or Symond), the former chantry priest is still living in the
"tenement" and paying 6 shillings 8 pence rent a year for the
house and garden. He signs a declaration that the certificate
accurately shows the total revenue from the property, but also
says that the Wentworth lease, supposedly dated in 1545 was

1. Certificate of Colleges and Chantries 20 No. 11., E.R.O. T/P 116/4, p.4.
2. *ibid.*, Certificate 30 No. 12, p. 5.

actually "made and delivered" only eight weeks before the commissioners arrived. Very strange.

From a book of rate of the sale of Chantry lands between 27 April and 29 September 1548, we read:

> Rental of lands of the chantry of the Blessed Mary in Bockinge
>
> Shows details ... with memorandum that they were rated at 25 year's purchase £161.0s.10d. for Tristram Fiche of Bocking gent.

Figure 52 - Possible Bricked up Gate in Church Wall
(Courtesy of Dorothy Pickford, Bocking Hall)

11 May 2 Ed. VI [1548] & that the bells & lead were to be excepted from the sale.[1]

And so, we finally learn the additional information that the "Mr. Fytche" is Roger's nephew Tristram, son of his oldest brother Richard (see Figure 41). It also appears that he may have paid about £161 for the property, a price which may have been determined by multiplying the yearly income by twenty-five (it's actually a bit less, so perhaps they used a present value calculation!). We also note that he didn't get the bells or lead from the chapel, since the King may well have wanted those to melt down for guns and cannon balls.

Since the chantry property eventually became part of Roger's estate, we can only conjecture that he bought it from Tristram sometime between 1548 and 1558. About a century later, the massive wall around the church was reinforced "and the gateway

1. *ibid.*, Misc. Bk. (Augmentation Office) 68 fo. 29., p. 6.

that once led to the chantry priest's house was filled in, there being no longer any use for it."[1] The filled area can be found "at the extreme end of the adjoining wall with the house and church that has been bricked in ... The bricks are laid in the old bond and it was obviously done 200 - 300 years ago."[2] (See Figure 52.)

But, there is more of interest about St. Mary's. During the period from 1490 to 1520, the church was largely rebuilt. In the process, some of the generous benefactors were commemorated in emblems and bosses and stained glass windows. Among these decorations in the richly carved ceiling is the leopard's head crest of the Fitch family. Unfortunately, the crest commemorates not Roger, but a much wealthier Fitch family which occupied Lyons hall nearby.[3] In 1548, a John Fitch, gentleman of London bought Lyons Hall and Bocking Hall from Roger Wentworth. He also bought another manor at Boones. Unfortunately, this John Fitch was just another of the stray twigs we have not been able to attach to a family branch. All we know about him is that his parents were named William and Margaret and that he had at least six brothers. After his death in 1569, the manors went to those brothers, one of whom, Oswald, is commemorated by a brass in the church. Another brother, Reverend James Fitch, Prebendary of Rochester—not to be confused with our immigrant ancestor who was also Reverend James Fitch and who also came from Bocking(!)—was evidently the rector of the church at Bocking.[4] He died in 1612, ten years before our James was even born.

But, to return to the main thread of our story, we have very few actual records, other than his will, to tell us about Roger Fitch.

1514 As noted in the previous chapter, Roger appeared in court in 1514 with his mother and his older brother William. The court granted him "one field called Herteshede, etc." to be held by Agnes during the rest of her life and then to be

1. Hoffman, *op.cit.*, p. 28.
2. Pickford letter, *op.cit.*
3. Hoffman, *op.cit.*
4. R. C. Fitch, *op.cit.*, pp. 29, 30.

passed on to Roger.[1] (One can only wonder what the "etc." might have comprised, though it might have been some structures on the field.)

We get a nice snapshot of the relative wealth of the four brothers in a tax record during 15 Henry VIII, which would have been sometime between April of 1523 and the same time the following year. At that time, they all paid the Lay Subsidy[2] for "Lyndsell" in the "Donmowe Hundreth" based on the value of their person property, as follows: 1523

	Value			Subsidy		
	£	s	d	£	s	d
Rychard Fytche	8				8	
Robert (Rich.'s servant)		26	8			4
William Fytche	20				20	
Richard (Wm.'s servant)		20				4
Thomas Fytche		66	8	3		4
Roger Fytche		53	4	2		8

Jennifer C. Ward writes:

From the late twelfth century, the levy on a man's personal property, his movable goods, developed into the most usual form of royal taxation ... The size of the tax varied, a twentieth of a man's movable property being granted in 1327 ... Knights and gentry often paid tax of about £1.[3]

For our purposes, though, the important information to note is that Roger clearly has the smallest estate. His oldest two brothers, Richard and William, even have servants who are well off enough to pay taxes themselves.

The next record we have regarding Roger is a land transaction. It was in 1531 when he, his brother William, and others bought some land from William Cotton and his wife. 1531

1. Court Rolls, Manor of Priors Hall, Lindsell, New College, Oxford.
2. Lay Subsidy Calendar, E.R.O. T/A 427/1/1, No. E179/108/151 m. 1
3. Ward, *op.cit.*, pp. i-v.

Michaelmas. 23 Henry VIII
File 60. County of Essex

30. Trin. and Mich. William Fycche, John Maxye the younger, Richard Lyndesell, Roger Fycche, Thomas Kyng, John
Mede, Nicholas Colyn, John Bendelowes and John Clerke,
pl. William Cotton, esquire, and Margaret his wife, def.
1 messuage, 1 garden, 100 acres of land, 9 acres of meadow,
21 acres of pasture, 5 acres of wood, 5s. rent and a rent of 3/4
lb. of pepper in magna Bardefeld and parva Bardefeld. Def.
quitclaimed to pl. and the heirs of William Fycche. Warranty
as in 18. Cons. 1001. (18 says: Warranty against John, abbot
of St. Peter, Westminster, and his successors.)[1]

This deed transfers about 135 acres including a domicile
together with the right to some rental income in Great Bardfield
and Little Bardfield from William and Margaret Cotton to a group
which includes both Roger and William Fycche. The next thing
we note is that the participants are referred to as "pl." (for
plaintiffs) and "def." (for *deforciants*). No one is suing anyone
here; *plaintiff* in this context simply means the purchaser. Another frequently used word for purchaser is *demandant*. The
deforciant is the seller, sometimes also called the *tenant*.

1533 On September 25, 1533, Roger appeared at Priors Hall,
Lindsell manor court to receive the land that had been willed
to him by his father.

Thursday before St. Michael Archangel, 25 Henry VIII

Roger Fiche admitted to one field called Hartshede, etc., on
death of his mother Agnes, as son of Thomas and Agnes
Fitch, in accordance with the will of said Thomas. William
Fyche assoined.[2]

---

1. Marc Fitch and P. H. Reaney, eds., *Feet of Fines for Essex*, vol. iv, 1423-1547
   (Colchester: Essex Arch. Soc., 1964).
2. Priors Hall, *op.cit.* Note: R. C. Fitch gives the recipient's name as "John" Fiche. There
   was no son named John, and Hertshede was clearly assigned to Roger in the court
   record of 23 December 1514, cited in the previous chapter.

The reference to brother William says that he "assoined," which means that he put in a legal excuse for not appearing.

Four years later, Roger was back in land court for another filing. [1535]

Michaelmas. 27 Henry VIII
File 63 County of Essex

50. William Fytche, Roger Fytche, William Bendlowes, gentleman, George Fytche, John Wynterflode the younger and William Botolf, pl. Thomas Lyndesell the younger def. 1 messuage, 24 acres of land, 4 acres of meadow and 16 acres of pasture in Lyndesell and Eystans ad montem. Def. quitclaimed to pl. and the heirs of William Fytche. Cons. £30.[1]

The interesting development to note here is that Roger appears again with brother William, but this time he is joined by a George Fytche. This cannot have been Roger's own son, George[B], who was probably not born until 1540 or later. Neither William nor Thomas had a son George. So he was probably Richard's son George, the one who was involved in the 1581 Brazen Head farm transaction, discussed in the last chapter.

Henry VIII dissolved the monasteries. The monks were largely pensioned off, the large estates were sold to wealthy landowners, and some of the monastery buildings were simply plundered for building materials. [1538]

The Priors Hall, Lindsell rental book (Figure 53) for 38 Henry VIII lists two properties under Roger's name. The first, "Templers," can be located on the map of Figure 30, on page 79, just north of Priors Hall (where it is spelled "Temples"). The other, "Hurryes," was the 24-acre tofts we have already encountered in the 1581 sale of Brazen Head. Roger must have sold the property to his brother Richard, perhaps in connection with his move to Panfield. [1546]

Edward VI, at the age of nine, succeeded his father Henry VIII on the latter's death in January 1547. This was [1547]

1. Fitch and Reaney, *op.cit.*

Figure 53 - Priors Hall, Lindsell, Rental Book
(Courtesy Charles Fitch-Northen, Paignton, South Devon)

also the year that the chantries were dissolved and may have been about the time Tristram Fitch acquired the house and land of St. Mary's chantry, which was later to show up in Roger's will.

Later that same year, Roger sold some land in Great Dunmow to one James Larke.

> 24 November. Dunmawe magna xij.d. Also (the jurors) present that James Larke has bought of Roger Fytche one tenement with the curtilage situated in Great Dunmow by rents therein annually. Wherefore it falls to the Lord the King by way of fine for the enrolled charter as appears in the head. And let him be distrained for fealty.[1]

It appears that James Larke may have fallen behind in his rent. The jurors have acknowledged that he bought the tenement and "curtillage" (the yard and outbuildings of a house) from Roger. But this may have been manorial land with an annual

1. M.F.C., *op.cit.*, Ewen Vol. C, f. 325, from Court Rolls in P.R.O. (General Series) Ref. S.C.2 171/65 Dunmow Edw. I - Edw.VI 67 mm.

"fine" of 12 pence ("xij.d."). So Larke is to be "distrained," i.e. forced by seizure of his property, to pay up.

Two years later, Roger teamed up with a William 1549
Gregyll to buy three houses and four gardens in Braintree from John Beeld and his wife.

> Final agreement made from Easter Day in 15 days, 3 Edw.
> VI. between William Gregyll and Roger Fitche, plaintiffs,
> and John Beeld and Margaret his wife, deforciants of 3 mes-
> suages and 4 gardens, etc. in Branketre J. and M. have
> acknowledged the said tenements, etc. to be the right of W.
> as those which W. and R. have of the gift of J. and M...And
> for this acknowledgment, etc. W. and R. have given to the
> said J. and R. £40 sterling.[1]

This is the first time we have come across what was called a *Deed of Gift*. As we learned in the previous chapter, it has the same meaning as a *Feoffment*, i.e. it is a deed, conveying freehold property. In this case, Roger Fitche and William Gregyll have the tenements through the "gift" of the Beelds. Of course, the gift cost them 40 pounds.

Edward VI died of tuberculosis and the crown passed 1553
briefly to Lady Jane Grey, daughter-in-law of Edward's regent, John Dudley, Duke of Northumberland. In the struggle that followed, Edward's half-sister, Mary I, became queen. Her marriage to Philip of Spain, the re-establishment of papal authority, and her persecution of the Protestants earned her the sobriquet, "Bloody Mary"—and the hostility of the English people.

The next year, Roger both bought and sold property. In 1554
fact, two transactions took place the same day. First, he bought a house, a garden, and 55 acres of land in Bocking from Roger Perker, gentleman, and his wife Anne.

> Final agreement made on the Octave of St. Michael, 1 & 2
> Philip & Mary. Between Roger Fytche, plaintiff, and Roger

---

1. *ibid.*, from Essex, Proclamations endorsed (57/420, no.67) Feet of Fines, Edw. VI C.P. 25(2)

Perker, gentleman, and Anne, his wife, deforciant of 1 messuage, 1 garden, 30 ac. of land, 6 ac. of meadow, 16 ac. of
pasture and 3 ac. of wood, etc. in Bokyng. Deforciants have
acknowledged the said tenements, etc. to be the right of
Roger Fytche as those which he has of their gift. And those
they have remised and quitclaimed from them and their heirs
to the said Roger Fytche and his heirs for ever. And for this
acknowledgment, etc. Roger Fytche has given to the Deforciants £80 sterling.[1]

The peculiar reference to "1 & 2 Philip and Mary" results
from it being the first regnal year for Philip but the second for
Mary. Again, it's a *Deed of Gift* with a price of 80 pounds. In the
second transaction, we meet Roger's wife Margery for the first
time, as they and two other couples, including the same Mr.
Perker, sell property to a Robert Pole.

Final agreement made on the Octave of St Michael, 1 & 2
Philip & Mary. Between Robert Pole, plaintiff, and Roger
Perker, gentleman, and Anne his wife, Roger Fytche and
Margery, his wife, and Thomas Woodam and Agnes, his wife,
deforciants of 1 messuage, 2 cottages, 2 barns, 1 garden, 52
ac. of land 6 ac. of meadow, 30 ac. of pasture, and 8 ac. of
wood, etc. in Lyndesell and Brokeshed. And those they have
remised and quitclaimed from them and their heirs to Robert
and his heirs for ever. Warranty (as to Lyndesell And tenements) by R. and A. and R. and M. for themselves and the
heirs of Roger Fytche and Margery and the heirs of Roger
Fytche. Like warranty (as to Brokeshed tenements) by T. and
A. and the heirs of Agnes to R. Pole and his heirs, against T.
and A. and the heirs of Agnes for ever. for the acknowledgment, etc. R. P. has given to Deforciants £80 sterling.[2]

Although this deed covers land in Lindsell and Brokeshed,
Roger's property was in Lindsell. The fact that the two transac-

---

1. *ibid.*, f. 328, from Essex. Proclamations endorsed. (70/579, no. 20) Feet of Fines, Mary
    C.P.25 (2).
2. *ibid.*, ff. 328,9 from Essex. Proclamations endorsed. (70/579, no.40) Feet of Fines, Mary
    C.P.25 (2).

tions that day involved the same amount of money makes one wonder whether this wasn't really a swapping of properties, with Roger making his move from the Lindsell-Great Dunmow area to the Panfield-Bocking-Braintree area.

In other transaction of 1554,

> Roger Fitch surrenders his copyhold lands into the hands of the Lord of Priors Hall manor in the presence of his brother Richard and other tenants of the Lord—who regrants the same to a lady called Christiana Fitch.[1]

Unfortunately, we know nothing of this Christiana Fitch, other than that a widow of that name died in Bocking.

The Will

Roger probably died in early 1559, less than 60 years of age. He was the first of the line to leave a will—at least one we know about. The transcript that follows was made from a copy of the original (Figure 54). As you can see in the illustration, the will was written as a single paragraph, starting on one page and ending on the next, with little or no punctuation. It has been subdivided here for easier reading. 1559

> **In the name of god Amen** the vii[th] daye of Januarye in the yeare of our Lord god 1558 I Roger Fyche of Panfeilde in the countie of Essex, yeoman beinge of good and perfect Remembrance god bee thanked doe ordeine and make this to bee my last will and Testament in manner and forme followinge First I bequeathe my soule to allmightie god and my bodie to bee buried wthin the churche yarde of Panfeilde aforesaid

> Item I bequeathe to Margery my wiffe my house and my free lande wthin the parishe of Bockinge in the countie aforesaid some tyme called Sainte marie chauntrie duringe her naturall lyfe and after her decease to John Fiche my sonne and to the heirs of his bodie lawfully begotten and yf he fortune to dye wth out heirs of his bodie lawfully begotten then I will that Richard my sonne shall have itt to him and to the heires

1.   New College Oxford Priors Hall manorial rolls. Courtesy of Charles Fitch-Northen.

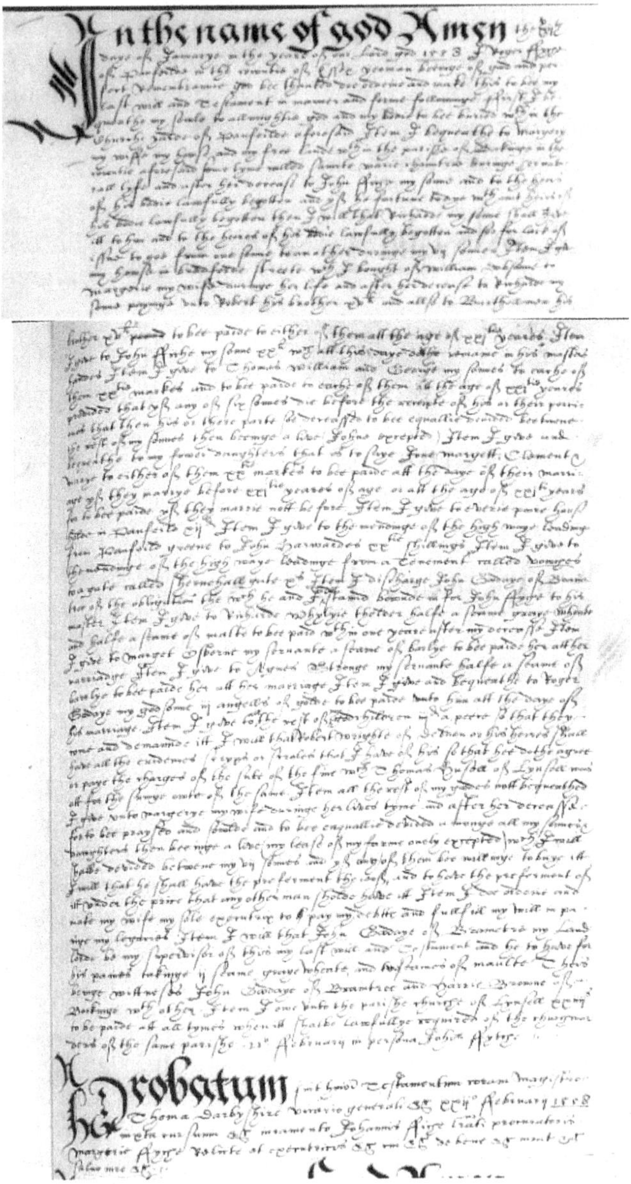

Figure 54 - Will of Roger Fyche, 7 January 1558/9
(Corporation of London, Greater London Record Office, DL/C/357/1, 193 Horn. Bishop)

of his bodie lawfully begotten and soe for lack of issue to goe from one sonne to another duringe my vij sonnes

Item I give my howse in bredferde streete wch I bought of William Dobsonne to Margerie my wife duringe her life and after her decease to Richarde my sonne payinge unto Robert his brother xv^t and allso to Barthollomew his brother xv^t pound to be paid to either of them att the age of xxi^{tie} yeares

Item I give to John Fiche my sonne xx^t wch att this daye doethe remaine in his masters handes

Item I give Thomas William and George my sonnes to eache of them xx^{tie} markes and to bee paide to each of them att the age of xxi^{tie} yeares provided that yf any of six sonnes die before the receipte of his or their porcions that then his or there parte soe deceased to bee equallie divided betwene the rest of my sonnes then beinge a live John excepted

Item I give and bequeathe to my fower daughters that is to saye Jone Margett Clement & Mary to either of them xx^{tie} markes to be paide att the daye of their marriage yf they marrye before xxi^{tie} yeares of age or att the age of xxi^{tie} yeares for to be paide yf they marrie nott before

Item I give to everie poore house holde in Panfeild xii^d

Item I give to the mendinge of the high waye leadinge from Panfeild greene to John Harwardes xx^{tie} shillinges

Item I give to the mendinge of the high waye leadinge from a Tenement called Vowches to a gate called shernehall gate x^s

Item I discharge John Goodaye of Braintree free of the obligation the wch he and I do stand bownde in for John Fyche to his master

Item I give to Richarde Whylyie th'elder halfe a seame gray wheate and halfe a seame of malte to be paid wthin one yeare after my decease

Item I give to Marget Osborne my servante a seame of barlye to be paid to her att her marriadge

Item I give Agnes Stronge my servante halfe a seame of barlye to be paide her att her marriage

Item I give and bequeathe to Roger Goodaye my godsonne iii angells of golde to be paide unto him att the daye of his marriage

Item I give to all the rest of my godchildren iiii^d a peece so that they come and demande itt

I will that Robert Wrighte of Debden or his heires shall have all the evidences scrypes or scroles that I have of his so that hee dothe agree or paye the charges of the sute of the fine whch Thomas Husell of Lynsell was att for the suringe owte of the same

Item all the rest of my goodes nott bequeathed I give unto margerye my wife duringe her lives tyme and after her decease for to be payed and soulde and to be equallie divided amonge all my sonnes & daughters then beinge a live (my lease of my farme onely excepted) wch I will shallbe divided betweene my vij sonnes and yf any of them be willinge to buy itt I will that he shall have the preferment thereof and to have the preferment of itt under the price that any other man sholde have itt

Item I doe ordeine and make my wife my sole executrix to pay my debttes and fulfill my will in payinge my legacies

Item I will that John Goodaye of Braintree my Land lorde be my supervisor of this my last will and Testament and he to have for his paines takinge ii seame gray wheate and two seames of maulte

Theis beinge witnessed John Goodaye of Braintree and Harrie Browne of Bockinge wth other

Item I owe unto the parishe churche of Lynsell xxiiii^s to be paide att all tymes when itt shalbe lawfullie required of the church wardens of the same parishe

22 February *in persona Johannes Fyche*

*Probatum fuit Testamentum coram Magistro Thoma Dar-
byshire vicario generali xxii February 1558 Johannes Fiche
[?] procuratori margerie Fyche Relicte et executrices*

The Latin text indicates that the will was "proved," i.e. its
genuineness was established, before Thomas Darbyshire, the
vicar general, by son John on behalf of his mother, Margerie, the
"relict" or widow. For modest estates like this, the will was
probated at the Consistory Court of London, because until 1846
Essex was part of the diocese of London. As we shall see in the
following chapters, the larger estates of Roger's son, George[B], and
grandson, Thomas[A], were probated at the Prerogative Court of
Canterbury. Not shown in the Figure is a separate notation as
part of the record:

Will of Roger Fitch late of Panfyld, Essex, Decd. was proved
February 22nd 1558, by the oaths of children Robert Maryanne and John.[1]

Thus, Roger appears to have been a reasonably well-off farmer.
He had a wife named Margery (also spelled Margaret later in the
will) and at least eleven *living* children—seven sons and four
daughters—all of them named and remembered in the will.

Next, Roger bequeaths to "Margaret" the house in "Bredforde" Street. Here, we must assume that Margaret and Margery
are one and the same and that Bredforde Street is the present
Bradford Street, a beautiful curved street lined with houses,
including the "Tudor" house (Figure 55), built during Roger's
lifetime. Now, since second son Richard was unlikely to receive
the first house, he was to be the ultimate recipient of the Bradford
Street house. But there was a stipulation that he must give 15
pounds each to two of his younger brothers, Robert and
Bartholomew when they reached the age of twenty-one. (The
little superscripted "tie" probably indicates that *twenty-one* was
thought of as "one and twentie." This house may well have been

1. Greater London Record Office DL/C/357/1. Consistory Court of London. 193 Horn.
    Bishop.

Figure 55 - Tudor House, Bradford Street, Bocking

one named *Blackhouse* on Bradford Street which a later record indicates did belong to Richard.

Oldest son John appears to be apprenticed to someone (from his later trade, it was probably a mercer). There are two references to this arrangement. In the next clause, Roger states that John is to receive 20 pounds which are presently being held by his "master." The second reference to the apprenticeship is later when Roger discharges John Goodaye, his "Land lorde" and evidently a close friend, "of the obligation which he and I do stand bound in for John Fyche to his master." We may also infer that this John Goodaye is the father of Roger's godson, also named Roger, who is to receive "3 angells at his marriage." According to Richardson, an *angel* was a gold coin worth 6 shillings 8 pence minted in 1464/5. It replaced the old version of the *Noble*, minted in 1344. It was thought to bring good health.[1]

---

1. Richardson, *op.cit.*, p. 218.

Next, a clause provides for sons Thomas, William, and George[B]. These last three are to receive "20 marks at 21." As we have seen, 20 marks would be equivalent to 13 1/3 pounds sterling. It's interesting to note that five of the sons have family names: John was the name of Roger's grandfather, Thomas was the name of both father and brother, and, of course, Richard and William were Roger's other brothers. The new names here are Bartholomew and George; perhaps they are from the maternal side of the family. On the other hand, George may have been named for the elusive George Fitch we have already encountered in two real estate transactions. If we can infer anything from the order of the names, then George was apparently the seventh and youngest son.

Then Roger provides for his four daughters, Jane, Margett, Clement and Mary (or Maryanne as she is identified on the back of the will). They are each to get 21 marks when they reach the age of twenty-one or when they are married.

At this point in the will, Roger turns to eleemosynary bequests: first, 12 pence to each poor household in Panfield, followed by two contributions to road mending projects.

There are several people who receive gifts of grain. The first of these, Richard Whylyie the elder is to receive half a seam of gray wheat and half a seam of malt. A *seam* in this context is loosely defined as a pack-horse load; in the case of grain, it was customarily equal to 8 bushels. The Fitch household was evidently affluent enough to have at least two servants (in fact from the juxtaposition of names one might speculate the elder Whylyie was also a family retainer). Marget Osborne, a servant, is to get a seam of barley on the occasion of her marriage, and Agnes Stronge is to receive half a seam at her marriage.

He takes care of some more godchildren who are to get 4 pence apiece, takes care of some unfinished business with Robert Wright of Debden and then leaves any "residue" of the estate to his wife and, eventually, to all the children equally. To this he makes one exception: his farm. I think we can assume that the farm is in Panfield (else why would he be "of Panfield"?). Recognizing perhaps that dividing it among seven sons will probably impoverish them all, he says that if any one of them is willing to buy it, he should be able to do so at its fair market value.

Margery is appointed executrix and John Goodaye supervisor. The latter is to receive two seams of wheat and two of malt for his trouble. The will is witnessed by Goodaye and Harry Browne of Bocking. Almost as a postscript, Roger mentions that he owes the parish church in Lindsell 24 shillings. The will was proved by son John, acting for his mother, the "relict" or widow, and by siblings Robert and Mary(anne). The will was dated 12 January 1558/9 and was "proved" or entered in the Consistory Court of London on February 22nd of that year.

The Children

We have only sketchy information about most of Roger and Margery's eleven children (Figure 56). The oldest, John, was a mercer, an occupation we shall examine in more detail in the chapter on Roger's son George[B]. John may have married an Anne Bucks.

Next was Richard. He and his younger brother, William (see below) are referred to in a 1593 will of one John Lagden of Wethersfield, yeoman, who mentions them in connection with houses and lands he wants to leave to his wife:

> To Anne my wife for life in consideration that she shall not claim any third or dower of my lands which Richard Fitche of Bocking clothier holdeth in Bocking except two tenements adjoining to the tenement wherein Richard Fitche dwelleth, which William Fitche and [blank] holdeth.
>
> To Sarah [presumably a daughter] at marriage or 21 my tenement with the house, yards and garden in Bocking in the tenure of William Fich of Bocking, clothier, ...[1]

1. F. G. Emmison, *Elizabethan Life: Wills of Essex Gentry & Yeomen* (Chelmsford, England: Essex County Council, 1980), p. 129,30.

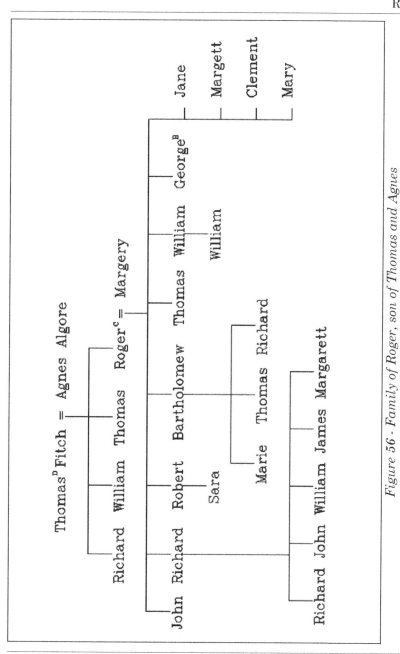

Figure 56 - Family of Roger, son of Thomas and Agnes

The condition that Anne "not claim any third or dower" was fairly standard practice in these wills. Before the 12th century, a *dower* meant the gift from a husband to his bride on the morning of their marriage. But, by the time of this will, it meant that part of the estate that the widow had the right to claim for life or until her remarriage. This portion was usually one-third. So, Lagden was saying (as did most testators) that she could have more than her third so long as she let him decide how the estate was eventually to be divided and not claim the third she had a right to. With this, we also learn that both Richard and William live in Bocking (perhaps next door to each other) and are clothiers, an occupation about which we will have more to say in the chapter on Thomas[A]. Another record indicates that Richard lived in the *Blackhouse* on Bradford Street.[1] Richard also held copyhold land in Braintree. He married an Anne, last name unknown. They had five children (Figure 56): Richard, an apothecary who lived in Chelmsford; John, a gentleman of Felstead; William; James, another Bocking clothier; and Margaret. Richard, John, and James all had large families. Richard, senior, was buried at Bocking, 13 June 1603, and his will, dated 11 June 1603, was proved on 24 June 1603.

Roger's third son was Robert, a husbandman of Burnham and Rainham. Again, we see how the last son is reduced in status; his father was a fairly wealthy property owner, a yeoman, and Robert was no more than a tenant farmer. He married a widow, Elizabeth Tymm Parker, and they had a daughter, Sara who married Roger Mayward. Robert received some land from his brother William in 1591. His will is dated 18 December 1592.

The fourth son was Bartholomew who lived in Chelmsford. He married, first, Alice Ayer on 8 February 1579/80. He married, second, Mary Chamberlain. He and his second wife had three children, Marie, Thomas, and Richard, all baptized in Chelmsford. Bartholomew was buried in Chelmsford on 4 November 1598.

1. Chancery Proceeding C54, 1220, m.22., in M.F.C., *op.cit.*, Ewen Vol. D, f. 423.

The fifth son was Thomas who died on 4 July 1595. There are several baptisms in the Bocking parish register for children of a Thomas about this time. He definitely had Mathew and Frances and may have had children named Rebecca (baptized at Panfield) and Jane. Mathew may have been the one of that name, who was master of a small ship who explored the James River in Virginia. He was "wounded by the Indians, but recovered and made home only to lose his life, ship and company in a further expedition to the Islands when all were wrecked in a hurricane."[1]

The sixth son was William, a mercer of Chelmsford (as we have seen, he was also mentioned as a "clothier" of Bocking—the terms are similar, and he may well have lived in both places). On 17 June 1583, he married Sarah Egiott. They had one child, named William, who was baptized in 1586 and died in 1597. The senior William is almost certainly the same man ("a mercer of Chelmsford") who was arrested in 1597 for poaching in the park of Sir William Walgrave. On 6 September, he was brought before Thomas Waldegrave and charged with hunting in Sir *William* Walgrave's park.[2] (No conflict of interest there, evidently!) On 12 to 14 January 1597/8, he appeared at the General Sessions in Chelmsford before Sir Thomas Mildmaye and others.

> ... William Fytche of Braintree, to appear at the Assizes; and the said Fytche to appear, by the sureties of Richard Fytche and John Higham of Chelmsford.[3]

It now appears that William must face a higher court and that his appearance is being assured by his brother Richard and a John Higham. On 4 November, the case of *Walgrave v. Fitch and others* came before the Star Chamber, said to have been so-called from a decoration of stars on its ceiling. It dealt with civil and criminal cases concerned with the interests of the crown. Noted for its arbitrary procedures, it gave rise to the name for any arbitrary or unfair hearing.

1. Letter of 4 Oct. 1994 to the author from Charles Fitch-Northen.
2. E.R.O. Q/SR 139/76.
3. E.R.O. Q/SR 140/2.

Bill 4 Nov. 40 Eliz. Sir William Walgrave, the elder, of Smallrydge, Suff. Kt., recites that for 40 years last past he had been lawfully seised to Wormyngford Park in Essex, etc. and complains that William Fitche, yeoman, John Clarke, laborer, Thomas Reignolde, laborer, John Scotte, the younger, laborer, all of Chelmsford, and five others named 'all men of bad behaviour and nothinge regarding the lawes', etc. on 29 August 39 Eliz. [1597] and other dates broke his park and killed his deer. Prays writ of subpena.

Joint and several answer of William Fitche and Thomas Kerington. Denial. Pray dismissal.[1]

5 Interrogatories to be ministered unto William Fitche.

Deposition of William Fytche of Chelmsford, mercer, sworn 24 Jan. 40 Eliz. He did not on 31 Aug. last year enter the park. The others with a brace of greyhounds killed a deer which they brought to the Bell Inn in Easterford, etc.[2]

So William says he didn't do it; the other fellows did it, and he just happened to be at the inn when the carcass was brought in! Incidentally, this last deposition is signed by William Fitche and may well be the earliest existing signature in this line.

The seventh son was George[B] who will be the subject of the next chapter. The other four children were the girls: Joan who married William Kent on September 2, 1596; Margaret, who may have married Thomas Preston; Mary; and Clement who was buried in Panfield on 22 May 1573.

---

1. Star Chamber 5, W3, 26, in M.F.C., *op.cit.*, Ewen Vol. D, f. 494.
2. Star Chamber 5, W16, 36, in *ibid.*

6

George[B]

George Fitch, son of Roger[C], was probably born at either 1551 Panfield or Bocking in Essex. We know that Roger's oldest son John was one of three "children" swearing oaths at the proving of the will. That and the fact that he was still apprenticed indicate that he was a minor in 1559. George was the youngest of seven sons who therefore must all have been under twenty-one, so we might guess that he was probably no more than about eight. That would put his birth date at around 1551 or even later.

From various references we will come to, we learn that he was variously called a *haberdasher* and a *mercer*. And, as we learned in the last chapter, three of his brothers were *clothiers* and/or *mercers*. These are all occupations having to do with the manufacture of and trade in cloth. Further, although we in America don't use the term mercer (the word *mercerized* comes from a man's name, not the trade), the other two have meanings for us that differ from what they would have meant to a sixteenth century Englishman. To us, clothiers and haberdashers are sellers of men's clothing, as in the chain of "Jos. A. Banks, Clothiers." Actually, the terms are seldom used today and, when they are, are likely to be affectations, meant to convey an image of Ivy League respectability.

In the sixteenth century, however, a clothier was an entrepreneur who farmed out the spinning of wool and the weaving of woolen cloth to local women, and sometimes operated a "factory" for the dyeing and "fulling" of the cloth. The Bocking-Braintree area of Essex was a major center for the production of woolens. But, we shall have much more to say about this in the next chapter when we deal with George's son, Thomas[A], who was himself a clothier. George, however, was first a haberdasher and later a mercer. John Bromley, writing about the Guilds of London has this to say about the haberdashers:

> The origin of the word 'haberdasher' and the early activities of the trade of haberdashery have provoked much speculation without reaching certainty. ... In two lists of custom dues on cloths and furs coming into London in the reign of Edward I appears the term 'hapertas' in one and 'haberdassherie' in the other. Apart from the obvious similarity of these two words, the context makes it probable that they are two renderings of the same word, or at least allied in meaning. Since hapertas is said to have been a coarse thick cloth or fustian used beneath armour, it would appear that the haberdasher's original function was that of a dealer in this material, and later, by extension, a seller of underwear of all kinds together with other articles of apparel and personal wear. The wide variety of a haberdasher's wares is revealed in an inventory of a haberdasher's shop made in 1378. This lists such goods as leather laces, numerous caps and hats, purses, spurs, beads, pencases, children's woollen boots, linen thread, etc. Of these, the most prominent articles mentioned are caps and hats, and the existence of separate misteries of cappers, hatters and hurers indicates that they were the manufacturers who supplied the haberdasher with these wares. ... By 1502, [they were known as] Merchant Haberdashers ... [which] marks a change in the functions of the members of the guild from small-scale shopkeeping to merchant trading.[1]

1. John Bromley, *The Armorial Bearings of the Guilds of London* (London: Frederick Warne & Co. Ltd., 1961), p 136.

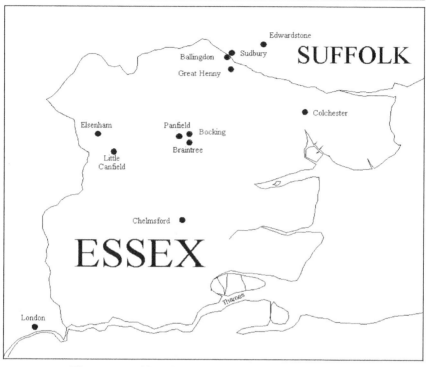

Figure 57 - Sites in Essex associated with George

By 1510, the haberdashers had evidently relinquished the term "merchant." So, it is likely that George had some sort of workshop and/or store and, thus, it is not surprising that he would settle first in Braintree (Figure 57), which, although it had only about 500 inhabitants, was growing faster than Bocking. Later he lived in Sudbury, across the border in Suffolk, and, eventually, in Edwardstone, a small village to the east of Sudbury.

Braintree

We have already mentioned Braintree in the previous chapter, because of its close connection to Bocking and even to Panfield. The name first appears in *Domesday* as *Branchetreu*, but there is little agreement as to its derivation. Ekwall says that the first syllable is probably a personal name, possibly related to *Branuc*, and the second syllable comes from the Old English *treo* the word for *tree.*[1] Quin, on the other hand, offers the explanation that the origin of the name is Celtic. The Celtic name for a settlement was *trev*, and their word for a judge or judgment was *brehon.* So, *Brehontrev* could have meant a place of judgment, later becoming *Branchetreu* and, ultimately, *Braintree.* Or, Quin adds, the name may derive from the Celtic term for rising ground, *bunk* or *bank,* so that *Banktre* would be a settlement on a hill. And that would be a fitting description for what is now the center of town.[2]

1550 We are also indebted to Quin for the following very brief history of Braintree. The main manor in Braintree, the Bishop's Manor of Raines, remained in the hands of the Bishops of London until 1550. The nine-year-old King Edward VI, who must have been about the same age as our George, had just succeeded to the throne on the death of his father, Henry VIII. Bishop Ridley gave the manor to the young king who, in turn, granted it to Lord Rich, who had played a part in the trial and execution of Sir Thomas More.[3]

1553 Edward VI died and the crown passed briefly to Lady Jane Grey. After just two weeks, Edward's half-sister, Mary I, became queen. The next year, she married Philip of Spain. It was she who had Bishop Ridley, the last bishop resident in Braintree, burned at the stake.

1159 In 1559, the year that George's father, Roger[C] died, Queen Elizabeth I succeeded Mary, and England entered a long period of wars, growth, and power. The population had doubled to four million since the days of William[F]. This was the time of William Shakespeare, Francis Bacon, and Sir Walter Raleigh. The Anglican church was re-established, and now it was the Roman Catholics who were persecuted.

1. Ekwall, *op.cit.*
2. Quin, *op.cit.*, p. 1.
3. *ibid.*, p. 15.

Figure 58 - St. Michael's Church, Braintree
(Photo courtesy of David Mansell Photography, Braintree, www.esseximages.co.uk)

There was important legislation affecting labor conditions, currency reform, agriculture, commerce, and manufacturing. And, in Essex, it was the time of Robert Devereux, second earl of Essex, first a favorite of the queen but finally executed for conspiring against her. Elizabeth was queen during almost all of George's adult life, dying only two years before he did.

Braintree's first church was on Chapel Hill near the Bishop's manor house. The present church, St. Michael's (Figure 58), dates from about 1200. There are even Roman bricks in the east wall of the chancel and in the base of the tower. Braintree also had a school taught by a teacher who received £5 a year for his services, which also included assisting the parish curate.[1] George was

1. *ibid.*, p. 30.

probably a parishioner of St. Michael's, but he wasn't married there.

1574 On 13 September 1574, George Fytche of "Braintrye" was granted a London license to marry "Johanna" Thurgood, spinster of "Ellesan."[1] "Johanna" means Joan and "Ellesan" is almost certainly Elsenham, a small village northeast of Stansted Mountfitchet (Figures 57 and 59). She was the daughter of Nicholas Thurgood of Battles in Manuden, another small

Figure 59 - St. Mary the Virgin Church, Elsenham
(Photo courtesy of David Mansell Photography, Braintree, www.esseximages.co.uk)

village slightly northwest of Stansted Mountfitchet. Thurgood is mentioned in several land transactions. The marriage took place at Little Canfield (Figures 57 and 15), home of George's uncle William, according to the parish register there.

1578 Four years later, George made the first of a great many property purchases; he bought a house and garden in Braintree.

13 Apr. 1578 Final agreement made from Easter Day in 15 days, 20 Eliz. between George Fytche, plaintiff, and Joseph mann, deforciant of 1 messuage and 1 garden, etc. in Branktre alias Brayntre. Whereupon a plea, etc. J. has acknow-

1. Little Canfield Parish Register.

ledged the said tenements to be the right of G. as those which he has of the gift of J. And those he (J.) has remised and quitclaimed from himself and his heirs to G. and his heirs against J. and his heirs for ever. And for this acknowledgment G. has given to J. £40 sterling. Essex. Proclamations endorsed.[1]

In the last chapter, we learned, from a will of one John 1585 Lagden, that George's brothers, Richard and William, were living in Bradford Street houses, owned by Mr. Lagden. Eight years before Lagden died, however, George also had dealings with him.

G. Fytche of Branktre, Essex, haberdasher, acknowledges himself to owe to John Lagden of Panfild, Essex, yeoman, and Margery L. his wife £140 23 Apr. 27 Eliz. Conditioned for voidance upon payment of an annuity of £15 during the lives of the said John and M. and the longer liver of them in two yearly payments (detailed) at the dwelling house of Richard Fytche commonly called the Blackhouse in Bredforde Streate in the parish of Bockinge.[2]

It appears that George has perhaps leased or bought property from the Lagdens and has promised to pay them with a twice yearly annuity or rent of 15 pounds. And the payments are to be made at brother Richard's house. Similarly, in February, brother William also acknowledged owing Lagden the same amount.[3]

In late 1586, George bought two properties in Bocking. 1586 The first transaction was in May, the second in December. From the descriptions, it sounds as though the two pieces may have been adjacent to each other.

To all the faithful in Christ to whom this present writing shall come Thomas Tylson of Bockyng in the county of Essex husbondman sends everlasting greeting in the Lord Know ye that I the aforesaid Thomas Tylson in consideration of £10

1. Bundle 120, East. 20 Eliz., no.6, Feet of Fines, Elizabeth C.P.25 (2), in M.F.C., *op.cit.*, Ewen Vol. C, f.343.
2. C54, 1220, m. 22., Recognizances On Close Rolls (C54), M.F.C., *op.cit.*, f. 423.
3. C54, 1222, m.26., *ibid.*, ff. 423,4.

paid to me by George Fytche of Branktrye haberdasher by these presents have given, granted, sold, bargained, enfeoffed, and by this present writing have confirmed to him All that piece of my land lying in the parish of Bockyng upon the Hill there namely between land now or lately of William Warde (as in the right of his wife) on the one part and the road there leading from the highway as far as the mill called 'Harry's Mylle' on the other part, one head thereof abuts upon land of Edward Thorsbye, armiger, called Chyleland, but the other head abuts upon a garden of John Hodge And it contains by estimation one rood of land or more or less which lately was of Robert Hodge deceased. And also I have given a parcel of my garden with a stable and one house called 'Le Shedd' lying in Bockyng between the tenement and garden of John Hodge and the road aforesaid on the other part, one head thereof abuts upon the highway leading from Branktrye towards Hawsted but the other head thereof abuts upon the piece of land aforesaid. Which certain piece of land and parcel of garden I had lately to me and my heirs of the gift of John Hodge the elder lately of Bockyng, clother and John Hodge the younger, his son, as by their charter. 7 Feb. 18 Eliz. (1576) more fully appears To have and to hold to the use of George Fytche for ever of the chief lords of that fee. (Warranty by Thomas Tylson against him and his heirs) Testimonium. Given 1 May 28 Eliz. (1586)

Endorsed: Estate, seisin and possession delivered and taken in the presence of John Davys, John Fytch, John Sp'hawke and John Baker.[1]

This property consisted of a rood of land, a part of Tylson's garden, a stable, and a house with the wonderful name of "Le Shedd." Since it bordered the road to "Hawsted" (Halstead), it must have been on the northwest side of Bocking. The "John Fytch" who was one of the witnesses may have been George's oldest brother. The feoffment was accompanied by a bond of 20 marks which Tylson put up,

1. *ibid.*, ff. 433,4.

... Conditioned for voidance upon saving George Fytche harmless from incumbrances, and for quiet enjoyment without disturbance of Margaret, wife of Thomas Tylson, etc.[1]

This probably doesn't mean that George should *expect* Margaret to disturb his quiet enjoyment. It just protects him from any claim she, as the wife of Tylson, might make on the property. Just nine days after buying the property, George turned right around and leased it back to Tylson.

Indenture made 10 May 28 Eliz. (1586) between George Fytche of Branktrye, Essex, haberdasher, of the one party and Thomas Tylson of Bockyng, husbondman of the other party Witnesses that George Fitche for good causes, etc. has demised, etc. to Thomas Tylson All that his tenement with the houses, etc. purchased from Thomas Tylson and in his tenure in Bocking (reserving trees, etc.) To hold to Thomas Tylson from the feast of the Annunciation of our Lady last past for fourteen years paying 20s. yearly, etc. Covenant by George Fytche to keep in repair and to pay outgoing rents. Covenant by Thomas Tylson to give George Fitche the first offer of buying the lease. Seal wanting. Endorsed.[2]

Since George himself lived in Braintree and Tylson evidently continued to occupy the property in question, it seems likely that George bought this Bocking property (and the next one) simply as an investment. In December, he bought the neighboring Hodge land.

To all the faithful in Christ to whom this present writing shall come. John Hodge of Bockyng, Essex, clother sends everlasting greeting in our Lord Know ye that I the aforesaid John Hodge in consideration of £16 paid to me by George Fytch of Branktre haberdasher by these presents have sold and enfeoffed and by this my present writing have confirmed to him All that my tenement with garden adjacent situate within the parish of Bockyng namely between the tenement

1. *ibid.*
2. *ibid.*, ff. 434, 5.

and garden of Thomas Tylson of the one part and the tenement and garden of William Warde (that he had lately and
holds in right of his wife) on the other part, one head thereof
abuts upon the Hill there but the other head abuts upon the
highway leading from Branktre towards Halstead And also
a gutter called 'le gutterwaye' for running water from a new
tenement there under 'le evesdroppe' on the south part of the
adjacent tenement Also all that annuity or yearly rent of 4d.
issuing from a tenement late of Thomas Tylson. All and
singular of which premises I had lately to me and my heirs
of the gift of Hercules Steven of Bockyng, clother as by his
charter 17 November last more fully appears. To have and
to hold to the use of George Fytch for ever of the chief and
lords of that fee (Warranty by John Hodge against him and
his heirs) Testimonium. Given 8 December 29 Eliz. (1586).
Mark H. Fragment of seal.

Endorsed: Estate, seisin and peaceable possession delivered
and taken in the presence of John Davye, Peter Ramse, John
Sp'hawke and others.[1]

This feoffment is accompanied by a bond of the same date
given by Hodge to George in the amount of 40 marks. It is
conditioned for voidance,

... upon saving George Fytche harmless from incumbrances
(dower of Mary Fayerwether, mother-in-law to John Hodge,
excepted); for further assurance by himself and Jane his wife;
delivery of deeds; and quiet enjoyment.[2]

This time, there is an exception to the bond to hold harmless:
Hodge and his wife, Jane, evidently cannot guarantee against a
possible claim by his mother-in-law for her widow's dower.

1586/7 At the turn of the year, George is involved in further dealing
with the Hodges, this time with Hercules Steven (mentioned
as the previous owner of the Hodge land) and the Fayerweth-
ers (whose claim Hodge could not bond against). The follow-

1. *ibid.*, ff. 435,6.
2. *ibid.*

ing document is a "final agreement," presumably clearing up the loose ends.

> Final agreement made from St. Hilary in 15 days, 29 Eliz. Between George Fytche, plaintiff, and John Hodge and Joan, his wife, Hercules Steven and Agnes, his wife, and Daniel Fayerwether and Mary, his wife, deforciants of 1 messuage, 1 garden, and 4 pence of rents, etc. in Bockynge. Whereupon a plea, etc. Deforciants have acknowledged the said tenements, etc. to be the right of G. as those which he has of their gift. And those they have remised and quitclaimed from them and their heirs to G. and his heirs for ever. Warranty of Deforciants for themselves and the heirs of John to G. and his heirs against Deforciants and the heirs of John for ever. And for this acknowledgment, etc. G. has given to Deforciants £40 sterling. Essex. Proclamations endorsed.[1]

George didn't hold on to the pieces he bought in 1586 from Hodge and Tylson. He sold them in 1588 to Robert Cotwyn of Colchester.

1588

> To all (men) faithful in Christ to whom this present writing shall come George Fitche of Branktry, Essex, haberdasher sends everlasting greeting in our Lord Know ye that I the aforesaid George Fitche in consideration of £40 paid to me by Robert Cotwyn of Colchester yeoman by these presents have given and granted enfeoffed and by this my present writing have confirmed to him
>
> Parcels as in Hodge to Fytch, 8 Dec. 1586
> Parcels as in Tylson to Fytch, 1 May 1586
>
> Which certain messuage I the aforesaid George Fitche lately had to me and my heirs by a fine levied in fifteen days of Easter, 29 Eliz. (1587) between me the aforesaid George Fitche, plaintiff, and John Hodge and Joan, his wife, Hercules Steven and Agnes, his wife, and Daniel Fayerweather and Mary, his wife, deforciants, as by the fine and a charter more fully appears. To hold of the lords of the fee (Warranty:

1. Bundle 122, Hil. 29 Eliz., no.32, *ibid.*, f. 347.

Testimonium) 10 June 30 Eliz. (1588) (Signed) Georg Fytch. Fragment of seal, device.[1]

1590 This feoffment was also accompanied by a bond for £60. Two and a half years later, George bought a fourteen acre farm in Bocking.

> 18 Nov. 1590 Final agreement made on the Octave of St. Martin, 33 Eliz. Between George Fitche, plaintiff, and Richard Ussher the elder and Joan, his wife, and Richard Ussher the younger, deforciants of 1 barn, 12 ac. of land, and 2 ac. of moor, etc. in Bockinge. Whereupon a plea, etc. Deforciants have acknowledged the said tenements, etc. to be the right of George as those which he has of their gift. And those they have remised and quitclaimed from them and their heirs to G. and his heirs for ever. Warranty by Deforciants for themselves and the heirs of Richard Ussher the younger to G. F. and his heirs against Deforciants and the heirs of R. U. the younger for ever. And for this acknowledgment, etc. G. F. has given to Deforciants £80 sterling. Essex. Proclamations endorsed.[2]

1591/2 George was summoned to serve on a jury panel at Chelmsford, for the Quarter Sessions to be held on 13 January 1591/2.

> Jury panel for Hundred of Hinkford
> Thursday after the feast of St. Michael, 1591. Writ, witnessed by Sir Thomas Mildmaye, knight, at Chelmsford to summon the chief constables and sub-constables of every hundred, 18 lawful men of every liberty and 24 lawful men of every hundred to the Epiphany Sessions next coming, and to make proclamation that all those should be there who wish to enquire concerning any cause. Endorsed by Richard Warren, esquire, Sheriff, that the writ has been executed as within-written.[3]

1. *ibid.*, ff. 436, 7.
2. Bundle 123m Mich. 32 & 33 Eliz., Feet of Fines, Elizabeth C.P.25 (2), *ibid.*, ff. 372,3.
3. E.R.O. Q/SR119/7 and /10.

The Quarter Sessions were county courts which, as their name implies, were held four times a year (at Easter, Midsummer, Michaelmas, and Epiphany) to hear cases of murder, riot, theft, assault, poaching, etc. They did not handle civil cases. George's name is listed among the "lawful" men, summoned for jury duty.

There is an interesting reference to George in the records 1594 of the General Sessions held on 4 and 5 July 1594 [36 Elizabeth].

> General Sessions of the Peace held at Chelmsford on Thursday and Friday after the feast of Saints Peter and Paul, before John, Suffragen Bishop of Colchester, Sir Thomas Myldmaye, knight, Henry Myldmaye, John Ive, Peter Tuke, Thomas Mildmaye of Barnes, William Towse, Edward Ellyott, Andrew Pascall and Robert Leight, esquires.
>
> Recognizances of those licensed to keep alehouses:
>
> 18 May 1594. ... and of George Fitch of Braintree, haberdasher, and Nicholas Wilbore of the same, draper, for Robert Ardlie of the same, clothier; ... Taken before Sir Edmund Huddilston, knight, Christopher Chibborne and Thomas Bendyshe, esquires.[1]

This probably does not mean that George added alehousekeeping to his list of jobs. What this document is saying is that at a session on 18 May before Huddilston, Chibborne, and Bendyshe, George Fitch and Nicholas Wilbore vouched for Robert Ardlie, a clothier who also, evidently, kept an alehouse. And the 4 and 5 July session was a higher level of court which simply approved the action of the Huddilston group.

A little more than seven years after he bought the house 1594/5 in Braintree, George sold it. In the interim, it seems to have added a stable.

> 20 Jan. 1594/5 Final agreement made on the Octave of St Hilary, 37 Eliz. between Joseph Manne, plaintiff, and George

1. E.R.O. Q/SR128/73-6.

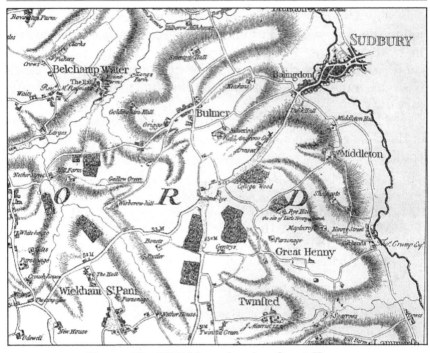

Figure 60 - 1777 Map, showing Great Henny
(1777 Chapman & André Map, reproduced courtesy of the Essex Record Office)

Fytche and Joan, his wife, deforciants of 1 messuage, 1 stable and 1 garden, etc. in Brancktrye. Whereupon a plea, etc. Deforciants acknowledged the said tenements, etc. to be the right of Joseph as those which he has of their gift. And those they have remised and quitclaimed from them and their heirs to Joseph and his heirs for ever. Warranty by Deforciants for themselves and the heirs of G. to Joseph and his heirs against G. and J. and the heirs of G. for ever. And for this acknowledgment Joseph has given to Deforciants £80 sterling. Essex. Proclamations endorsed.[1]

1599 It may be that at about this time, George and Joan were moving to Sudbury in Suffolk, because first he sold the

1. Bundle 124, Hil. 37 Eliz., M.F.C., *op.cit.*, Ewen Vol. C, ff. 374,5.

property in Bocking and the next year bought some land near the Essex-Suffolk border.

> 11 June 1599. Final agreement made on the Morrow of Holy Trinity, 41 Eliz. between Jonas Windell, pl., and George Fitche and Joan, his wife, def. of 1 messuage, 1 barn, 1 garden, 10 ac. of land, 2 ac. of pasture, and 2 ac. of moor, etc. in Bocking. Deforciants have acknowleged the right of Jonas as of their gift. And those, they have remised and quitclaimed from them and their heirs to Jonas and his heirs for ever. Warranty of Deforciants and the heirs of George for ever. And for this acknowledgement, etc., Jonas has given to G. and J. £60 sterling.[1]

In 1600, George bought land in the manor of Great Henny (Figures 57 and 60) from a London grocer, Roger Gwynne who had bought the manor from the Cornwallis family.[2] Figure 61 shows just the upper left of this large document, the earliest one we have for this line. The entire transaction is set out in an Appendix to this volume, but the highlights are as follows:

> Indenture made 30 November, 43 Eliz. between Roger Gwynne, citizen and grocer of London and lord and owner of the Manors of Great Heney and Pebmershe, Essex, of the one part and George Fitche of Sudburie, Suffolk, mercer, of the other part. In consideration of £26 13s. 4d. the said Roger Gwynne has demised to George Fitch All those four several pieces of meadow in Great Heney and Pebmarshe. To have and to hold the said four pieces of meadow, etc. to George Fitche, etc., from the feast of the Annunciation of the B.V.M. last (25 Mar.) for one thousand years without impeachment of waste yielding 3s. per annum, and suit of court, etc. or in default 3d. Covenant for quiet enjoyment. Covenant by George Fitche to pay 12d. at every alienation.[3]

1. Essex. Proc. (Bundle 125, Trin. 41 Eliz.), *ibid.*, f. 379.
2. Morant, *op.cit.*, p. 273.
3. E.R.O. D/DH VI.C.57.

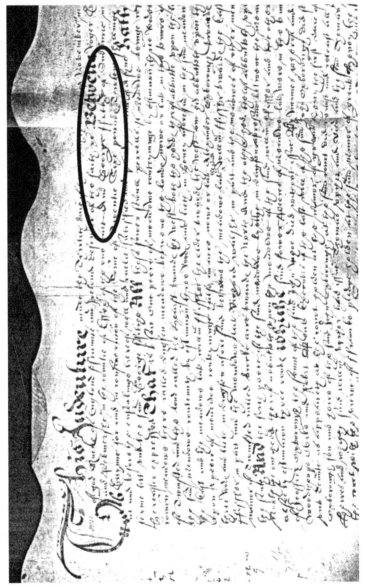

Figure 61 - 1600 Deed, Manor of Great Henny
(Cat. No. D/DH vi.c.57 reproduced by courtesy of the Essex Record Office)

The 1600 Map

In the same year that George acquired the four parcels described above, a map (Figure 62) was drawn up, showing the lands that Roger Gwynn held in the manors of Great Henny and Bulmer. Comparing this map to the 1777 map of Figure 60, it is quite easy to match landmarks; for example, the village of Bulmer on Figure 60 is the area at the upper left of Figure 62, and one can follow the road down and to the right into the larger area of Great Henny. Further south, on both maps, is Twinsted. The remarkable 1600 map shows twenty parcels of land that were leased by George Fitch. Although indecipherable in this small reproduction of the complete map, these assignments can more easily be seen in the enlargements of Figures 63 and 64. The four that are cited in the 1600 transaction (Figure 63) are in the southeast next to the river. You can easily find *Springolds*, and there is what appears to be a house at the eastern end of the upper part of *The Pilgrim Springoldes*. Further east are at least two more pieces with George's name in them; one vertically from the Upper corner of the large dark area, and the other runs horizontally out to the river. Unfortunately, we do not have the deeds for the other sixteen plots, shown in Figure 64.

The document from which these reproductions were made was not the actual map itself. Though at one time deposited at the Essex Record Office, the original has long since been withdrawn by its owner. It is described as:

> Great Henny and Bulmer, 1600
> The Mannor Henny Magna percell of the Possessions of Roger Gwin of London, gent. W[us] Sands descripsit. 13.3 in. to 1 m. 35 X 50. About 1500a.[1]

The Latin phrase "W[us] Sands descripsit" means "drawn by William Sands." The map is remarkable in several respects. When the author visited the area, we had no road map that showed as

---

1. Essex Record Office, D/DU 332/9A Photograph: Ph 3/10A. Withdrawn by depositor Jan. 1965.

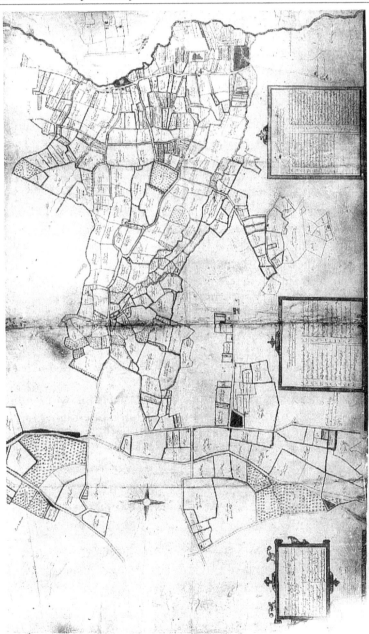

Figure 62 - 1600 Map, Manor of Great Henny

(Cat. No. D/DH vi.c.57 reproduced by courtesy of the Essex Record Office)

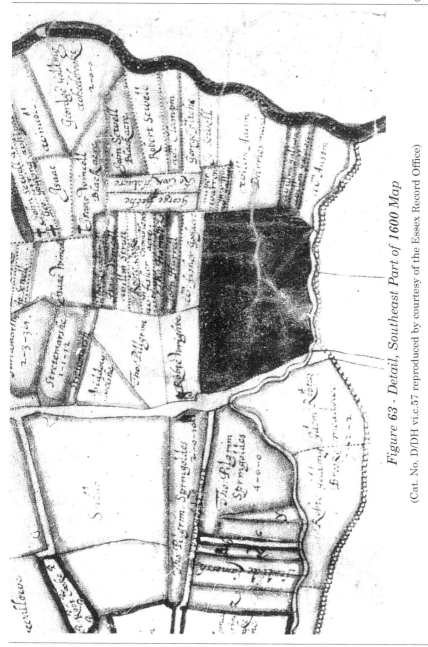

Figure 63 - Detail, Southeast Part of 1600 Map

(Cat. No. D/DH vi.c.57 reproduced by courtesy of the Essex Record Office)

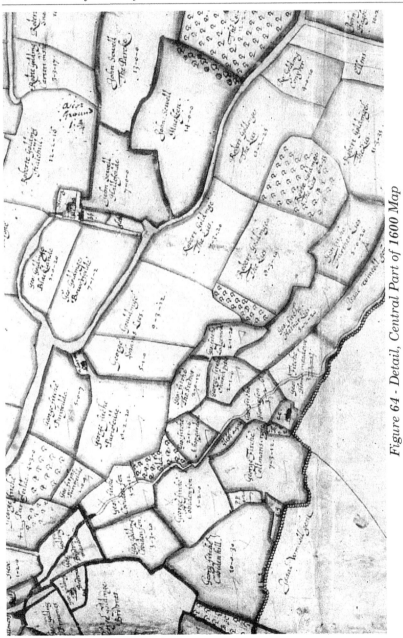

Figure 64 - Detail, Central Part of 1600 Map

(Cat. No. D/DH vi.c.57 reproduced by courtesy of the Essex Record Office)

Figure 65 - St. Mary's Church and Entry Gate, Great Henny
(Photos courtesy of David Mansell Photography, Braintree, www.esseximages.co.uk)

much detail as the 1600 map. So we used *it* to navigate the small roads through the hedgerows of Great Henny! Nothing appears to have changed in the ensuing nearly 400 years. We were able to find the small church of St. Mary's (Figure 65), shown on the maps at the upper right of the large "loop" (see Figures 60 and 63). We were even able to stand—without any doubt as to where we were—in one of George Fitch's fields (at the southwest corner of the loop road, where "a barn" is shown). The bucolic view down toward the stream that drains into the Stour can be seen in Figure 66.

Each parcel on the map is marked with its size in three numbers. Thus the piece called *Collmans crofte* at the lower left of Figure 64 is marked "7-3-12." The first number indicates it contains 7 acres. The second number means 3 roods, where a rood is a fourth of an acre. And the last number means 12 perches, where a perch is a fortieth of a rood, or 1/160th of an acre. In addition to the larger parcels with names like *Parifeilde* (which may be derived from *praiere* or meadow land), *Cobiden fen*, and *Collmans crofte*, two are marked *Hether Lies* and *Further Lies*. *Hether* is actually *Hither*, and *Hether Lies* meant *near field*.

Figure 66 - Field and River, George's Land, Great Henny

Further Lies meant *far field*. On the bank of the river there is a piece marked *hopgarden* and next to it, *The Stewes*. A *hop* was an enclosed piece of marshy land, a *stewe* could mean either a pond in which fish are kept until needed for the table or, more likely in this case, a breeding place for pheasants. Below that are a couple of acres called *Church pitle*. A *pitle* (also spelled *pightle*, *pigtail*, and *pingle*) is a small piece of land in the open fields or a small enclosed plot. Straddling the river itself or running alongside it are two pieces called *Cobiden fen* and one called *Home fen*. A *fen* is a low area subject to flooding, in other words a marshy area.

At the lower left, between *Collmans croft* and *Home meadowe* are two small parcels, the one on the left showing some trees and labeled *E*, and the one on the right showing a house and labeled *c.c.* To the lower right of *Cobiden fen* is one labeled *d.d.*, and between *Cobiden hill* and *Collmans croft* is a fourth, labeled *p.p.* These are so labeled because they are too small to contain a complete description. Two boxes of keys at the bottom of the map

(Figure 52) identify "The names of the Owners of the percells of land which the letters underwritten are inserted [?] the names also and contents of the saide percells." The key identifies *E* as "Geo. Fitche orchard by his tenemente co:," *c.c.* as "Geo. Fitche tenemente Colliers co: cont: 0-3-20" *d.d.* as "Idem Geo. Cobidenfen co: cont. 2-0-10," and *p.p.* as "George Fitche a hopgarden co: by Cobiden hill," where the abbreviation "co:" undoubtedly means the land is copyhold of the manor. Thus, in addition to *Springolds*, George also owned a house called *Colliers*. Near the house lot are the *Home meadowe* and aforementioned *Homefen*.

Sudbury

The 1600 lease says that George was now a mercer, living in Sudbury, across the border in county Suffolk. Bromley has this to say about the occupation of mercer:

> Mercery was formerly a generic term, derived from the Latin *merx* (merchandise), which covered a wide variety of small goods, mostly for apparel and personal use. In the Middle Ages these were hawked by the pedlar and chapman who sold them from village to village and displayed them at fairs. Fine fabrics, damask, satin, silk, linen, hats and trinkets were originally among their stock-in-trade. ... The activities of the Mercers impinged especially upon those of the Haberdashers, to an extent that their wardens are found jointly challenging the bona fides of a freeman of another guild who had used the "art of Mercers and Haberdashers".[1]

There is no way to know why George moved from Braintree to Sudbury, but we can speculate that it may have had to do with changing his business from haberdasher to mercer, or it may have been because of his real estate transactions in the manor of Great Henny, which is much closer to Sudbury than to Braintree (see Figure 57). And, since by 1600 George was about fifty years old, it's even conceivable that he had retired to live off the income from his various properties. Even though this document and his will

1. Bromley, *op.cit.*, p. 168.

Figure 67 - St. Gregory's Church, Sudbury

refer to him as a *mercer*, his son Joseph's entry in a Cambridge University alumni book a few years later referred to George as a *yeoman*, which as we have seen, was a land-owner, just beneath the rank of gentleman. At any rate, he does appear to have moved to Sudbury, county Suffolk, some time prior to 1600.

The Sudbury name goes back to Saxon times when it was *Sudberi* in the Anglo-Saxon Chronicle of 798. It became *Sudbyrig* by about 995 in the *Cartularium saxonicum*, and it was *Sutberia* in the *Domesday* book of 1086. The meaning appears to be *Southern burg* where *burg* is the Old English for a fortified place.[1] The town is in the south of Suffolk, and there are traces of earthwork surrounding the town.

St. Gregory's church (Figure 67) also goes back to Saxon times. Two wills, dated 970 and 993, mention it by name. It was

1. Ekwall, *op.cit.*

named for Pope Gregory (590-604) who sent missionaries to Saxon England under St. Augustine, the first Archbishop of Canterbury. In *Domesday*, the church possessed 50 acres of arable land and 25 of meadow. After the Conquest, the manor of Sudbury eventually passed to the de Clare family, whose seat is at Clare not far to the West. They had the advowson of St. Gregory's; that is, they had the right to appoint its vicar and the responsibility to support him. This right eventually passed to Simon of Sudbury, then Bishop of London, who with his brother gave it to the Fellow and Wardens of the College they were founding. The restored brick gateway of the College can still be seen opposite the west end of the church.[1]

It is not clear when George sold the greater number of 1602 lots at Great Henny. But, he sold the four small parcels, including "the tenement Springoldes," not long after acquiring them, to a John Wilkins on 24 December 1602.[2]

Remarriage

We can speculate that by this time George's wife Joan had died. And he may have sold the Great Henny lands because he was moving to Edwardstone, a few miles to the east of Sudbury (Figure 57). Edwardstone was an old village (it was *Eduardestuna* in *Domesday*, probably from *Eadweard's tun*, or 'Eadward's village'[3]). There he remarried. His second wife was Bridget, the widow first of John Goss of Edwardstone and then of John French of the same village. Since French's will is dated 21 January 1601/2, she and George must have been married sometime after that.

This second marriage for George lasted only about a year, because Bridget died on 29 August 1603 and was buried the next day at Edwardstone, perhaps in the churchyard of the parish

1. *St. Gregory's Sudbury*, (Lavenham, Suffolk, England: The Lavenham Press Ltd.), pp. 1,2.
2. E.R.O. D/DC 23/377.
3. Ekwall, *op.cit.*

Figure 68 - St. Mary the Virgin Church, Edwardstone

church shown in Figure 68. George then married for a third time
— another widow, named Joane Taylor.

1604 On 13 April 1604, George and his son Thomas sold to one
John Sampford, some land in Elsenham that George's first
wife, Joan, had inherited from her father, Nicholas Thurgood. The indenture[1] is of particular interest because it bears
the signatures of both George (Figure 69) and Thomas (Figure 70). Note that George, in a cursive hand, uses the older
"*ff*" and Thomas, who prints his name, uses an "*F*" —and a
very fancy flourish.

The Will

1605 George was probably in his early fifties when he died. His
will is dated 12 May 1605 and was probated in the Preroga-

1.   Courtesy of the Marc Fitch Collection, Essex Record Office.

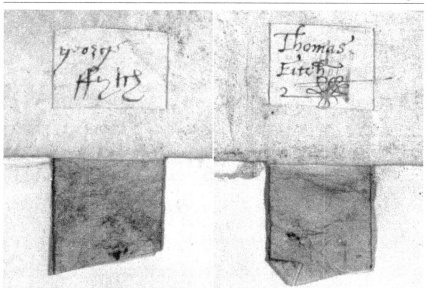

Figure 69 - Signature of George Fytch   *Figure 70 - Signature of Thomas Fitch*

tive Court of Canterbury on June 18th.[1] In the court copy, the first few lines of which are reproduced in Figure 71, the will is one continuous paragraph—with very little punctuation. Because the text is so long, so difficult to read, and so replete with legalisms, we will include a transcription of only the first few lines here, together with a summary of the various bequests, and to put the complete text in an *Appendix* corresponding to this chapter.

> In the Name of God Amen The twelveth day of May in the yeare of our Lorde god one thousand six hundred and five I George Fytch of Edwardston in the County of Suff:" Mercer beinge sick in body but yet of perfect mynde and memory Thanks be to god therefore; utterly renouncing all former wylls and Testaments whatsoever heretofore by me made, doe nowe ordayne make and declare this my present testament...[2]

---

1. 49 Hayes.
2. Prerogative Court of Canterbury (P.C.C.) 49 Hayes. Cat. No. PROB 11/105.

Figure 71 - Will of George Fytch
(Courtesy of the Public Record Office)

One thing to note is that this is another death-bed will; it was evidently not the custom to make a will ahead of time. The first paragraph confirms our speculation that George was living in Edwardstone, county Suffolk, and he was still a mercer. He was clearly a trinitarian Christian and wanted to be buried as such. He then starts his bequests—first to his last wife, Joane. She is to get £40 in two installments. But, she is also to receive an annuity of £5 a year for the next seven years, again in six-month installments. This latter is to be drawn from the income earned by his estate in Edwardstone. If £5 a year doesn't sound like very much, remember that the school teacher only earned that much and that a maid servant's wages were only three shillings a year. Next in the will, George returns to Joane the "downe bed" and other household things she brought with her to their marriage. Then comes the standard catch: she is to receive these legacies on the condition that she does not make a widow's claim for a third of his estate.

Next we learn that Thomas is the oldest son and, after twelve years, he is to receive the entire Edwardstone estate. Since the "landes pastures meadowes" are not specified as located else- where (e.g. Great Henny), we must assume that George had more than just a house, i.e. an estate of some size, in Edwardstone. One might wonder why Thomas would have to wait twelve years for his legacy. It may be that George wanted to ensure that the

Figure 72 - Essex-Suffolk Border near Sudbury

younger children would be able to continue to live there with their mother until they were old enough to be on their own.

The will mentions these four younger children: George, Joseph, Arthur, and Fraunces, and we can reasonably assume that at least the sons are listed in order of age. They are to get a total of £73 ("threscore thirtene") 6 shillings and 8 pence. This odd amount is divided up so that George, Arthur, and Fraunces each get £20 and Joseph gets the balance: £13, 6 shillings and 8 pence. Perhaps Joseph had received an advance on his inheritance. At any rate, none of them is to see the money until Thomas takes over the estate twelve years hence.

If Thomas defaults on his filial duty, then George, junior, is to sell the estate, pay the children their due, and turn over the surplus to Thomas. And if George fails to do it, then the other children are to take over. Finally, the intent is not to sell the estate but to pay these legacies plus the funeral and probate expenses for George, senior, out of current income. If there isn't enough to do that, however, then the executors are to sell off the estate to satisfy these needs.

Next, George asks his executors to sell his house and out buildings in Ballingdon, county Essex, a place he bought from Mr. Sheppard there. If you look for Ballingdon on a map, you'll find it in Suffolk, virtually a suburb of Sudbury. But, in those days, Ballingdon *was* in Essex, on the south side of the River Stour which generally formed the boundary between Essex and Suffolk (Figure 57). As Sudbury expanded, however, into a major city, it bridged the river, and in 1905 the county boundary was changed (see Figure 72). Now Ballingdon (or the parish of Ballingdon-cum-Brundon) is in Suffolk.[1] At any rate, the money from the sale is to be used for paying George's debts and legacies.

In addition to the moneys already bequeathed to the younger children, they are to receive still more when they reach adulthood. To his namesake, George, he gives £80, two pairs of sheets, and his own gold ring (with his name) at age 22. Joseph is to receive £50 and two more pairs of sheets, when he reaches 24. Arthur is to get £80 and still another two pairs of sheets at 22. And Fraunces gets the £80, a featherbed, two down pillows, two pairs of sheets, and "my biggest brasse pot"—all at the age of 21. Furthermore, Fraunces gets an annuity of £5 a year until she reaches 21 or gets married, whichever comes first. There is no explanation as to why Joseph is short changed again, nor why he has to wait two more years than his brothers. One possible explanation is that (as we shall see) Joseph was already at Cambridge University by this time and may have had an advance for his tuition and expenses there. A bit later, we learn that the children get the silver spoons that were given to them at their christenings.

George also states that his wife, Joane, and the two youngest children, Arthur and Fraunces, are to continue to live in his

1. Essex Parish Records 1240-1894, Essex Record Office No. 7.

"messuage" (presumably the one at Edwardstone) and that they are to receive sufficient funds for the maintenance of their "diet." After the first six months, Fraunces should continue to live with her mother until she can be "placed in some good and convenient service." And Arthur is to be "bound an apprentice to some good trade or occupacon."

Having taken care of his own wife and children, George turns to others. First, there is a small three shilling, four pence gift to Robert Stebbing, not otherwise identified, but possibly a faithful retainer. Next, the father of his second wife's second husband, i.e. the father of Bridget's second husband John French, will continue to receive the annuity of £6 a year that his son willed to him. John and Robert French (presumably Bridget's children by John French) each get a silver spoon and a "tipped" pot which their father had bequeathed to them. And to Bridget and Suzan Goss, (presumably Bridget's children by her first husband, John Goss) he assigns each a ring according to the will of their step-father, John French.

Then, there is a grandchild, Marie Burgis, who gets £16 and a brasse pot. It isn't clear how this girl comes to be his grandchild. She cannot be the daughter of any of his own children, so it seems likely she is the grandchild of his second or third wife (e.g. if one of the Goss girls had married a Burgis, she could have a child named Marie that George might well consider a grandchild). And there is a final bequest to Sara Taylor, Joane's daughter by her first husband. Sara is to receive 30 shillings.

Everything else, "yardes rights credites cattles and chatteles readye money and plate" are to go first to pay for his funeral and probate and then to be divided up in some way between son Thomas and George's brother William, who are also to be the executors. George evidently signed each page of the will and set his seal on the last page. Unfortunately we cannot see these (could he sign his name or only make a mark?), because what we have is a *copy* of the will in the court record books—copied, in fact, in more than one hand. (It wasn't so long ago that wills and deeds in this country were still laboriously copied over by scriveners in our own Probate Courts.) The will is witnessed by a George Culpeck; a man with only one name–Christopher, yeoman; Phillip Clark, who wrote the will; and Sara Taylor, George's step-daughter. Then the document lists some additions and corrections, made after the will was written, and it is attested to again. The court adds its own coda in Latin that son Thomas and brother William submitted the will for probate.

The Children

George and his first wife, Joan, had five children: four boys and a girl (Figure 73). We know the sequence of the boys: Thomas[A], George, Joseph, and Arthur, but we don't know where Fraunces fits in. She was always listed last in the will, but that may only be because she was a girl. The only birth year we can estimate with any accuracy is that of the third son, Joseph, because we know he was sixteen when he was admitted to college in 1603. That means he was born about 1587. And that means that his two older brothers, Thomas and George had to be born before that. George and Joan were married in 1574, so Thomas must have been born after 1574 and before 1583, because we know he was already at least twenty-two when his father died in 1605.

The second son, George, was still under the age of 22 in 1605, so he could not have been born earlier than 1583. He lived in Much Dunmow. In 1612, he sold his father's estate in Edwardstone to William Ponde for £41. Because he must have been at least 21 for such a transaction, he could not have been born later than 1591. In the transaction we learn that George had "two messuages, one dovecote, two gardens, one orchard, 16 acres of land, 3 acres of meadow, and 10 acres of pasture with appurtenances."[1] George, junior, died, unmarried, in 1614. His younger brother Joseph administered his estate in the Prerogative Court of Canterbury.

---

1. P.R.O., C. P. 25 (2) 356, Mich. 10 James I.

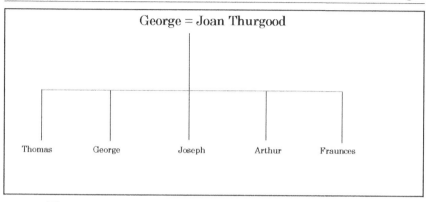

Figure 73 - Family of George, son of Roger and Margaret

The daughter, Fraunces, married 5 February 1606/7, James Stracey. Joseph, the third son, as we have determined, was probably born in 1587. His entry in *Alumni Cantabrigiensis* reads:

> Fitch, Joseph. Adm. pens. (age 16) at Caius, Oct. 7, 1603. S.
> of George, yeoman, of Braintree, Essex. School, Boxford
> Suffolk (Mr. Huggen). Scholar, 1604-6.[1]

Expanding the abbreviations, we learn that, after attending Boxford School in Suffolk (we even learn his teacher's name!), he was admitted at the age of sixteen as a "pensioner" of Caius College, Cambridge. Being a *pensioner* meant simply that he was paying his own way. Later, from 1604 to 1606, he was a "scholar," which meant that he received financial aid toward his costs as a result of merit. It appears, then, that he was the first member of the family to attend a college or university. Note that his father, George, is referred to as a "yeoman," which seems a bit odd, since he spent his life as a haberdasher and mercer.

We know absolutely nothing about the fourth son, Arthur, except that he must have been very young at the time of his

---

1. John Venn and J. A. Venn, *Alumni Cantabrigiensis*, Vo. II (Cambridge, England: University Press, 1922), p. 145.

father's death. His father wanted him to be bound as an apprentice to a trade. In such an arrangement, his family would probably have had to pay an adult workman, a weaver for example, to take on young Arthur as an apprentice. Arthur then would learn the craft or trade under the guidance of his master for as long as it took to learn to do satisfactory work.

7

Thomas^A

T homas Fitch, the eldest son of George^B and Joan, was
born, probably in Braintree, some time between 1574
when his parents were married and 1583 (because his father's will in 1605 treats him as an adult of at least twenty-
two). He inherited his father's property in Edwardstone and,
presumably, shared in proceeds from the sale of another
house in Ballingdon. By that time, however, he himself was
living and working in Bocking, just north of Braintree.
Figure 74 locates these and a number of other towns with
which Thomas would be associated. There are a number of
records that indicate that Thomas was a clothier, like three
of his uncles before him—and several of his children after
him—so we should now look more closely at why so many
members of the family were engaged in this business.

Wool Cloth Manufacture in Essex

We are indebted to Bowden,[1] Hoffman,[2] and Quin[3] for the
following information on the woolen cloth industry in southeast
England, particularly in the Bocking-Braintree area of Essex and
in Sudbury, the main Suffolk center. It is likely that from Saxon

---

1. Peter J. Bowden, *The Wool Trade in Tudor and Stuart England* (London: Macmillan, 1962), pp. 47-55.
2. Hoffman, *op.cit.*, pp. 44-47.
3. Quin, *op.cit.*, pp. 50-75.

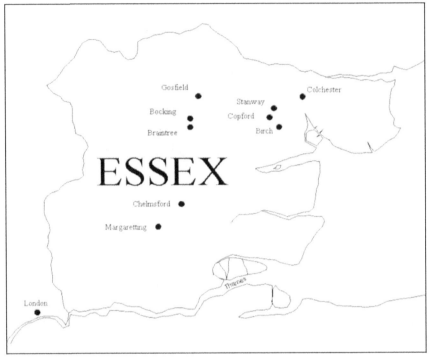

Figure 74 - Sites in Essex associated with Thomas

times onward there was a native cloth industry; there were certainly plenty of sheep recorded in the *Domesday* survey. As early as 1303, Bocking had a "fulling" mill (see right edge of Figure 48) for treating woven cloth. In the late fifteenth century, Essex possessed a considerable woolen industry, and Suffolk was the largest cloth-producing county in England. The products made in Essex were largely broadcloths—not the cotton shirting we think of today, but a wool fabric, tightly woven in a plain or twill pattern, and having a sheen. In Suffolk, the materials ranged from good-quality broadcloth to very inferior fabrics known as "sett clothes." By 1556, there were three fulling mills in Bocking. During the late sixteenth and early seventeenth centuries—the period we are particularly interested in—the broadcloth industry had been largely replaced by the manufacture of worsted, made from long-staple wool that had been combed and then firmly twisted into yarn.

Most of the work was carried out in people's homes. First the raw wool had to be combed. Then the combed wool was spun into yarn, and the yarn, in turn, was woven into cloth. The cloth then went out of the home to a mill for "fulling," which Bromley describes as follows:

> After the weaver had produced the raw cloth it was subjected to a process of cleansing and thickening, or fulling. This was effected by trampling the cloth in water, cleansing with grease-absorbent fuller's earth, and scouring with teasel, or thistle heads to remove loose particles and raise a nap. The material was then passed to the shearman who cut the raised fibres to produce a fine, even finish to its surface.[1]

Figure 75 shows the use of teasels. Finally, it was sometimes dyed. Over time, these several steps in the manufacturing process began to be coordinated by enterprising men, known as *clothiers*, who bought the raw wool, parceled it out to the workers in their homes, collected the woven cloth, and put it through the fulling mill and dye works. As Sir Anthony Wagner describes it:

> The change came gradually, by several roads, but in the 16th century it was complete and a wealthy class of capitalist clothiers, who organized the whole manufacture was seen to have reduced the weavers, fullers, spinners and shearmen to dependence.[2]

This was a period in which many cloth merchants made vast fortunes and turned themselves into "landed gentlemen." Certainly, both George the father and Thomas the son were very well off, considering the evidence provided in their wills. Unfortunately, while the clothiers grew rich, many of their workers starved. There were rules protecting these workers—mostly

1. Bromley, *op.cit.*, p. 45.
2. Wagner, *op.cit.*, p. 151.

Figure 75 - Raising the Nap of Wool Cloth with Teasels
(From *The Armorial Bearings of the Guilds of London* by J. Bromley,
courtesy of Frederic Warne & Co. Ltd.)

women—from some of the more venal clothiers. The Colchester
corporation, for example, passed a regulation that stated:

> Further for the benefit of the trade and the town, it is and
> has been a custom that any inhabitant exercising the afore-
> said art or mystery [cloth-making] and desiring to expose
> before his own dwelling, wool, either for combing or spinning,
> ought to expose such wool according to certain weights em-
> ployed in the town during the whole time aforesaid, namely
> for women combers of wool, by the weight there commonly
> called a kembyng ston [combing stone] of five pounds and not
> more; and for women spinners, by the weight there called a
> spynning ston, of four pounds and a half and not more, and
> that for each kembyng ston, the price for combing be 2d, and
> for each spynning ston 6d. for spinning.[1]

1.   Quin, *op.cit.*, p. 52.

It would be difficult to estimate how long it takes to comb five pounds of wool or spin four-and-a-half pounds of yarn, but the evidence is that the daily earnings were on the order of sixpence—insufficient to support a family without supplementary produce from the land. Some clothiers sought to evade even these low piece-rates by having their work done outside the towns, where the rules didn't apply. They employed hundreds of spinners and weavers from the surrounding hamlets. An act in 1552, amended in 1557, nearly put Bocking out of the cloth-making business, because to enforce the corporate town standards no work was to be done outside the corporate or market towns. Bocking was neither (though Braintree qualified as a market town). By dint of heavy lobbying, however, Bocking was exempted from the act in 1558. Bocking was described as a "fayre large Towne ... inhabited of a long time with Clothe makers which have made and dayle do make good and trewe clothe." So Bocking clothiers could continue to exploit the cheap labor of the countryside.

Even with the exemption, however, more and more of the workers were drawn into the town, so that by 1575, the population had reached 1,500, and Bocking was considered second in importance only to Colchester. The problem for these new workers was that the wages had been fixed in terms of the worker who still had a strip of land to farm. The new town dwellers had no such resources, and complaints to the Essex Quarter Sessions were frequent. In April 1599, the Court ordered:

> ... the matter in variance between the clothiers and weavers of Bocking and Braintree shall be referred to my Lord Suffragen, Francis Harvye, John Tyndall, Ralph Wyseman, Henry Maxey and Thomas Walgrave, esquires, to end and determine all controversy between them if they can, and to certify their proceedings at the next Sessions.[1]

---

1. Hoffman, *op.cit.*, p. 45.

About the time Thomas was born, that is in the latter part of the sixteenth century, there was an influx of Flemish and Dutch Protestant craftsmen who were fleeing Spanish religious persecution. They brought with them a new type of cloth—actually called the *New Draperies*. The more formal names for these products were *bays* and *says*. They were lighter in texture than the "old" cloths, and some had been of a chestnut color—hence the name *bays*—although Essex cloth was white. *Bay* was a coarse kind of blanket cloth or *baize*. *Say* was a much finer product, the earliest form of serge. In fact, the Bocking clothiers manufactured a special sort of bay which was famous enough to be called "Bockings," and was regularly exported for sale abroad. Parliament even passed an act in 1557 which referred to the counterfeiting of Bocking (and Braintree) cloth and, in 1572, granted the town the right to use a distinctive seal on its finished product.[1]

Bocking cloths may have been famous, but they were not of very high quality. A London clothworker, in 1632, tried to pass off some bays "of a meaner condition," i.e. Bocking bays, by affixing counterfeit Colchester seals to the goods. He was caught, fined £1,000 (a very large sum of money), condemned to stand in the pillory, had his crime published at Bocking and Colchester, and sent to prison until he should reveal who had made the fake seals. During the trial it was disclosed that Bocking bays fetched a lower price than the Colchester bays, both at home and abroad.

1603   Queen Elizabeth I, "the Virgin Queen," died childless, thus ending the Tudor period in England. She was succeeded by James VI of Scotland, son of Mary Queen of Scots, whom Elizabeth had had beheaded. He became James I of England, Scotland, and Ireland, beginning the Stuart reign that lasted until 1714. Although James was forever memorialized in the King James Version of the Bible, he managed to offend both Protestants and Roman Catholics. He saw the beginnings of colonization in America by some of the same

---

1. E.R.O. Museum Class 37.

Puritans he had persecuted. He asserted his divine right to rule, dissolved Parliament in 1611, and ruled without it for ten years. His extravagance and his refusal to recognize the importance of Parliament furthered discontent and led to the Civil War that followed during the reign of his successor. James was king during much of Thomas' life.

In late May or early June 1605, Thomas' father George **1605** died at Edwardstone in Suffolk. By this time, Thomas was already a young man and, presumably, living and working in Bocking. He was not to receive his inheritance, however, for another twelve years, probably to allow his mother and younger siblings to have the use of the estate.

Thomas is mentioned in the will, dated 10 October **1606** 1606, of his first cousin, once removed, Thomas of Margaretting.This latter Thomas was the son of Roger's brother, Thomas, and the grandson of Thomas and Agnes (See Figure 76). He was married, but had no children. He left his estate to his nephew Thomas, son of his brother Robert or to that Thomas' son Thomas(!), whom he called his "godsonne." In the event neither of them survived, the estate was to go to *our* Thomas. And, finally, if our Thomas wasn't available, the estate was to go to his cousin Thomas, son of his cousin Richard. Since the Thomases ahead of ours were alive and well in 1606, evidently nothing devolved upon Thomas^A. [Note: With all these Thomases about, it is small wonder that an earlier family historian attached our family line to the fifth generation Thomas shown at the bottom center of Figure 76. The only problem was that that Thomas not only didn't live in Bocking—he probably lived in Great Dunmow—but he would have been only twelve years old when he married. Our historian was clearly Bocking up the wrong family tree.]

Other than the mention in his father's and his cousin's **1608** wills, the first record we have for Thomas is an unusual court

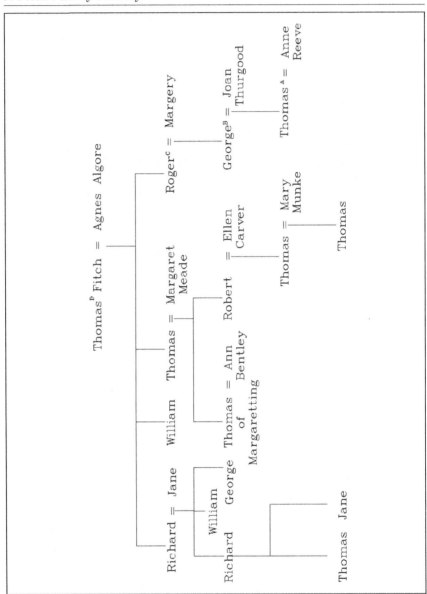

Figure 76 - The "Thomases" of Essex

Figure 77 - Bocking and Gosfield
(1777 Chapman & André Map, reproduced
by courtesy of the Essex Record Office)

*Figure 78 - St. Catherine's
Church, Gosfield*
(Photo courtesy of David Mansell
Photography, Braintree,
www.esseximages.co.uk)

record in which he has been called—probably as a juror—in
an assault and battery case against a fellow clothier:

> Session held on 7 July 6 James I
> Examinations taken before Sir Edward Boteler, knt. and
> Richard Franck, esq.
> 4 July. Gaol Delivery of Colchester Castle, before Sir Thomas
> Walmesly, knt. Justice of Common Pleas, and Sir John
> Croke, knt. Justice of the king's Bench, held at Chelmsford
> on Monday the 4th day of July, by the oath of John Barron
> ...Thomas Fitch ... and Robert Allen, gentlemen who say on
> their oath that the bill annexed to this schedule is true.
> Indictments of 2 June. Henry Roberts of Bocking, clothier,
> for assaulting and beating Katherine, wife of Stephen Reary
> of the same, clothier, so that she despaired of her life. En-
> dorsed, fine assessed at 10s. and to the within-named Kath-

Figure 79 - Bocking Parish Register
(Pointer indicates entry for marriage of Thomas Fitch and Anne Reve)

erine 10s. Witnesses, Susan Ansell, Stephen Reary, Mary Bennett.[1]

What has happened evidently is that on 2 June, one Henry Roberts was indicted for assaulting the wife of another clothier, Stephen Reary, so badly that "she despaired of her life." Roberts was fined 10 shillings, and the money was awarded to poor Katherine. Then on 4 July, Thomas and the other jurors meeting in Chelmsford approved the charges (Roberts was almost certainly in the Colchester castle jail while awaiting trial). Finally, the "gaol delivery" record was reviewed again on 7 July.

1611 Our next record for Thomas is a bit more cheerful. On 8 August 1611, Thomas Fitch married Ann Reve (or Reeve) of Gosfield, a few miles northeast of Bocking (in the map of Figure 77, it is spelled *Gossfield*). They were married, how-

1. E.R.O. Q/SR 184/67,8

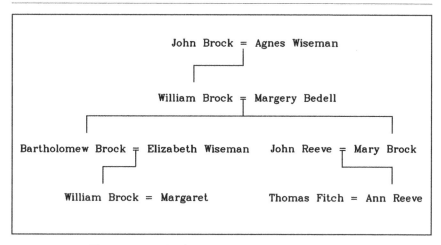

Figure 80 - The Brock Pedigree of Anne Reeve

ever, at the Church of St. Mary in Bocking. The rector at the time was Zaccheus Pasfield and the marriage was duly recorded in the parish register (Figure 79).[1]

Reve (or Reeve)

As the heading indicates, Ann's family name was spelled either *Reve* or *Reeve*. And her own Christian name was spelled both as *Ann* and *Anne*. Her father was John Reeve of Bocking and later of Gosfield. (He is listed as a *yeoman* along with Thomas' uncle Richard the clothier and Richard's son, James, as trustees for a Bocking charity.[2]) Actually, we know a little more about Ann's mother, Mary Brock. As shown in Figure 80, a simplified pedigree, we can go as far back as John Brock of Little Leighs in Essex, who married (the mind reels) another Agnes Wiseman. They had seven children, one of whom was Mary's father, William Brock of Boxted and Colchester, both in Essex. This William married Margery Bedell of Nottey in Essex; they had three children, including Mary. William's will is dated 17 July 1598.

1. Parish Register, Church of St. Mary, Bocking, Essex. E.R.O. D/P 268/1/1.
2. Close Rolls, C54, 1633, M.F.C., *op.cit.*, Ewen Vol. B, f. 278.

We have shown Mary's brother Bartholomew on this skeleton pedigree as well as his son William, because (a) they bought Priors Hall, Parsonage Farm, Stebbing from William Fitch (page 106) and (b) they will figure prominently in a 1630 purchase of land by Thomas[A].

Mary Brock married John Reeve at Gosfield on 24 October 1588. Figure 78 is a photograph of St. Catherine's church in Gosfield. Mary and John had five children, including Ann, who was born in 1590.[1] Ann had two brothers, John and Jeremy, and two sisters, Sarah and Susan. They are all mentioned in their father's will, dated 23 September 1620.

1612 Thomas and Ann had eleven children. The first was a boy, named Thomas for his father, who was born on 24 October 1612.[2]

1613 In September 1613 Thomas and Ann paid £41 to Thomas, John, and Sarah Gosse (who may have been relatives of his step-mother, Bridget) for "two messuages, two gardens, one orchard, 8 acres of land, 5 acres of meadow, and 11 acres of pasture with appurtenances" in Little Waldingfield, just north of Edwardstone in Suffolk.[3] This is the same sum received by his brother George the year before for their father's Edwardstone estate.

1614 The next record we have for Thomas senior involves a criminal proceeding. This time, however, he is not a juror; he is the victim. On 23 September 1614, "Tho. Fitche of Bocking clothier" appeared before Justice Wm. Wroth (what a wonderful name for a judge!) to "prefer an indictment against Mary Goodwyn for stealing a 'pillow-beere' out of his house."[4] A *pillow-beere* is a pillow-case, worth, the record states, 11 pence, the stealing of which would not seem to be a particularly heinous crime. Nevertheless, less than a month later, on the Thursday after Michaelmas, 6 October

1. Parish Register, Gosfield.
2. R. C. Fitch, *op.cit.*, p. 105.
3. P.R.O. C.P. 25 (2) 356, Mich. 11 James I.
4. Q/SR 208/109.

1614, Mary Goodwyn, "spinster," had to appear before the General Sessions at Chelmsford. There she confessed and was sentenced to be *whipped!*[1]

In September 1615, Thomas sold "one messuage, one 1615 garden, one orchard, 14 acres of land, 3 acres of meadow, and 6 acres of pasture with appurtenances," in Little Waldingfield to Edward Alston—again for £41.[2] But, as Charles Fitch-Northen points out in correcting an error in the pedigree provided to R. C. Fitch by the College of Arms, the sale was not a "wash;" Thomas bought 24 acres and sold 23 and, more importantly, was able to keep one messuage and one garden, which he apparently got for free!

Now, twelve years after the death of his father, Thomas 1617 should have fulfilled the terms of his father's will. The estate in Edwardstone was already sold and he should have sold the house in Ballingdon. He himself continued to live in Bocking in Essex. Unlike his grandfather Roger's will which specifically mentions a house on Bradford Street, Thomas' will doesn't tell us just where in Bocking he lived. It would not be surprising, however, to believe he lived on the same street of large, well-kept homes. Figure 81 shows the three-gabled "Woolpack" Inn, the "Bay" house (named not for its bay windows but for a *bays* factory in the back), and other houses on Bradford Street.

We don't know when the second son, John, was born, 1622 but the third was James[1]. He was born on 24 December 1622. We shall, of course, have a great deal more to say about him in his biography. There were eight more children, four sons and four daughters, but we do not have birth dates for any of them.

Thomas is mentioned in, and was probably the executor 1623 of, the will of a fellow clothier, Moses Wall of Braintree, dated 16 September 1623, and probated 23 January 1623/4.

1. E.R.O. Q/SR 208/27.
2. P.R.O. C.P. 25 (2) 357, Mich. 13 James I.

Figure 81 - Bradford Street, Bocking
(Reproduced by kind permission of the Braintree and Bocking Heritage Trust)

Wall was a churchwarden and therefore a member of the "Company of Four-and-Twenty," an exclusive group of influential townspeople who ran the parish of Braintree. The will mentions "My friend Thomas Fitch of Bockinge."

1625   Charles I succeeded his father James I as King of England, Scotland, and Ireland. Because the religious struggles that characterized his reign will be of greater importance when we take up James[1], we shall wait until the next volume to discuss this aspect of his reign. But the political debacles caused by King Charles, obtuse even by monarchial standards, included dismissing Parliament his first year on the throne, curtailing civil rights, and allowing his personal favorite, the Duke of Buckingham, to embroil England in disastrous wars with France and Spain—activities which eventually cost Charles his head. The wars, in particular, were evidently having severe economic impacts on the wool trade of southeast England. Much of the product, you will remember, was made for export, and war with one of their principal customers, Spain, was not good for business. One report to the Privy Council summarized the situation in Bocking:

> In and by, this towne by the Manufacture of Bayes are sett on worke 7,000 persons. Within this seven yeares, they were wont to make fower [four] hundred peeces a weeke. Since, they fell by little and little, to three hundred; and lately, they have not been able to make above One hundred a weeke, and within this five or six weeks, not above fortie a week, for having had little or noe sale, a great number have been undone and forced to give over their trade quite. Theire remaine upon theire hands, unsold, above two thowsand peeces, whereof seven hundred are in the towne; and theire warehouses beeinge full, they forebeare to bring up any more. That towne abounds with poor, whereof many are very unrulie; and having noe employment, will make the place veree hazardous for men of better Ranke to live amongst them.[1]

On 30 Oct. 1628, Thomas served as a Grand Juror.   1628

> Names of such as we have nominated to have the view of the accounts for several sums disbursed and to be paid for several employments for the county, delivered up by us the Grand Jurors: ... Hundred of Hinckford—Tho. Fitch.[2]

Bocking lay in the *Hidingafort* Hundred, a name which was later shortened to *Hinckford*. So, in this case, it appears that the court has nominated Thomas, among others in his Hundred, to approve the accounts for county hirings.

The depression in the Bocking-Braintree area was   1629
growing worse. Unemployment was endemic. A letter to the Privy Council in May of 1629 reported on what might be called hunger riots. Two or three hundred people from Braintree and Bocking had marched to Maldon, the nearest

---

1. Quin, *op.cit.*, p. 56.
2. E.R.O. Q/SR 263/98.

river port, where they seized supplies of corn from a ship, a house, and a warehouse. The mob was dispersed, and four of its leaders were tried and sentenced to be hanged. In the winter of 1629/30, a petition was delivered to the Justices meeting in Quarter Sessions at Chelmsford complaining about the unemployment. The petition alleged that some clothiers were taking on apprentices despite the fact that many adult weavers had no work. Some of the workmasters had increased the length of bays by fifty percent without paying anything extra; in other words, the piece rates had been cut by a third.

It is interesting that the signatories to this petition included several prominent clothiers, among them a John Fitch, who may have been Thomas' second son, although he would have been quite young. It also included another clothier, William Stacie, the father-in-law of Thomas' oldest son, Thomas junior. Quin thinks the inclusion of these men indicates that there may have been a rivalry between established Bocking clothiers concious of the needs of the township (they were also paying "rates" for support of the poor) and outside clothiers.[1]

1630   Whether or not the depression was affecting Thomas Fitch or not, the record shows that on 27 September 1630, he bought 130 acres of land, including several houses, from William Brock of Thelnetham in Suffolk, his wife's first cousin (see pedigree of Figure 80). He paid £660—a very large amount of money—for a meadow in Copford, another in Stanway, and a "messuage" called Nevers or Pages in Great Birch (see maps of Figures 74 and 82). The documents—four of them—covering this transaction are all transcribed in the *Appendix* for Thomas[A]. If we think lawyers today tend to nit-pick, we should be thankful we do not live in the seventeenth century; these deeds are mind-numbing in their detail and repetition. First there is a document covering the "bargain and sale," presumably what we would call a "purchase and sale" agreement, i.e. a contract. Then

1. Quin, *op.cit.*, pp. 57,58.

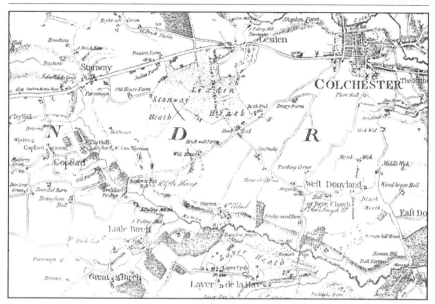

Figure 82 - Copford, Stanway, and Great Birch
(1777 Chapman & André Map, reproduced by courtesy of the Essex Record Office)

there is an "enfeoffment," putting the tenant legally in possession
of the property. Next, a bond on the part of the seller, holding
Thomas harmless should something turn up that would prevent
him from enjoying his new lands.[1] And, finally, nearly two years
later, during the Easter Term of the court in 1631/2, there is a
"final concord," basically affirming that the transfer took place.
This last summarizes the agreement:

> Final Concord (Counterparts)
> Tho. Fitch v. Wm. Brocke, gent. and w. Margt..
> 1 messuage, 1 garden, 1 orchard, 66a. of land, 12a. of
> meadow, 46a. of pasture, 12a. of wood, and 4/6 rents in Great
> and Little Birch, Copford and Stanway.[2]

1. D/DU 161/171-173.
2. D/DU 161/174,175.

The Will

1632   Thomas Fitch died in late 1632 or early 1633. If he was born, as we have estimated, about 1580, then he would have been only about fifty-two or fifty-three years old. His will is dated 11 December 1632, and it was probated in the Prerogative Court of Canterbury on 12 February 1632/3. Figure 83 shows the first page of the court copy of the will, which runs for three pages without paragraphing or punctuation. The will is transcribed in full, using the idiosyncratic spelling of the day, in the *Appendix* for Thomas[A], but we shall also describe the bequests in some detail here. The quotations, however, are in present day spelling.

Being "weak and sick of body yet of good and perfect mind and memory, God be praised therefore and calling to mind the uncertainty of life and the certainty of death" Thomas wanted to "set in order that portion which God hath trusted me withall." He asked to be given a Christian burial, "believing that after this separation of soul and body in this life, they shall both be raised when Christ shall come in judgment and be united again together, to life with God and Christ forever in that immortal kingdom which never shall have end." Thomas clearly died a wealthy man by the standards of the day, but his first bequest is a small one: three pounds "to the poor people of Bocking."

He owned two houses in Bocking: the one he lived in and one next door, occupied by his eldest son Thomas who had just married Anne Stacie. He left both houses to Thomas as well as more houses, buildings, and lands which he had purchased from William Collin in Bocking and still more tenements and lands which he had bought from Edward Poppen and John Amptill. To this he added a barn in Panfield Lane (Figure 84) that he had purchased from Thomas Trotter. Out of the income from all this, Thomas was to pay "my Sister Stracey twenty shillings yearly during her natural life." Despite the similarity of names—Stacie and Stracey—these are two different families. His sister, Frances (or "Fraunces" as it was usually spelled at the time), had married

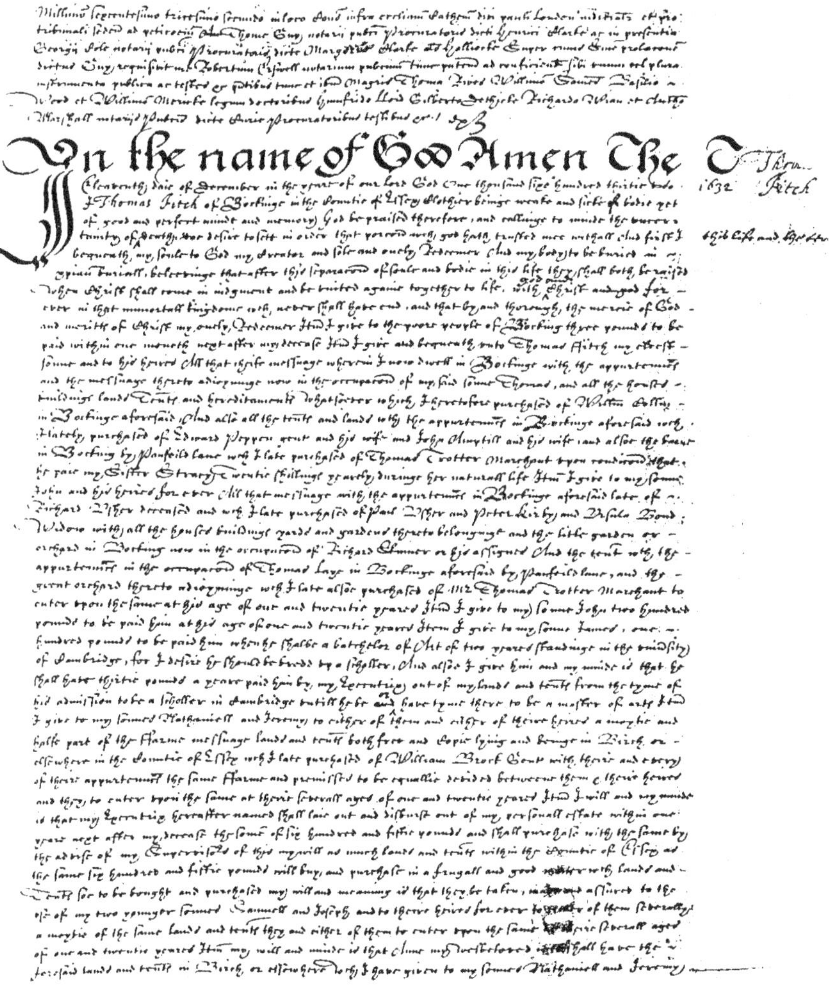
In the name of God Amen The Eleventh daie of December in the yeare of our lord God One thousand six hundred thirtie two I Thomas Fitch of Bocking in the Countie of Essex Clothier beinge weake and sicke of bodie yet of good and perfect minde and memory God be praised therefore

Thom. Fitch 1632

Figure 83 - Will of Thomas Fitch of Bocking
(Cat. No. PROB 11/163, courtesy of the Public Record Office)

Figure 84 - Panfield Lane
(Reproduced by kind permission of the Braintree and Bocking Heritage Trust)

James Stracey. And, she is also to have the right to take anything in the barn in Panfield Lane should Thomas default on her annuity.

Next, the senior Thomas turned to his second son, John, who we learn is not yet twenty-one. He gives him another "messuage" in Bocking that he had bought from Paul Usher, Peter Kirby, and the widow Ursula Bond. This place included houses, buildings, yards, and gardens. He also gave John a garden or orchard, now being used by Richard Skinner, the other churchwarden (we have already mentioned Moses Wall). In addition, he gave him part of the same properties in Panfield Lane that he had bought from Thomas Trotter; these included a tenement, occupied by Thomas Laye, and the great orchard adjoining it. Finally, he gave him £200, all of the above when John turned twenty-one.

Of greatest interest to us is the next bequest—to James, his third son. We know that in 1632, James was just ten years old. He must have been a rather precocious ten-year-old, though, because his father had already decided that James was to be a university graduate. He was to receive £100 when he had been enrolled for two years in a bachelor of arts program at Cambridge "for I desire he should be bred up a scholar." To see young James through school, he was also to receive £30 a year from his mother until such time as he would become a "master of arts."

Then come two more of the sons, Nathaniel and Jeremy. Each of them is to receive half of the farm, messuage, land, and rents in Birch and elsewhere in Essex that Thomas had bought from William Brock. Since they are also minors, this bequest is to take effect as each becomes twenty-one. It is evidently up to Ann, the executrix, to divide the property equally.

There are still two more sons, Samuel and Joseph. But, since the lands and houses have all been given away, Thomas asks that Anne (with the advice of "Supervisors") buy £650 worth of additional land and houses in Essex for the youngest boys. This amount closely matches the £660 he had paid for the Brock lands, which he had now given to Nathaniel and Jeremy.

The next paragraph tells us that Ann is to have all the lands given to the four youngest boys and that she is to use the income therefrom to bring up the boys and their sisters. When each of the boys reaches the age of sixteen, however, she is to separate out the income from each lad's share for his own particular benefit.

Next, we come to the girls. Although the will mentions only three by name, Thomas and Ann had an elder daughter, named Elizabeth; she had died 11 November 1615.[1] Each of the other three, Mary, Anne, and Sara, are to receive £300, two hundred to be paid them when they are eighteen, and the other hundred when they reach twenty-one. Incidentally, if one of these girls should marry without Anne's consent, she is to lose £100 of her legacy.

After the children are taken care of, there are several other small bequests to some of Thomas' friends. He gives 20 shillings

1. R.C.F. *op.cit.*, pedigree opposite p. 6.

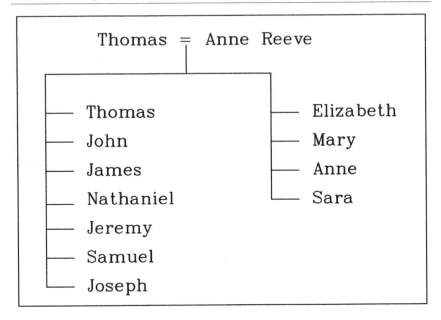

Figure 85 - Family of Thomas Fitch of Bocking

each to Mr. Hooker, Mr. Nathaniel Rogers, Mr. Daniel Rogers, and Mr. Collins. The "Mr. Hooker" was undoubtedly Thomas Hooker, the Rector of Chelmsford. We shall have a good deal more to say about him, because he was the mentor of James[1]. Nathaniel Rogers was the curate at Bocking, and we shall come back to him as well. Daniel Rogers may have been a brother; he was neither the father nor the son of Nathaniel Rogers. And Mr. Collins is almost surely Samuel Collins, Vicar of Braintree from 1610 to 1656.

A couple of lead cisterns for oil are given to Thomas and John. Then 20 shillings each to "my brother John Malden and my sister his wife." The way "sister" is used here suggests that he really does mean his only real sister, Fraunces. Also £5 to Henry Stracey "my kinsman." Here again, "kinsman" is probably being used in the same sense as "sister" in the earlier reference to "my Sister Stracey." It is unlikely that these are Stacies, for there is no *Henry* Stacie on that family pedigree. To add evidence of this, a bit later, Thomas specifically mentions "my brothers John Reeve and William Stacy" and gives them and "my brother Jeremy Reeve" 20 shillings each as "a token of my love." John and Jeremy Reeve are, of course, Anne's brothers, and William Stacie is Thomas junior's father-in-law.

Thomas concludes the will by leaving everything else to his wife, binding her under a £2000 bond to John Reeve and William Stacie to carry out his wishes. Furthermore, if she should decide to re-marry, he wants her next husband—on the day before their marriage—to put up another £2000 bond to make sure all the legacies are handed out. Otherwise, Reeve and Stacie are to take over as executors.

Anne and the Children

Anne never did re-marry. She accompanied three of her sons to America, lived for at least another 37 years, and probably died in Hartford, Connecticut. In England, Charles the first was ruling without Parliament. When he tried to force the Church of England's episcopacy on Scotland, there was a "Bishop's War." In 1640, there was the "Long Parliament," a government in parallel with the king's. Civil war broke out in 1642, and Essex took the Parliamentary side. There was a terrible and bloody siege at Colchester in 1648, after which the royalist commanders were put to death by the parliamentarians. Finally, at the end of January 1649, after repeated defeats, the king was tried, convicted, and beheaded. England, for the next eleven years, was a Commonwealth.

As we have seen, Thomas and Anne had eleven children (Figure 85), including Elizabeth who pre-deceased her father and mother. Rather than take up the children in chronological order, we can dispose of four of the sons as a group, because they all left England for America. These were James, the first to leave in 1638, and then Thomas, the oldest, together with Samuel,

Joseph, and their mother Anne about 1650. We shall deal here only with those who stayed in England.

John, the second son, was a clothier like his father, though his business was in Braintree rather than Bocking. He may have participated in the Civil War because he was also known as Captain John Fitch. In the Great Plague of 1665, when people in Braintree were dying at the rate of fifty or more a week, he was one of the Overseers, one of those who "bestowed their charity towards the maintayning the poor of Braintree the time of the Plague."[1] Unfortunately, he was also one of its victims and the *Essex Review* mentions "gallant Capt. John Fitch of Braintree, clothier, the leading overseer" who died in the plague.[2] He probably died in 1666, toward the end of the plague. Altogether, Braintree lost 665 people—nearly a third of its population—before the plague finally abated in 1667.

Next we come to the two sons, Nathaniel and Jeremy, who were to share the estate at Birch. Nathaniel never married and died in late 1648 or early 1649. His will was dated 15 August 1648 and was probated on 8 May 1649. Jeremy was a stapler, which, if he had stayed in Bocking might have meant one who sorted wool according to the length or courseness of its "staple" or pile. But, he was a citizen of London, so "stapler," in his case, may have meant someone who dealt in staples or commodities. He is also recorded as a grantor of lands in Stanway, evidently part of his inheritance. There appears to be no information about the daughters, Mary, Anne, and Sarah.

And so we follow the four older sons and their mother to the new world, to America.

---

1. Quin, *op.cit.*, p. 94.
2. *Essex Review*, vol. 36, p. 22.

8

Genealogy

The genealogy that follows is in Register Plan, i.e. English forbears are lettered in reverse chronology, and American descendants are numbered chronologically. Abreviations used are:

b.	birth, born	d.s.p.	decessit sin prole
bp.	baptized		(died without issue)
bro.	brother	d.y.	died young
bur.	buried	g.s.	gravestone
ca.	circa	m.	married, marriage
co.	county	sis.	sister
d.	death, died	v.r.	vital records
dau.	daughter	w.	wife
div.	divorced	wid.	widow, widowed

1. WILLIAM[F] FECCHE, FICCHE, FYCCHE, FICHE, FYCHE, FYTCHE, FITCHE of Wicken Bonhunt, county Essex. Born about 1400. Death reported at Widdington, county Essex, court on 24 April 1466[1]. Wife's name unknown. First mention is on the Plea Rolls in 1428. Received grants of land at the manor court of Widdington in 1440/1 and in 1458/9. The court post mortem inquisition also states that "John Fytche is son and next heir of the same William"[2].

1. Court Rolls, Manor of Widdington, New College Oxford
2. *ibid.*

Child (may have been others), surname *Fitch*:

2. i. JOHN[E], b. probably at Wicken or Widdington, ca. 1437; d. before 9 April 1468; m. JULIANA _____.

2. JOHN[E] FYCH, FYCCHE, FYTCHE (*William*[F]) was born no later than 1437, because in 1467 he was said to be "aged 30 years and more"[1] Death reported at Widdington court 9 April 1468. He married JULIANA _____ about 1464. First mention was on a Court Plea in 1458 which says he was "of Wicken." At the time that his father's death was reported at the manor court of Widdington on 24 April 1466, he was acknowledged to be the son and next heir[2] On 14 May 1467, he was again acknowledged as son and next heir and admitted to his father's estate and received additional grants of land[3]. At the court session of 9 April 1468, it was stated that "Thomas is his son and next heir and aged three years"[4]. Custody of the land was given to JULIAN(A), who remarried Richard Westley and died about 1475[5].

Child (may have been others), surname *Fitch*:

3. i. THOMAS[D], b. probably at Wicken or Widdington, ca. 1465; d. 21 April 1514; m. ca. 1490 AGNES ALGORE.

3. THOMAS[D] FITCHE, FYTCHE, FITCH (*John*[E], *William*[F]) was born about 1465, because he was said to be three years old at the time that his father's death was reported at the manor court of Widdington in 1468[6]. He died in Lindsell, county Essex, on 21 April 1514 as commemorated on a brass in the Church of St. Mary the Virgin. He married AGNES ALGORE before 22 December 1490 when they received land from her parents[7]. She died before 3 May 1527[8]. They probably had eleven children—six sons and five

1. *ibid.*
2. *ibid.*
3. *ibid.*
4. *ibid.*
5. *ibid.*
6. *ibid.*
7. Court Rolls, Manor of Priors Hall, Lindsell, New College Oxford
8. Widdington, *op.cit.*

daughters—as pictured on the church brass. He was admitted to his inheritance at Widdington court on 9 November 1487 when the clerk referred to the session of 9 April 1468 which reported his father's death[1]. Agnes was the heiress of her father, Robert Algore[2], and brought to the marriage Brazen Head Farm in Lindsell. In 1497, Thomas received an additional grant of land at the manor court of Priors Hall, Lindsell[3] and in November 1505, he took possession of land that his father John had left in custody of his widowed mother, Juliana. That same year, Agnes received more land when her mother, Margaret Algore, died.

In addition to the church brass, Thomas and Agnes are also commemorated in a stained glass window in the same church. All the following children are mentioned in Widdington and Priors Hall, Lindsell court records. Richard was named son and heir.

Children (these and probably four others), born at Lindsell, surname *Fitch*:

i. MARGARET, b. abt. 1494.

ii RICHARD, son and heir, bur. Lindsell 26 Jun. 1579; m. (1) ELIANOR STORKE, d. abt. 1533, dau. and heir of Tristram Storke of Trent, Somerset; m. (2) JANE _____, bur. Great Leighs, Essex, 25 Jun. 1593.

Children by first wife, Elianor, surname *Fitch*:

1. Tristram, m. Margaret _____.
2. John.

Children by second wife, Jane, surname *Fitch*:

1. Richard.
2. William.
3. George.

iii. WILLIAM, b. ca. 1496; d. 20 Dec. 1578 at age 82, bur. Little Canfield[4]; will dated 13 Oct. 1577, proved 12 Jan. 1578/9; m. (1) ELIZABETH _____, bur. Little Canfield; m. (2)

1. Widdington, *op.cit.*
2. Priors Hall, Lindsell, *op.cit.*
3. *ibid.*
4. From brass in church.

ANNE WISEMAN, d. 3 Dec. 1593, dau. of John and Joan (Lucas) Wiseman of Felsted, Essex. After William d. Anne m. (2) City of London, 28 May 1597, Ralph Pudsaye of Grays Inn, Gent.

Children (these three, one other daughter, and one other son) by first wife, Elizabeth, surname *Fitch*:

1. William, bur. All Saints, Little Canfield, 5 Nov. 1561.

2. Elinor, d. bef. 1578; m. Rooke Greene, Esq., d. Little Sampford, Essex, 9 Apr. 1602, eldest son and heir of Sir Edward Grene and Margery (Allington) Rooke (or Rocus).

3. Mary, d. before 1578; m. Francis Manock, Esq. of Stoke Nayland, Suffolk, d. 3 Nov. 1590, son of William and Audry (Allington) Mannock.

Children (these and one other son) by second wife, Anne, surname *Fitch*:

4. Thomas, son and heir, b. abt. 1560; d. bur. Church of St. Mary, Great Canfield, 29 Nov. 1588; m. Great Canfield, 22 Jun. 1579, Agnes Wiseman, dau. of John and Agnes (Waldegrave) Wiseman. After Thomas d. Agnes m. (2) George Wyngate of Harling, Bedford, Essex.

5. William (Brother Benedict Canfield), b. ca. 1562, d.s.p. Paris, 21 Nov. 1611 at age 49.

6. Sir Francis, bp. Little Canfield, 5 Sep. 1563; d.s.p. 12 Oct. 1608; m. (as 2nd husband) Margaret Tyrrell, dau. and co-heir of Edmund Tyrell, Esq. of Beches, Rawreth, Essex, and wid. of John Daniell of Acton, Suffolk. After Sir Francis d. Margaret m. (3) Francis Joselyn.

iv. THOMAS, m. MARGARET MEADE.

Children, surname *Fitch*:

1. Thomas, d. ca. 1606; m. Ann Bentley.

2. Robert, bur. 22 Aug. 1589; m. Ellen Carver.

3. Margaret, m. _____ Taylor.

  4. v. ROGER[C], d. 1559; m. MARGERY _____.

  vi. KATHARINE

  vii. JOAN

4. ROGER[C] FYTCHE, FYCCHE, FICHE, FITCHE, FYCHE (*Thomas*[D], *John*[E], *William*[F]) was born in Lindsell prior to 1514 and died in Panfield, county Essex. His will was dated 12 January 1558/9 and probated in the Consistory Court of London, 22 February 1558/9[1]. He married MARGERY _____, who was sole executrix of his will. Mentioned as son of Thomas and Agnes Fitch in Priors Hall, Lindsell court record of 23 December 1514[2]. Mentioned in land transaction of 1531[3]. Received land "on death of his mother Agnes, as son of Thomas and Agnes Fitch, in accordance with the will of said Thomas" on 25 September 1533.[4]

In his will, he was listed as "of Panfeilde in the countie of Essex, yeoman." He asked to be buried in Panfield churchyard. He left two houses in Bocking, county Essex, and "free lands" to Margery during her life, after which they were to go to sons John and Richard. The other children received money bequests. All the following children are mentioned in his will.

Children, born at Panfield or Bocking, surname *Fitch*:

  i. RICHARD, bur. at Bocking, 13 Jun. 1603, will dated 11 Jun. 1603; m. ANNE _____.

    Children, surname *Fitch*:

    1. Richard, bp. at Bocking, 8 Jul. 1565; m. (1) Margerie Gray; m. (2) Elizabeth Picker.

    2. John, bp. 8 Mar. 1560/1; will dated 3 Jul. 1628, m. Margaret _____.

    3. William, bp. 7 Jan. 1570/1; m. (?).

1. 193 Horn. [Bishop]
2. Lindsell, *op.cit.*
3. Marc Fitch and P. H. Reaney, eds. *Feet of Fines for Essex*, vol. iv, 1423-1547
4. Lindsell *op.cit.*

      4. James, will dated 4 Aug. 1616; m. Margarett Beale.

      5. Margaret, bp. 23 Jan. 1568/9; m. (1) Rev. Edward Gutter; m. (2) John Smilts.

  ii. JOHN, m. ANNE BUCKS(?).

  iii. BARTHOLOMEW, bur. Chelmsford 4 Nov. 1598; m. (1) at Chelmsford 8 Feb. 1579/80 ALICE AYER; m. (2) MARY CHAMBERLAIN.

  iv. THOMAS, d. 4 July 1596.

  v. WILLIAM, bur. 5 Dec. 1588; m. 17 June 1583, SARAH EGIOTT.

      Child, surname *Fitch*:

      1. William, bp. 1586, d. 1597.

5. vi. GEORGE[B], will dated 12 May 1605, probated 18 June 1605; m. (1) at Little Canfield, 14 Sept. 1574, JOAN THURGOOD; m. (2) BRIDGET (____)-GOSS FRENCH; m. (3) JOANE (____) TAYLOR.

  vii. ROBERT, will dated 18 Dec. 1592; m. ELIZABETH (TYMM) PARKER.

      Child, surname *Fitch*:

      1. Sara

  viii. JOAN, m. 2 Sept. 1596, WILLIAM KENT.

  ix. MARGARET

  x. CLEMENT, bur. Panfield 22 May 1573.

  xi. MARY

5. GEORGE[B] FYTCHE, FYTCH, FITCHE, FITCH (*Roger[C], Thomas[D], John[E], William[F]*) was probably born about 1551, because he is the last of seven sons mentioned in his father's will in 1558/9 as being under 21. His own will was dated 12 May 1605 and was probated at the Prerogative Court of Canterbury on 18 June 1605[1]. The will names his son Thomas and his brother William as executors. He married first at Little Canfield, 14 Sept. 1574, JOAN THUR-

---

1. 49 Hayes

GOOD, daughter of Nicholas Thurgood of Eisenham. He married second BRIDGET _____, widow, firstly, of John Goss of Edward-stone, secondly of John French of Edwardstone. She died 29 Aug. 1603 and was buried in Edwardstone. He married third JOANE _____, widow of _____ Taylor.

George lived in Braintree, county Essex, and later in Sudbury and Edwardstone, both county Suffolk. He was a mercer by profession, but was also a land holder and is referred to as a yeoman in an entry for his son Joseph in *Alumni Cantabrigiensis*. All the following children are mentioned in their father's will.

Children, probably born at Braintree, surname *Fitch*:

6. i. THOMAS[A], will dated 11 Dec. 1632, probated 12 Feb. 1632/3; m. at Bocking, co. Essex, 8 Aug. 1611, ANN REEVE.

ii. GEORGE, administration 14 Nov. 1614.

iii. JOSEPH, admitted pensioner Caius College, Cambridge, 7 Oct. 1603; Scholar 1604-6; administered effects of his bro. George.

iv. ARTHUR

v. FRAUNCES, m. Bocking, 5 Feb. 1606/7, JAMES STRACEY.

6. THOMAS[A] FITCH (*George*[B], *Roger*[C], *Thomas*[D], *John*[E], *William*[F]) was mentioned in his father's will in 1605 as "my eldest son." He was also mentioned in the will of his first cousin once removed, Thomas of Margaretting. His own will was dated 11 December 1632 and probated in the Prerogative Court of Canterbury 12 February 1632/3[1]. He married at Bocking, 8 August 1611, ANNE REVE daughter of John Reve of Gosfield, County Essex. She moved to America with her sons and was reported as living in 1669. Thomas lived in Bocking and was a clothier by profession. He was involved in a number of land transactions. The following children (except Elizabeth) are mentioned in their father's will.

---

1.   20 Russell

Children, born at Bocking, surname *Fitch*:

i. THOMAS[1], b. 14 Oct. 1612; d. Norwalk, Connecticut; m. Bocking, 1 Nov. 1632, ANNE STACIE.

ii. JOHN, d. England.

iii. JAMES[1], b. 24 Dec. 1622; d. Lebanon, Connecticut, 18 Nov. 1702; m. (1) 1 Oct. 1648, ABIGAIL WHITFIELD, d. 1659; m. (2) 1664, PRISCILLA MASON.

iv. NATHANIEL, b. 26 Dec. 1623; d. England, 1649; will dated 15 Aug. 1648, proved 8 May 1649.

v. JEREMY, b. 5 Aug. 1625; d. England.

vi. SAMUEL[1], b. 9 Nov. 1626; d. Milford, Connecticut, 1659; m. SUSANNAH _____ WHITING.

vii. JOSEPH[1], living Windsor, Connecticut, 1713; m. MARY STONE.

viii. ELIZABETH, bp. 7 Nov. 1615; bur. at Bocking, 11 Nov. 1615.

ix. MARY, b. Mar. 1629.

x. ANNE, b. 6 Aug. 1630.

xi. SARA, b. 24 Jul. 1631.

9

Bibliography

Several early histories of Essex have been referenced in this book, and it may be helpful to note the sequence of these manuscripts and books. I am indebted to G. W. Martin for the following explanation.[1] The earliest historian was Thomas Jekyll (1570-1652) who worked as a court clerk and thus was able to create a large collection of extracts of ancient records. He did not publish, but much of his material found its way into the British Museum, where other historians made use of it. Among these, and the first to complete an actual history (though unpublished), was probably the Reverand William Holman of Halstead. His "sketch history" of Essex from about 1710 is at the Essex Record Office. The vicar of Great Waltham, the Reverend Nicolas Tindal obtained Holman's manuscript for publication. The project was short-lived, however, and abandoned after only two parts were produced. Next, Dr. Nathaniel Salmon purchased the Holman manuscripts (for £60) in 1739 and began to publish a history in parts. He died in 1742 after nineteen parts had been printed, and the work stopped again. The material was eventually bought by the Reverend Philip Morant in about 1750. He first thought to complete the Salmon project, but decided instead to start over from scratch. He spent twelve years working on his own version, based heavily on the Holman manuscript, before the first part

1. G. W. Martin, "How the history of Essex came to be published" in Essex Countryside, Vol. 11, No. 75, April 1963.

appeared in 1763, and another five years before he completed his two massive volumes in 1768.

_____, *Heraldry in Essex.* County Council of Essex, ERO Publications 19, 1953.

Bowden, Peter J., *The Wool Trade in Tudor and Stuart England.* London, England: Macmillan, 1962.

Bromley, John *The Armorial Bearings of the Guilds of London.* London, England: Frederick Warne & Co. Ltd., 1961

Burke, Sir Bernard, *The General Armory.* London, England: Burke's Peerage Ltd., 1884.

Cheney, C. R., *Handbook of Dates for Students of English History.* London, England: Offices of the Royal Historical Society, University College London, 1978.

Christy, Miller, "The 'Brazen Head' at Lindsell," in *The Essex Review*, vol. i, 1892.

Christy, Miller, "On Some Interesting Essex Brasses," in *The Essex Review*, vol. vii, 1898.

Christy, Miller, "On Some Early Bronze Knockers and Sanctuary Rings Existing in England," in *Proceedings of the Society of Antiquaries*, vol. xxii, Feb. 11, 1909.

Edwards, A. C., *A History of Essex.* London, England: Philamore & Co. Ltd., 1985

Ekwall, Eilert, *The Concise Oxford Dictionary of English Place-Names*, 4th ed. Oxford, England: Oxford University Press, 1985.

Emmison, F. G., *Elizabethan Life: Disorder.* Chelmsford, England: Essex County Council, 1970.

Emmison, F. G., *Elizabethan Life: Morals & The Church Courts.* Chelmsford, England: Essex County Council, 1973.

Emmison, F. G., *Elizabethan Life: Wills of Essex Gentry & Merchants.* Chelmsford, England: Essex County Council, 1978.

Emmison, F. G., *Elizabethan Life: Wills of Essex Gentry & Yeomen.* Chelmsford, England: Essex County Council, 1980.

Fitch, John G., *Genealogy of the Fitch Family in North America.* Olmsted, Ohio: Printed for Private Distribution, 1886. Included for its historical position as, apparently, the first published Fitch genealogy in the United States. Largely irrelevant to the line under study here.

Fitch, Marc and Reaney, P. H. (Editors), *Feet of Fines for Essex*, vol. iv, 1423-1547. Colchester, Essex, England: Essex Archaelogical Society, 1964.

Fitch, Roscoe Conkling, *History of the Fitch Family: 1400-1930*, 2 vols. Haverhill, Massachusetts: By the Author, 1930. Contains the results of 1929 research conducted by the College of Arms into the antecedents of Thomas and Agnes Fitch and, thus, corrects all earlier genealogies, including the College's own official version of the 1615 Visitation of Essex. Aside from this valuable research, contained in the first chapter, the two volumes are, for the most part, an incoherent jumble of facts, fantasies, and fulsome sketches of turn of the century Fitches.

Garraty, John A. and Peter Gay, editors, *The Columbia History of the World.* New York, New York: Harper & Row, Publishers, 1984.

Gentleman, A, (pseudonym for Peter Muilman of Great Yeldham), *History of Essex*, Vol. 3, 1749 (or 1771?).

Hey, David, *Family History and Local History in England.* London, England: Longman Group UK Limited, 1987.

Hoffman, Ann, *Bocking Deanery, The Story of an Essex Peculiar.* London, England: Phillimore & Co. Ltd., 1976

Holman, Rev. William, *History of Essex*, 1710. This manuscript is the earliest of the Essex histories. It is deposited at the Essex Record Office, Catalog No. T/P 195/15.

McKinley, Richard, *Norfolk and Suffolk Surnames in the Middle Ages.* Leicester University Press.

Metcalfe, Walter C. (editor), *The Visitations of Essex by Hawley, 1552; Hervey, 1558; Cooke, 1570; Raven, 1612; and Owen and*

Lilly, 1634, vol. xiii (1878). London, England: The Harleian Society, 1878. The College of Arms cautions that these are unofficial copies of the original documents and contain errors.

Morant, Rev. Philip, *The History and Antiquities of the County of Essex.* Originally printed London, England: 1763-1768. Republished by EP Publishing Limited with the Essex County Library, 1978. The two volume Morant history is taken (some have said shamelessly copied) largely from the earlier work of Rev. William Holman and Nathaniel Salmon *q.v.*

Osborne, Arthur F., *Lindsell, A Record of its People, Parish and Church.* Lindsell, Essex, England: 1944.

Pugh, R. B., ed., *A History of the County of Essex,* vol. 4. London, England: Oxford University Press, 1956.

Quin, W. F., *A History of Braintree and Bocking.* Lavenham, England: The Lavenham Press Limited, 1981.

Rackham, Bernard, "The Ancient Stained Glass at Lindsell Church," in *Transactions of the Essex Archaeological Society,* XX New Series 1933. Colchester, Essex, England: 1933.

Reaney, P. H., *A Dictionary of British Surnames.* London, England: Routledge and Kegan Paul.

Reaney, P. H., *The Place-Names of Essex.* Cambridge, England: University Press, 1935.

Richardson, John, *The Local Historian's Encyclopedia.* New Barnet, Herts, England: Historical Publications Ltd., 1983.

Salmon, Nathaniel *History and Antiquities of Essex,* 1740.

Swinbank, Peter, *Lindsell.* Parish of St. Mary the Virgin, Lindsell, Essex, England.

Wagner, Anthony Richard, *The Records and Collections of the College of Arms.* London, England: Burkes Peerage Ltd., 1952.

Wagner, Sir Anthony, *English Genealogy.* London, England: Oxford University Press, 1960.

Ward, Jennifer C., ed., *The Medieval Essex Community: The Lay Subsidy of 1327.* Essex Record Office Publication No. 88, 1983.

10

Glossary

The definitions here are compiled from a number of sources including the *Oxford English Dictionary, New Webster's Dictionary*, John Richardson's *The Local Historian's Encyclopedia*, Henry Campbell Black's *Black's Law Dictionary*, and John Bouvier's *Bouvier's Law Dictionary*.

acre, 4 roods, or 160 square rods, or 4840 square yards.

adeo tarde, The name of a return by a sheriff to a writ, when it came into his hands too late to be executed before the return date.

advowson, The right of *presenting* or appointing a clergyman to a *benefice*, an ecclesiastical post. The appointment includes an endowment of property or income. Normally the bishop could not refuse the choice. An advowson *appendant* is one which is annexed to an estate or manor.

alienate, To transfer title, property, or other right to another.

amercement, A fine for misdemeanors. The phrase *in mercy* meant *fined*. Originally in manorial court, the convicted offender was "in the King's mercy" and was liable to a monetary penalty.

angel, A gold coin worth 6 shillings 8 pence, minted in 1464/5 and replacing the old version of the *Noble* minted in 1344.

appurtenance, A minor property, right, or privilege, belonging to another more important, and passing in possession with it.

armiger, Originally one who attended a knight to bear his shield, etc. In later usage, one entitled to bear heraldic arms.

assoin, A legal excuse entered at court for a non-appearance.

assize, Judicial proceedings.

assurance, Securing of a title of property; the conveyance of lands or tenements by deed; a legal evidence of conveyance of property.

bay, A course kind of blanket cloth or *baize*. Usually used in the plural, i.e. *bays*. Also called "New Draperies." Introduced to England in sixteenth century by Flemish and Dutch immigrants. Lighter in texture than "old" cloth. Originally, a chestnut color; hence, "bay."

behoof, Use, benefit, advantage.

boss, A knob, often richly ornamented, at the intersection of beams in a ceiling.

capital pledge, One of the leading or richest villagers who could participate at manor court sessions for the purpose of electing village officers.

capite, (Usually used as *in capite*) Tenant-in-Chief who held his land immediately from the Crown.

chancel, The part of a church, usually containing the altar, divided from the nave by a screen. From Latin *cancelli* meaning "lattice bars."

chantry, (also **chauntrey**, or **chauntrie**) A side chapel in a church together with an endowment for the maintenance of one or more priests to sing daily mass for the souls of the founders or others specified by them. From French *chanter*, to sing.

chapman, A man whose business is buying and selling; a merchant, trader, dealer.

charter, A document recording a grant, usually of land.

clerestory, The portion of the nave walls rising above the aisles, usually provided with windows.

close, An enclosed place.

Close Rolls, (1204/5 to 1903) Literally vellum rolls containing grants of the Crown closed with the Great Seal. Private instructions, mainly to officers of the Crown, were enrolled on the face of the rolls. Their main content was enclosure awards, deeds, polls, quit claims, provisioning of garrisons, aids and subsidies, and pardons. The reverse side of the membranes were used for the enrollment of deeds, conveyance of land and records of livery of seisin, charities, and wills.

clothier, One engaged in the cloth trade: (1) a maker of woollen cloth; (2) esp. one who performs the operations subsequent to the weaving (arch.) (3) a fuller and dresser of cloth (4) (U.S.): a seller of cloth and men's clothes.

conveyance, Written instrument or document by which transference of property is effected; the transference of property, especially real property, from one person to another.

copyhold, Originally the tenure of land dependent upon custom and the lord's will and carrying with it obligations to perform certain services for the lord. After 1400, the services were commuted to money payments. The tenant was protected not by national law but by title written into the court rolls. To transfer the property the tenant surrendered it to the lord, who then admitted the new tenant. Alternatively called *tenancy by copy* and *tenancy by the verge*.

cordwainer, A shoemaker.

cotillage, Cooperative tillage, as practiced in ancient village communities.

cotiller, (See cotillage.)

cottar, After 1400, one who held 3 to 5 acres and paid 3 pence, 3 farthings a year rent. See also *forelander* and *villein*.

court baron, A manorial court which dealt with land transactions.

court leet, A manorial court which dealt with petty offenses.

court of augmentation, Created in 1535 to administer the property of the dissolved religious houses. Abolished in 1554.

croft, A small piece of enclosed ground for tillage or pasture; a very small agricultural holding.

cross-crosslet, In heraldry, a cross the top and arms of which also have cross-like terminations.

curtilage, The yard and out-buildings of a house.

damnify, To cause damage or injurious loss.

deforciant, The seller in a property transaction. Also see *tenant*.

demandant, The purchaser in a property transaction. Often abbreviated *dem*. Synonymous with *plaintiff*.

demise, To transfer a right or landholding, usually by a lease.

dissolution, The breakup of the monasteries, beginning in 1536, by Henry VIII. The monks were pensioned off, their lands were granted to others, and many of the buildings were canibalized for building materials.

distrain, To constrain or force by seizure or detention of a chattel.

distress, Can have same meaning as *distrain* (q.v.). The taking of possessions, generally livestock, in lieu of rent.

dower, After the 12th century, that part of the estate the widow had the right to claim for life or until her remarriage. This portion was usually one-third and sometimes one-half.

enfeoff, Either to put a tenant legally in posession of a holding, or to surrender a holding. See also *feoffment*.

enseal, Affix with a seal; to close with a seal or seal up.

fealty, The obligation of fidelity on the part of a feudal tenant or vassal to his lord.

feedings, Grazing ground or pasture lands.

feet of fines, Copies of agreements made after land disputes. Some disputes were artificial, just to register the ownership of the land.

fen, Low land covered wholly or partially with shallow water, or subject to frequent flooding; a tract of such land, a marsh.

feoffment, Freehold tenures were conveyed in earlier times by *livery of seisn* (q.v.). It was the custom for the vendor, before a witness, to hand over a piece of turf from the holding to the purchaser. It was unnecessary to mark the conveyance with a deed, called a *Feoffment* or *Deed of*

Gift, but usual, and after 1677, compulsory.

fess point, In heraldry, the central point of an escutcheon.

fine, A money payment made by a tenant to his lord on the transfer of property to him.

fitch, Vetch, the plant *Vicia sativa* or its seed. Early forms: fecche(e), fechche, fetche, fetch, veitch.

force and arms, Phrase used in common law pleadings in declarations of trespass to denote that the act complained of was done with violence.

forelander, After 1400, one who may have held strips of land around the edges of large fields. May not have paid any rent.

freehold, A free tenure and not subject to the custom of the manor or the will of the lord. Its disposal after death was without restriction. Alternatively called *frank tenement* or *freeland*.

full, To clean and thicken cloth by moistening and beating processes. From Old French, *fouler*.

gaol delivery, Records kept of prisoners who were delivered from jail to stand trial at the Quarter Sessions. These records included the indictment, the jurors names, and the verdict.

gules, Red; depicted in engravings by perpendicular lines.

haberdasher, Formerly a dealer in a variety of articles now dealt with by other trades, including caps, and probably hats. In the course of the 16th cent. the trade seems to have been split into two, those of (1) a dealer in, or maker of, hats and caps, a hatter (obs.); (2) a dealer in small articles appertaining to dress, as thread, tape, ribbons, etc.

hereditatament, Any kind of property that can be inherited; anything descended to the heir at common law.

hop(e), An enclosed piece of land, especially in marshy areas.

hostler, One who took care of horses at an inn.

husbandman, A tenant farmer.

imparl, An abbreviated form of *imparlance*. In early practice, the time given to answer pleadings of the other party or time for parties to try to reach settlement.

indenture, Originally a document cut through the middle, the authenticity of one part being proved when matched with the other. The text of the document was written twice, above and below a word such as *indenture*. A jagged cut was made through the word. Used for contracts, title deeds, etc.

joynture, (form of *jointure*) Holding of an estate by two or more persons in joint tenancy or holding of property for the joint use of husband and wife for life and as provision for the latter in the event of her widowhood.

knight's fee, (1) A variable land area (depending on the quality of the soil) which was thought to be enough to support a knight and his family for one year. (Also knight's service) (2) A feudal tenure which obliged the holder to provide military assistance to the Crown, normally a fully-armed knight and his servants for 40 days a year. Later commuted to a money payment and abolished in 1660.

Lady day, (1) March 25, *die feste Sanctae Virginis Mariae*, the feast day of the Blessed Virgin Mary. (2) The blessed Billie Holiday

latten, (Old French) A brasslike alloy, commonly made in thin sheets, formerly much used for church utensils; iron plate, tinned over; any metal in thin sheets.

manor, The land held by a lord. It could be a subdivision of a parish or spread over more than one parish.

mark, In England, after the Conquest, the ratio of 20 sterling pennies to the ounce was the basis of computation; hence the value of the mark became fixed at 160 pence = 13s. 4d. or 2/3 of the £ sterling.

medieval, Equivalent to the Middle Ages, the time period from the 8th to the middle of the 15th century.

mercer, One who deals in textile fabrics, esp. a dealer in silks, velvets, and other costly materials (in full silk-mercer). Note: 1696 Phillips: "Mercer, in the City one that deals only in Silks and Stuffs;

in Country Towns, one that Trades in all sorts of Linen, Woollen, Silk, and Grocery Wares."

messuage, Originally, the portion of land intended to be occupied, or actually occupied, as a site for a dwelling-house and its appurtances ... Capital messuage: that occupied by the owner of a property containing several messuages. Probably originally, a graphic corruption of *mesnage* from French *menage*, house.

Michaelmas, September 25, *feste Sancti Micaelis*, the feast day of St. Michael.

moiety, A half, one of two equal parts, in legal or quasi-legal use.

muniments, A document, such as a title deed or charter, preserved as evidence in defense of rights or privileges belonging to a person or family.

nihil, Nothing. An abbreviated form of return made by a sheriff when he has been unable to serve a writ.

non est inventus, He is not found. The sheriff's return to a writ when the defendant is not found within his jurisdiction.

outlaw, In English law, one put out of protection or aid of the law, a fugitive.

pain, That which one is liable to pay or forfeit, e.g. *pain of 10 shillings*.

pensioner, At Cambridge University, an undergraduate student who is not a *Scholar* (q.v.).

perch, A linear measure of land which could vary between 9 and 26 feet, but later standardized to 16½ feet. Also used as a square measure, each side of which was one perch, equal to 1/40th of a rood or 1/160th of an acre.

perpetuana, A durable fabric of wool, manufactured in England from the 16th century.

pightle, A small piece of land in the open fields, or else a small enclosed plot. Alternatively spelled *pigtail, pingle*. Note that in the 1600 map of Great Henny, it is spelled *Pitle*.

pillow-bere, Pillow-case.

plaintiff, In a property transaction, the purchaser. Often abbreviated *pl.* Also see *de-*

mandant.

pledges, Persons who become sureties for the prosecution of a suit.

pole, Name of a lineal measure, esp. for land: in Statutory Measure, equal to 5½ yards or 16½ feet, but varying locally.

postfine, A duty formerly paid to the Crown for the royal license to levy a fine.

pound, Originally a pound weight of silver from which 240 pennies could be minted. Later there were 12 pennies or pence to a shilling and 20 shillings to the pound.

praiere, Meadow land.

presentation, The nomination of a clergyman to a benefice (an ecclesiastical post) by the holder of the advowson. The *presentation* was made to the bishop, who normally could not refuse the nomination.

primogeniture, The system by which, in the absence of a will, the oldest son (or his issue) was heir to the estate of his father, to the exclusion of other siblings . Abolished in 1925.

prove, To establish the genu-

ineness or validity of a will; to obtain probate of the same.

quarter, (as a measure) One fourth of a ton or eight bushels.

Quarter sessions, Four times a year the County Justices met to discuss local matters, including industrial relations, transmit the orders of the Crown or central government, and try all manner of offences against the law.

raze, To erase or obliterate writing by scraping or otherwise. Also scratched, cut, slit.

regrant, The giving back, by the manor lord, of copyhold land to the heirs of a deceased tenant. Often required payment, such as a *relief* (q.v.).

relict, A widow or widower.

relief, A payment by an incoming tenant to succeed to his ancestor's land. The payment varied with the size of the estate, typically a year's rent for a small holding.

reredos, A carved screen at the rear of an altar. From Anglo-French *reredos.*

reversion, A freeholder could lease his land, usually for a year, to an occupier who had a deed of grant or release, keeping for himself a future interest, i.e. a reversion. It could also be sold to a purchaser.

rod, A measure of length, equal to 5½ yards or 16½ feet; a pole.

roll, Court (and other) records were made on sheets of vellum, called membranes. These were stitched together end to end and rolled up.

rood, A square measure containing 40 square poles or perches, equal to 1/4th of an acre, but varying locally. Also a plot of land this size.

rood screen, The screen carrying a cross separating the chancel from the nave of a church.

sable, Black; depicted in engravings by horizontal and perpendicular lines crossing each other.

St. John's day, June 24, *feste Sancti Johannis*, the feast of St. John the Baptist.

Sts. Philip & James day, May 1, *die feste SS Philippi et Jacobi*, the feast day of Sts. Philip and James.

saxon, North German invaders of England in the 5th and 6th centuries.

say, The earliest form of *serge*. Much finer product than *bay* (q.v.). Usually used in the plural, e.g. *bays and says*.

scholar, At Cambridge University: a student who receives funds towards defraying the cost of education as a result of merit.

seam, (as a measure) A packload; of grain, 8 bushels.

seisin, A term meaning possession rather than ownership. A grant of land was only valid when the tenant had given the lord *livery of seisin*, usually a symbolic gift. A tenant was then 'seised in deed.' Probably dates from before the Norman Conquest. Opposite of *disseisin*.

sistern, Large vessel for water or liquor, often richly ornamented, used at the dinnertable.

socage, The tenure of land by certain determinate services other than knight-service.

stewe, (1) A pond or tank in which fish are kept until needed for the table. (2) A breeding place for pheasants.

surrender, In the transfer of copyhold land, the seller *surrendered* the property to the lord of the manor who then re-granted the land to the buyer.

tenement, Any type of permanent property, such as lands, houses, or rents. Lands and *tenements*: lands and all freehold interests in things immovable.

tenant, In a property transaction, the seller. Often abbreviated *ten*. Also see deforciant.

toft, A house or the site of a house and its outbuildings; a homestead or messuage; a knoll or hillock. Certain rights might still attach to the house even though it had long disappeared.

underwood, Small trees or brush growing beneath timber wood.

verge, (Usually used as in *by the verge*) See *copyhold*.

vestry, A room used for dressing or for parish meetings. From Old French *vestiare* a dressing place.

villein, In the 11th century feudal system, the highest of three social gradations, a comparatively free villager. Below the villein were the *bordar* and the *serf*. Later, after 1400, one who held about 30 acres and who paid 17 shillings 9 pence a year for the rental of the land.

wage law, To give a pledge or security for the performance of an act.

way, In legal documents, sometimes equivalent to a right-of-way.

yeoman, A man holding a small landed estate; a freeholder under the rank of gentleman; hence vaguely, a commoner or countryman of respectable standing, esp. one who cultivates his own land, worth at least 40 shillings a year. A yeoman was qualified to serve on juries and vote for shire representatives.

11

Appendix: George[B]

The first document is the 1600 deed by which George Fitch obtained four parcels in the manor of Great Henney from Roger Gwynne of London. This is followed by the 1605 will of George Fitch. All documents, which in the original are written as a single paragraph with little or no punctuation, have been subdivided for ease of reading. The original spelling, however, has been preserved wherever possible. Most unfamiliar words not defined in earlier chapters will be found in the *Glossary*.[1]

1600 Deed

This Indenture made the Thirtith daie of the moneth 1600
of November in the Thre and fortith yeare of the Raigne of
our Soveraigne ladie Elizabeth by the grace of god Quene of
England Fraunce and Ireland Defender of the faith etc.
Betwene Roger Gwynne Citizen and Grocer of London and
lord and owner of the meadowes of great Heney and Pebmar-
she in the countie of Essex of the one part And George Fitche
of Sudburie in the countie of Suff. Mercer of the other part
Witnesseth that the said Roger Gwynne for and in consid-
eracon of the Some of Twentie Sixe poundes and Thirtene shillinges and fower pence of lawfull monye of England unto him by
the said George Fitch and before the ensealinge hereof well and
trulie satisfied and paied in name of A fyne **hath** devised

1.   All documents transcribed from copies of the originals by Edith Fitch Swapp.

graunted and to ferme letten and by theis ferme lett unto the said George Fitche

All these fower sevrell parcells of meadowe beinge coppy-holde parcells of the said manore of great Heney and Pebmarsh them herafter expressed

That is to saie One peece of meadowe conteyninge by esti-macon three Roodes late graunted with the tenement Springolde as it lieth in Great Heney in the comon meadowes there called Dugfen meadowe betwene the lande nowe as late in the tenure of Willm Fissher at Brownes towardes the East And the manor of Twinsted and the land called the Hearst towardes the West both the heddes thereof abbutte upon the landes sometime Thomas Goblond towardes the south and north

And a piece of the lands in the said Meadowe contenith by estimacon three Roodes and lieth in Heney aforesaid in the said meadowe called Dugfen betwene the meadowe sometime of Ed-ward Cressener towardes the East and the meadowe late Willm Fissher the elder towardes the West one hed abubutteth upon the Meadowe called longe acre towardes the South and the other hed abbutteth upon a peece of meadowe conteyninge a halfe acre nowe or late Alexander Oxborough towardes the North

And the Third peece of the said meadowe conteyninge alsoe by estimacon three Roodes and lieth in Dugfen afore said betwene the meadowe late the said Willm Fissher towardes the East and the meadowe of Isaack Wincoll gent in part and the meadowe late of the said Willm Fissher in part and the meadowe late Richard Walshe in part and the meadowes of other men in part towardes the West one hed therof abbutteth upon the land belonginge to the manor of Twinsted called brocke acre towardes the North And the other hed therof abbutteth upon a peece of meadowe of Willm Fissher conteyninge by estimacon one Roode towardes the South

And the forth peece of the said meadowe lyeth in Dugfen aforesaid betwene the meadowe of John Sewall towardes the South and the meadowe of John Pollye towardes the North the one head therof abbutteth upon the meadowe of the said Willm

Fissher and the other hed threof abbutteth upon the comon River there towardes the East and conteyneth also by estimacon three roodes

Whiche said fower Peeces of meadowe late were in the tenure or occupacon of one John Oxborough deceased and alsoe in the tenure or occupacon of Jeoffrey Oxborough the sonne of the said John Whoe died without issue By meanes wherof and by force of the last will and testament of the said John Oxborough one John Woodthorpe Clerke and Robert Poule Executers of the last will of the said John Oxborough did sell the said premisses unto one Willm Upcher and his heires whoe Was admitted therunto tenant as appeareth at the courte holden at the Manor of great Heney the first daie of Aprill in the thirtith yeare of the Quenes hieyhnes Raigne that nowe is And John Oxborough son and heire of the said John Oxborough at the said courte did devise and release all his right and title in and to the premisses unto the said Willm Upcher and his heires and whych said Willm Upcher had issue Thomas Upcher and Died and the said Thomas Upcher was admitted Tenante to the said premisses And the said Thomas Upcher at the courte with the view of Franke pledge holden at the said manor of great Heney the forth Daie of December in the [two?] and fortith Yeare of the Quenes hieyhnes as did surrender and release his right till and [?] and to the said Roger Gwynne then lord of the said Manor and beinge then and there present at the said court to the propre behest and [?] of the said Roger Gwynne and his heyres as by the roules of the said courtes [?]

To have and to houlde the said Fower peeces of meadowe withall and singular their Appurtenances with the said George Fitche his executors administrators and assignes from the feast of the Annunciacon of the blessed virgen Marie nowe last past before the date hereof unto the ende and terme of one thousand Yeares from Nowe next ensuinge fullie to be complete and ended withut Impeachement of enye maner of waste

Yealdinge and payinge threfore yerlie duringe the said terme unto the said Roger Gwynne his heires and assignes to the manor of great Heney three shillinges of lawfull monie of England at the feasts of Ste michiell the Archangell and the Annunciation of the blessed Virgin marye by equall and even porcons and to doe fealty to the court of the Manor of great Heney once evry yeare upon reasonable Warninge or this to forfett for eney Defalt three pence of lawfull monye

And the said Roger Gwynne doeth covenant for him his heires executors and administrators to and with the said George Fitche his executors and administrators and assignes for the Rentes and [?] aforesaid shall and maie peaceblie and ymetlie have hold and occupie the said fower peeces of meadowe every part therof with the Appurtenances without anye lawfull eviccon or recovery therof or of anye part therof to be had or made by the said Roger Gwynne and Beatrix his wife or either of them their or either of their heires or assignes or by or under [?] Chamberleyne Esquire his heyres or assignes or by anye other person or persons lawfullie clamyinge by from or under them or anye of them

And my [?] discharged or from time to tyme upon reasonable request shalbe saved and kempt harmless by the said Roger Gwynne his heires executors or administrators of and from the rentes services and [?] due or to growe due to the chiefe lords of the Manor whereof the premisses bene houlden as of and from all maner of chardges statutes reversions indegentes fynes executions issues and Amercements from interests titles and encombrances had moved or growne by from or under the said Roger Gwynne and Fitch [?] Ruffe Chamberlayne or to be therafter had moved or growne by from or by meanes of the said Roger Gwynne his heires and assignes duringe the said terme

And finallie the said George Fitche doeth graunte for him his executors administrators and assignes unto the said Roger Gwynne his heires and assignes That when and as often as the said estate interest and terme of yeares of in and to the said parcells of meadowe or any part therof shalbe aliened assigned setover or tenement therof altered That then upon eney suche

assigninge setover or alteracon of Tenement therof The said
George Fitche his executors administrators heires or assignes to
whose possesson the same shall [?] or be convaied or assured shall
paie and allowe (out of the presmisses soe to be aliened) unto the
said Roger Gwynne and his heires or issue Landes or proprieties
therof for every acre that soe shalbe aliened assigned setover or
tenement altered Twelve pence of lawful monye in name of A fyne
or Income and soe after that rate for more or lesser penaltie or
anye part therof whiche soe shalbe aliened assigned forever or
tenement altered, And that for not payment therof yt shalbe
lawfull to and for the said Roger Gwynne his heires and Assignes
to enter into the said parcelles of meadowes or anye part therof
whiche soe shalbe aliened assigned settover or tenement altered
and therto distreyne for the said fyne or Income whiche soe shalbe
behinde and not paiyed and the distres there soe taken to drive
lead and carrye awaie and to detaine and keape untill of the said
fyne or monye he the said Roger Gwynne his heires and assignes
shalbe fullye satisfied and paied

In witnes wherof [?] to this present Indenture have hereunto enterchangeablie sett their handes and seales the daie [torn
away]

Sealed and delivered in the presens of
Robert Thompson[1]

The Will

In the Name of God Amen The twelveth day of May in   1605
the yeare of our Lorde god one thousand six hundred and
five I George Fytch of Edwardston in the County of Suff:[c]
Mercer beinge sick in body but yet of perfect mynde and
memory Thanks be to god therefore; utterly renouncing all
former wylls and Testaments whatsoever heretofore by me
made, doe nowe ordayne make and declare this my present

1. E.R.O. D/DH vi.c.57.

testament conteyninge therein my last wyll in manner and forme followinge

First and principallye I commende my soule unto almightie god my creator and to Jesus Christe my onely saviour and redemer and to the holie ghoste my sanctifier and comforter thre persons and one god, And my body to be buried in christian buriell

Item I give unto Joane my welbeloved wife the somme of fouretie poundes of lawfull money of England to be paied unto her by myne executors in manner and forme following That is to saie, twentie pounds within six monethes next after my decease And the more Twenty poundes within one whole yeare next and imediatly after my death and decease Also I wyll and devise unto the saide Joane my wief one Annuity or yerely rent or yerelie payment of five poundes the yeare for and during the full terme and tyme of seven yeres next ensuinge after my death half yearely to be paid her equall porcons out of my messuage or tenement landes and hereditaments withe their appurtenances scituate and beinge in Edwardstone aforesaide (if she shall so long live) The first payment thereof to beggin within one half yeare next after my decease, Moreover I give and bequeath unto the saide Joane my wiefe one downe bed and all other the household stuf and implements of household which I received with her by marriage, All which saide severall legacies Annuities and bequests I give and bequeath unto her uppon condicon That she shall nott challenge any Thirdes or Dowrye out of any my landes or tenements whatsoever and nott otherwise,

Item I do devise and bequeath unto Thomas Fytch my eldest sonne after the end and determynacon of twelve yeares next ensuinge after my death and departure out of this life All That my messuage or tenement lienge and beinge in Edwardstone aforesaide And all the wainscoat and glasse now standinge and beinge uppon any windoes belonginge to the same; Together with all and singular my landes pastures meadowes feedinges and hereditaments whatsoever with their appurtenances, To have to hould the same after the tyme aforesaide to him and to the heires of his body lawfully begotten uppon this Condicon following and not otherwise That is to saie, that the saide Thomas shall and will well and truely content and pay or cause to be paied unto my foure children viz. George, Joseph, and Arthur my sonnes and Fraunces my daughter the full and whole somme of threscore thirtene poundes six shillinges and eighte pence of lawfull English money in manner and forme followinge, viz. unto George, Arthur and Fraunces and to eyther of them the somme of twentye poundes, And to Josephe the somme of thirtene poundes six shillinges and eighte pence within one whole yeare next after the saide Thomas shall by force of this my saide wyll enter into the foresaide messuage or tenement landes meadowes pastures feedinges and hereditaments with their appurtenses, Provided always that if it shall happen the saide Thomas my sonne to make defalte of paymente of and in the foresaide somme of threscore thirtene poundes six shillinges and eighte pence or of any parte or parcell thereof contrary to the forme before expressed Then I will and further devise that the saide George my second sonne shall enter into the foresaide messuage or tennement landes meadowes pastures feedings & hereditaments with all and singular their appurtennes And the same to the best advantage shall sell And the money thereof arisinge and commynge shall firste pay or cause to be paide unto the said Joseph Arthur and Fraunces their aforesaide severall sommes, of the which saide severall sommes with his saide somme of twentie poundes being paide and discharged shall pay and yeild up or cause to be paied yeilded up or delivered unto the saide Thomas my sonne all the surplufage or overplus of the money that shall be and remaine in the handes and custody of him the saide George for the sale of the saide messuage or tennement and other the premisses and yf the sayd George shall cause to make sale of ye foresaide messuage or tennement & all other the premisses as is afore menconed then I will and further devise That the saide Joseph Arthur and Fraunces or for many of them as shall then be livinge shall by force of this my will enter into the aforesaide messuage or tenne-

ment as aforesaide, And the same to the best advantage shall sell,
And the money thereof arisinge and comminge shall first paie and
discharge them selves their saide severall sommes And the surplufage or overplus as beforesaide shall yeild up and deliver unto
the saide Thomas Provided further and nevertheless my true
intent and meaninge is That if there shall nott be founde sufficient goodes which I now have or by any manner of wayes or
meanes of right are due unto me to pay all such debts as (?) and
discharge all such legacies (?) the charges of my funerall and
Probate of my wyll then I will and further devise that my
executors hereafter named shall by force of this my will sell the
foresaide messuage and tennement and all other the premisses
(which my sonne Thomas before in this my will given upon
condicon to the best advantage for and towarde the payment of
all my saide debts and legacies discharging of my funerall and
probate of my will, the which all beinge performed the surplus or
overplus of which money uppon the saide sales shall be yeilded
up and delivered unto the saide Thomas my sonne;

Also I wyll and devise that my saide executors hereafter
named shall sell my messuage and tennemente with th'appurtenances as it is scituate and beinge in Ballingdon the County of
Essex and which I late purchased of one Sheppard of Ballingdon
aforesaide, to the best advantage within a convenient tyme at
their discrecone for and towards the payment of my debts and
legacies as is aforesaide

Item I give and bequeath unto George Fytch my saide sonne
the somme of fourscore poundes of lawfull English money to be
paid unto him at his age of two and twentie yeares and two paire
of sheetes and my gould ringe that my name is uppon to be
likewise delivered unto him at his age aforesaide,

Item I give and bequeath unto Joseph Fytch my saide sonne
the somme of fiftie poundes of lawfull money of England to be
paied unto him at his full age of foure and twentie yeares; And
two paire of sheetes to be delivered unto him at his age aforesaide
Item I give and bequeath unto Arthur Fytch my saide sonne the

somme of fourescore poundes of lawfull English money to be payed unto him at his age of two and twentie yeares And two paire of sheetes to be delivered unto him at his age aforesaide

Item I give and bequeath unto Fraunces my saide daughter the somme of fourescore pounds of lawfull English money And one featherbed in the great chamber with all that belongeth unto it, And two downe pillowes And two paire of sheetes And my biggest brasse pot, to be paied and delivered unto her at her full age of one and twentie yeares

Item I give and bequeath unto the aforesaide Fraunces my daughter out of my foresaide messuage or tennement and all other the premisses unto my sonne Thomas in this wyll before given one Annuitie or yearely rent or yearely payment of five poundes the yeare half yearely to be paied by even and (?) porcons untill she shall accomplish here saide full age of one and twentie yeares or the day of her marriage which shall first happen, the first payment thereof to beggin with six moneths next after my decease

Item I will and it is my true meaninge that father french shall have his Annuitie or yerely rent of sixe poundes a yeare payed unto him accordinge to his sonnes will, Also I will that my children shall have their silver spoones that were given them at their Christeninges

Item I will and my meaninge is that Joane my wife shall contynue in my messuage or tennement wherein I nowe dwell and Arthur my sonne and Fraunces my daughter there with her duringe the terme of sixe monethes next ensuinge after my decease And that they shall have during all the saide tyme sufficient maynetenance for their diet, And after the saide six monethes ended I will that my saide daughter Fraunces shall contynue with my saide wife untill she shall be fit to be placed in some good and convenient service, And that my sonne Arthur in the meane tyme or soe soone as conveniently may be shall be bound an apprentice to some good trade or occupacon,

Also I give and bequeath unto Robte Stebbing three shillinges foure pence of lawfull English money

Item I give unto John French one silver spoone, Item I give and bequeath unto Robte French one silver spoone Moreover I wyll and bequeath the saide John French and Robte French shall have their tipped pottes given unto them with their fathers will and testament

Also I will that Bridget Gosse and Suzan Gosse shall eithere of them have one ring accordinge to the last will of French

Item I give and bequeath unto Marie Burgis my grande child the somme of sixtene poundes of lawfull English money to be paied unto her at her full age of one and twentie yeares, Also I give unto the saide Marie Burgis one brasse bot to be delivered to her father to her use (?) after my decease

Item I give unto Sara Taylor my wifes daughter the somme of thirtie shillinges,

Finally all the residue of my yardes rights credites cattles and chatteles readye money and plate whatsoever which I now have in myne owne custodye or which be or remaine in any other place unbequeathed my debts and legacies beinge first paied my funerall and the Probate of my (will) togeather withall charges concerninge the same borne and susteyned I give them wholly to Thomas my sonne and William Fytch my brother, which saide Thomas and William I make constitute and ordeyne executors of this my last will and Testament, desiringe them in good behalf to see the same truely executed performed and doon according to my true intent and meaninge herein as my sure truste is they will. In witness whereof to every leaf of this my last wyll and testament beinge foure leaves in number I have set my hande and to the last my seale the day and yeare first wrytten.

George Fytch.

Read sealed and delivered in the presence of George Culpeck Christofer yeoman and of me Phillip Clark Sara Tayler the marke of George Culpeck.

Memorandum these wordes of his bodye lawfully begotten beinge in the first leaf and xxvi[th] lyne were interlyned before th'ensealinge and delivery hereof, And also these wordes one feather bolster two pillowes one coverlet two blanckets beinge three tymes repeated in the second leaf towards the later end thereof of the same leaf, And almost thre lynes in the third leaf were razed before th'ensealinge and delivery hereof, as almoste five lynes in the said third sheet or leaf nowe likewise razed: before th'ensealinge and delivery hereof in the presence of the aforenamed parties, viz. George Culpeck Chrystofer yeoman and of me Phillip Clarke wryter hereof the marke of George Culpeck Sara Talar Christofer yeoman

Probatum fuit suprascriptu - (?) London coram venebili - domeno Johanne Bennet milete logum - Thomae Fytch filij - et prime dicti - et Willem Fitch -[1]

---

1. Prerogative Court of Canterbury (P.C.C.) 49 Hayes.

12

Appendix: Thomas[A]

The first four documents all describe the same 1630 transaction between Thomas Fitch and his wife's cousin, William Brock for 130 acres of both freehold and copyhold land in Copford, Stanway, and Great Birch. The last document is the 1632 will of Thomas Fitch. All documents, which in the original are written as a single paragraph with little or no punctuation, have been subdivided for ease of reading. The occasional insertion of a string of x's in the text appear to cover over an area that has been scratched to remove the ink from the vellum.[1]

Bargain and Sale

This Indenture made the Seaven and Twentieth Day 1630 of September in the Sixth Yeare of the Reigne of our Soverine Lord **Charles** by the grace of god of England Scotland Fraunce and Ireland Kinge defender of the fayth **Betweene** Willm Brock of Thelnetham in the Countye of Suff gent brother and heire of John Brock deceased sonne and heire whilest he lived of Bartholmewe Brock gent deceased of th'one parte And Thomas Fitch of Bockinge in the countye of Essex clothier of th'other parte

Witnesseth that the said Willm **As well** for and in consideration of the sume of six hundred and Threescore poundes of lawfull money of England to him in hand att and before th'enseal-

---

1. All documents transcribed from copies of the originals by Edith Fitch Swapp.

inge and deliverye of these presents by the said Thomas well and truely paid whereof the said Willm doth acknowledge the receipte And thereof and of anye parte thereof doth cleerely aquite and discharge the said Thomas his heires executors administrators and assignes and every of them forever by these presents

As alsoe for divers other good causes and consideracons him the said Willm thereunto spedallie movinge **hath** bargayned sould and granted And by these presents doth fullie freely and absolutely bargayne sell and grante unto the said Thomas his heires and assignes forever **All that** little enclosed customary and coppyhold Meadowe conteyninge by estimacon three Roodes more or lesse with th'appurtenances called Goose Meade lyinge att the Southend of a Meadowe called Holemeade in Copford in the said Countye of Essex and holden by coppie of Courte Roll of the Mannor of Copford in Copford aforesaid the same coppiehold premisses to be assured accordinge to the Custome of the said Mannor and not otherwise

And alsoe the said Willm for the consideracons aforesaid **hath** granted bargayned sould xxxx and confirmed And by these presents doth grante bargayne sell xxxx and confirme unto the said Thomas Fitch his heires and assignes forever **All that** freehold Meadowe late of Robte Warde North conteyninge by estimacon three Roodes be it more or lesse xxxx lyinge and beinge in the p'she of Stanwaye in the said County of Essex That is to saye betweene the landes late of Chrystopher Jemmy Elginer in the Righte of Bridgett his wife called Stubbings in the East and North parte and the Meadowe late of the said Bartholmewe Brooke and nowe of the said Willm upon the South and West part And was sometymes parcell of the possessions of the late Monastery of St. Johns in Colchester in the said County of Essex and nowe is in the occupacon of one John Phillipps or his assignes **And all** and all manner of Woods underwoods comons mewes rents Revercons remaynders comodityes & profitts to the saide freehold belonginge or apperteyninge with their and every of their appurtenances

And alsoe all that Messuage or tenement with th'appurtenances called Nevers alsoe Pages or by wt other name or names soever the same is called or knowen wherein the said John Phillipps nowe dwelleth scituate & beinge in the p'ishe of Much Birch in the said Countye of Essex **And alsoe** all the houses buildings barnes stables tofts orchards gardens landes tenements & hereditaments meadowes pastures feedings rents woods and underwoods to the same Messuage or tenement belonginge or in ainewise apperteyninge unto or with the same used or occupied or accepted reputed taken or knowne as parte parcell or member of or belonginge to the said Messuage or tenement with their and every of their rights members and appurtenances nowe in the oqupacon of the said John Phillipps or his assignes conteyninge together by estimacon One hundred and thirty acres more or lesse And alsoe all other Messuages landes tenements and hereditaments whtsoever of him the said Willm Brock scituate lyinge and beinge in the p'ishes or Feildes of Much Birch Copford and Stanwaye aforesaid in little Birch in the said county of Essex or in anie of them with th'appurtenances nowe in the occupacon of the said John Phillipps or his assignes **And alsoe** all woods underwoods comons wayes waters & rents thereunto belonginge or in anie wise apperteyninge **And the** Revercon & revercons remaynder & remaynders estate right title interest clayme & demannd wtsoever of him the said Willm Brock of in & to the above bargayned xxxxx premysses and enye parte & parcell thereof **And alsoe** all coppies of Courte Rolls deeded evidences xx writings and muniments concerninge th'above menconed bargayned premysses onlye or onlye aine parte of them **Together** with true coppies to be coppied out at the Coste and charges of the said Thomas Fitch his heires or assignes of all such other coppies of Courte Rolls Deedes evidences and writings whatsoever as doe concerne the same above menconed bargayned premysses of aine parte thereof joyntlye with anie other landes or tenements of the said Willm Brock **To have to hold** all and eny th'above menconed bargayned Freehold premysses with their &

every of their rights members & appurtenances unto the said Thomas Fitch his heires and assignes for ever **To & for** th'onelye sole and proper use and behoofe of him the said Thomas Fitch and his heires and assignes forever **Of** the Cheife Lords xxxx of the Fee thereof by the advices thereofre formlie due and of right accustomed xxxx

And the said Willm Brock for himselfe his heires executors administrators and assignes and every of them doth by these presents Covenant promyse and grante to and wth the said Thomas Fitch his heires executors administators assignes and enye of them in manner and forme followinge (that is to saye) **First** that he the said Willm Brock nowe is & soe att the tyme of the executinge or vestinge of the First estate of & in th'above menconed bargayned Freehold premisses witheir appurtenances unto and in the said Thomas Fitch for the vestinge of the same premysses & enye parte & parcell thereof in the said Thomas & his heires shall & will stand & be lawfullie seised of & in the same Freehold premysses and eney parte of them wth their appurtenances of & in a good sure lawfull estate of inheritance in Fee simple

And alsoe att the tyme of the rendringe & assuringe of the said Coppiehold premysses wth th'appurtenances unto the use of the said Thomas Fitch & his heires shall and will stand & be lawfullie seised of and in the same coppiehold premysses with th'appurtenances of the like estate accordinge to the Custome of the said Mannor to the use of him and his heires without anie revercon or revercons Remaynder or remaynders and wthout any condicon or limytacon of anie further or other use or uses wch maye anie wayes alter change encomber or de[?]neyne the same estate or estates

And alsoe that he the said Willm nowe hath full powers good right and lawfull authoritye in his alone right to grante and convey the same coppihold and freehold premysses accordinge to their severall natures & qualityes unto the said Thomas and his heires accordinge to the intente and true meaninge of these presents

And alsoe that the the said Thomas his heires and or assignes shall or lawfullie maye from tyme to tyme & att all tymes hereafter peaceablie & quietly have hold use occupie possesse & enjoye all and every th'above menconed bargayned coppihold & freehold premysses wth their and enye of their appurtenances **Freed** and discharged or otherwise upon reasonable request to him the said Willm Brock his heires executors administrators by the said Thomas Fitch his heires or assignes to be made he the said Thomas Fitch his heires and assignes and the said landes tentements hereditaments & premysses above bargayned & enye of them shall be from tyme to tyme & att all tymes hereafter well and sufficiently served & kepte harmles by the said Willm Brock his heires executors administrators of from all former and other [quists?] grants bargaynes sales leases joyntures Dowers and namely of & from the Joynture & dower of Margarett nowe wife of the said Willm and of Elizabeth mother of the said Willm and of & from all mortgages entayles Anuities rents charges Rents [lock?] arrerages of rents Intrucons meane rates Liveryes [Onstre le maines[a]?] fynes postfynes yssues amercements recognizances statutes [?]chante & of the staple payments debts Judgements execucons and extents & of & from all other titles troubles charges and encombrances whatsoever had made comitted done or xxxxxxx suffered by the said Willm Brock and Bartholimewe Brock or either of them (the ancient and accustomed rents hereafter to growe due or payable to the cheife Lord or Lordes of the Mannor or Mannors of whome the same premysses are holden in free & comon socage Tenure or by coppie of Courte Rolle onely excepted)

And alsoe that the same bargayned freehold premysses and enye parte and parcell of them are holden in free and comon socage tenure and not in capite nor in socage in capite nor by Knights [fee?] or thereof the Kings Magistie or of anie other meane Lord or Lordes wtsoever

And further alsoe that he the said Willm Brock and xxxx Margarett his wife and the heires of the said Willm and the said Elizabeth and anye of them all and every other person and persons wtsoever nowe havinge or lawfullie clayminge to have or will att anie tyme hereafter shall or maye have or lawfullie clayme to have anie lawfull estate right title interest clayme or demand wtsoever of to or out of th'above menconed bargayned freehold and coppiehold premysses or of or out of anie parte or parcell of them by from or under him the said Willm Brock and the said Bartholmewe his father or either of their estate or estates right title or interest shall and will from tyme to tyme & att all tymes hereafter for & duringe the space of Ten whole yeares next ensuinge the Date of these presents unon the reasonable request and att the coste and charges in the lawe of the said Thomas his heires or assignes wthin the Countyes of Suff North or the Citty of Norwich Make doe acknowledge suffer execute levy and furnish unto the said Thomas his heires and assignes All and enye such further & other acte & acts thinge and things devyses conveyannces and assurances in the lawe whatsoever for the further better and more perfecte conveyinge assuringe Sure makinge of the above menconed bargayned freehold & coppiehold premysses respectfullye with their & enye of their appurtenances accordinge to theire severall natures & quallityes unto the said Thomas Fitch his heires and assignes for ever wth warrantye onlye of him the said Willm and his heires agaynst him & his heires and agaynest the heires of the said Bartholmewe and every of them & agaynst all persons clayminge by from or under anie of the estate right title or interest As by the said Thomas his heires or assignes or by his or their counsell learned in the lawe shall be reasonable advised or advised & required

And it is by these presents fullie & absolutely condiscended concluded & agreed unto uppon by and betweene all & enye of them their & enye heires **That** aswell all and enye tyme & tymes feoffments conveyances & assurances wtsoever had made levyed or suffred or to be had made levyed or finished of the above menconed bargayned freehold premysses wth their & enye of their appurtenances shall be & shall enure & shall be deemed expounded and taken to be & enure to and for th'onely sole and proper use and behoofe of him the said Thomas Fitch and of his heires & assignes for ever And to or for none other use or uses intents or purposes wtsoever

In witnes whereof the parties above named in these presents Indentures Interchangablie have sett their hands & seales the daye & yeare first above written.

[Signature of] Willyam Brock[1]

Enfeoffment

To all [?] people to whome this shall come Willm Brock of Thelnetham in the Countye of Suff gent sendeth greetinge in our Lord god everlastinge Knowe yee that the said Willm **As well** in parte of performance of certeyne Covenants and agreements menconed and expressed in certeyne Indentures of bargayne and sale bearinge date wth these presents made betweene the said Willm of th'one parte And Thomas Fitch of Bockinge in the Countye of Essex Clothier of th'other parte

As alsoe for divers other good causes and consideracons him thereunto spidallie movinge **hath** granted enfeoffed and confirmed And by these presents doth grante enfeoffe and confirme unto the said Thomas Fitch his heires and assignes for ever

All that freehold meadowe late of Robte Warde North conteyninge by estimacon Three Roodes be it more or lesse lyinge and beinge in the parishe of Stanwaye in the said Countye of Essex sometymes parcell of the possessions of the late Monastery of St. Johns in Colchester in the said County of Essex and nowe in the occupacon of one John Phillips or his assignes And all and all manner of woodes underwoods Comons wayes rents revercons Remaynders comodities and profitts to the said freehold meadowe

---

1. E.R.O. Colchester & North East Essex Branch, D/DU 161/171.

belonginge or apperteyninge wth their and enye of their appurtenances

And alsoe all that Messuage or tenemente with the appurtenances called Nevers also Pages or by wt other name or names soever the same is called or knowne wherein the said John Phillipps nowe dwelleth scituate and beinge in the parishe of Much Birch in the said Countye of Essex And alsoe all the houses buildings barnes stables tofts orchards gardens landes tenements hereditaments meadowes pastures feedings rents [fines?] woods and underwoodes to the same Messuage or tenemente belonginge or in anie wise apperteyninge or to or with the same used or occupied or accepted reputed taken or knowne as parte parcell or member of or belonginge to the said Messuage or tenemente with their enye and enye of their rights members and appurtenances nowe in the occupacon of the said John Phillipps or his assignes conteyninge together by estimacon One hundred & Thirtie acres more or lesse

And alsoe all other the Freehold Messuages landes tentements and hereditaments wtsoever of the said Willm Brock scituate lyinge and beinge in the parishes or feildes of Much Birch Copford and Stanwaye - and in Little Birch in the said Countye of Essex or in anie of them wth th'appurtenances nowe in the occupacon of the said John Phillipps or his assignes And also all woods underwoods comons wayes waters and rents thereunto belonginge or in anie wise apperteyninge **And** the Revercon & revercons Remaynder and remaynders estate right title interest clayme and demand whatsoever of him the said Willm Brock of in and to the premysses above granted and enye parte and parcell thereof wth their and enye of their rights members and appurtenances

To have & to hold th'above granted Messuage or tenemente and all and singler other th'above granted premysses unto the said Thomas Fitch his heires and assignes for ever **To & for** th'onely sole and proper use & behoofe of him the said Thomas Fitch his heires and assignes for ever **Of** the cheife lord or lords of the Fee or Fees thereof by the [fines?] therefore due and of right accustomed

And the said Willm Brock and his heires all and enye the premysses above menconed to be granted or assured wth th'appurtenances unto the said Thomas Fitch his heires & assignes agaynst him the said Willm and his heires and Margarett his wife and agaynst the heires of Bartholmewe Brock deceased his father and agaynst Elizabeth mother of the said Willm and enye of them shall and will warrant and for ever defend by these presents

In witnes whereof the said Willm Brock hath hereunto sett his hand and seale the Seaven & Twentieth daye of September Anno Dm 1630 Anno - regni Dm - Caroli nunc Regis Anglie - Sexto xxx [remainder torn away]

Sealed and delivered in the presence of us

[Signatures of] W. Lyngwood   Robt. Douer   Cambell Coamer   Gregory Jenner   Wm. Hammonde

Memorandi that full peaceblie and quiett thate [?] & posession of & in the freehold Messuage landes & tenements wth th'appurtenances with [?] to be bargayned were [?] had taken by the wthin named Wm Brock and by him delivered to the wthin written Thomas Fitch accordinge to his firme fine & effect true intent and meaninge of these presents in the presence of us

[Signatures of] W. Lyngwood   Robt Douer   John Clarke the mke [X] of John   William marcey   Phillippes [?]   George [X] Littlebury   Wm Hammonde[1]

Note: William Lingwood was a lawyer and a member of the "Four and Twenty," a close-knit fraternity of the elite of Braintree.[2]

Bond

The condicon of this Obligacon is such that yf the wthin Bonnden Willm Brock his heires executors administrators & all assignes and enye of them shall and doe from tyme to tyme and

---

1. E.R.O. Colchester & North East Essex Branch, D/DU 161/172.
2. Quin, *op.cit., p. 89.*

att all tymes hereafter well and truely observe perform fullie and keepe all and singler the covenants grants Articles & agreements wtsoever conteyned & specified in a payre of Indentures of bargayne and sale bearinge the Date within written made betweene the said Willm of th'one parte and the within named Thomas Fitch of th'other parte with aine the parte and on behalfe of him the said Willm his heires executors administrators and assignes & enye or and of them is or ought to be observed performed fullfilled or kepte accordinge to the intent and true meaninge of the same Indentures that then this presents Obligacon to be void or els to stand & abide in full force effect & vertue.

[Followed by a second page in Latin with same signatures as above, adding Willyam Brock.][1]

Final Concord

1631/2 The fourth document, in Latin, is dated Easter Term 1631/2.

Tho. Fitch v. Wm. Brocke, gent., and w. Margt.

1 messuage, 1 garden, 1 orchard, 66a. of land, 12a. of meadow, 46a. of pasture, 12a. of wood, and 4/6 rents in Great and Little Birch, Copford and Stanway.[2]

The Will

1632 The following is the complete text of the will of Thomas[A] Fitch. Although reproduced here with its original spelling and punctuation, it has been divided into paragraphs to facilitate finding specific bequests.

In the name of God Amen The Eleaventh daie of December in the yeare of our Lord God One thousand six hundred thirtie two I Thomas Fitch of Bockinge in the Countie of Essex Clothier beinge weake and sicke of bodie yet of good and perfect minde and memory God be praised therefore and callinge to minde the uncertainty of this life and the certainty of Death doe desire to

1. E.R.O. Colchester & North East Essex Branch, D/DU 16/173.
2. E.R.O. Colchester & North East Essex Branch, D/DU 16/174, 175. Note: 175 is a "counterpart" or copy of 174.

sett in order that porcon wch God hath trusted mee withall And first I bequeath my Soule to God my Creator and sole and onely Redeemer And my bodie to be buried in Xtian buriall believinge that after this separacon of soule and bodie in this life they shall both be raised when Christ shall come in judgment and be united again together to life with God and Christ for ever in that immortall kingdom wch never shall have end and that by and through the mercie of God and meritte of Christ my onely Redeemer

Item I give to the poore people of Bockinge three pounds to be paid within one moneth next after my decease

Item I give and bequeath unto Thomas Fitch my eldest sonne and to his heires All that chiefe messuage wherein I now dwell in Bockinge with the appurtenances and the messuage thereto adjoyninge now in the occupacon of my said sonne Thomas and all the houses buildinges landes tenements and hereditaments whatsoever which I heretofore purchased of Willm Collin in Bocking aforesaid And alsoe all the tenements and lands with appurtenances in Bockinge aforesaid wch I lately purchased of Edward Poppen gent. and his wife and John Amptill and his wife and alsoe the barne in Bockinge by Panfield Lane wch I late purchased to Thomas Trotter Marchant upon condicon that he pay my Sister Stracey Twentie shillinges yearely duringe her naturall life

Item I give to my sonne John his heires forever All that messuage with the appurtenances in Bockinge aforesaid late of Richard Usher deceased and which I late purchased of Paul Usher and Peter Kirby and Ursula Bond Widow with all the houses buildinges yards and gardens thereto belonginge and the litle garden or orchard in Bockinge now in the Occupacon of Richard Skinner or his assignes And the tenements with the appurtenances in the occupacon of Thomas Laye in Bockinge aforesaid by Panfield lane, and the great orchard thereto adjoyninge wch I late also purchased of Mr. Thomas Trotter Marchant to enter upon the same at his age of one and twentie yeares

Item I give to my sonne John two hundred poundes to be paid him at his age of one and twentie yeares

Item I give to my sonne James one hundred poundes to be paid him when he shalbe a bachelor of Art of two yeares standing in the univ(er)sity of Cambridge, for I desire he should be bredd up a scholler and alsoe I give him and my minde is that he shall have thirtie pounds a yeare paide him by my Executrix out of my lands and tenements from the tyme of his admission to be a scholler in Cambridge untill he be or have tyme there to be a master of arts

Item I give to my sonnes Nathaniell and Jeremy to either of them and either of their heires a moytie and halfe part of the Farme messuage lands and tenements both free and copie lyinge and beinge in Birch or elsewhere in the Countie of Essex wch I late purchased of William Brock Gent with their and every of their appurtenances that same Farme and premisses to be equallie divided between them & their heires and they to enter upon the same at their severall ages of one and twentie yeares

Item I will and my minde is that my Executrix hereafter named shall laie out and disburse out of my personall estate within one yeare next after my decease the some of six hundred and fiftie pounds and shall purchase with the same by the advise of my Supervisors of this my will as much land and tenements within the countie of Essex as the same six hundred and fiftie pounds will buy and purchase in a frugall and good manner wch landes and tenements soe to be bought and purchased my will and meaninge is that they be taken, made and assured to the use of my two younger sonnes Samuell and Joseph and to theire heires forever to either of them severally a moytie of the same lands and tenements they and either of them to enter upon the same at theire severall ages of one and twentie yeares

Item my will and minde is that Anne my welbeloved wife shall have the foresaide lands and tenements in Birch or elsewhere wch I have given to my sonnes Nathaniell and Jeremy - and the lands and tenements wch I have appointed to be purchased for the use of my sonnes Samuell & Joseph untill every of my said foure sonnes shall herewith accomplish theire ages of sixteene yeares for and toward the bringinge of them and my other younger children up and after theire severall ages of six-teene yeares attayned then my will and minde is that the rents issues and profitts of theire severall lands and tenements shalbe severally imployed by my said wife for the use and benefitt of my said foure younger sonnes till theire severall ages of one and twentie yeares and that then my wife doe paie the same unto them for a severall stocke for them

Item I give to my three daughters Mary, Anne, and Sara three hundred pounds apeece whereof two hundred pounds apeece to be paid at theire severall ages of eighteene yeares and th'other hundred pounds apeece at theire severall ages of one and twentie yeares

Item my will and minde is that if any one of my three daughters doe die and depart this mortall life without issue of theire bodies lawfullie begotten before such tyme as theire sever-all porcons and legacies are appointed to be paid to them as aforesaid that then the legacie and porcon of her soe dyinge shalbe equallie paid to the other two surviving at such tyme as the same should have beene paid unto her deceased if she had lived

Item my will and minde is further that if any of my younger sonnes doe happen to die and depart this life before theire severall ages of one and twentie yeares without issue of theire bodies lawfullie begotten That then the land and tenements With the appurtenances before given and willed to them or any of them shall equallie goe and remaine amongst the rest of my sonnes that shalbe then livinge and to theire heires for ever part and partlike

Item my will and minde is alsoe that if my sonnes John or James doe happen to die before such tyme as they or either of them have or ought to have received theire severall legacies of two hundred pounds and one hundred pounds to them given and appointed as aforesaid That then the legacies of him or them soe dyinge shalbe paid and equallie divided amongst the rest of my sonnes that shalbe then livinge and be paid at such tyme as it should have beene if they or either of them had lived

Item my will and minde is that if any more than one of my said daughters doe happen to die before theire or either of theire legacies be paid or due to be paid as aforesaid that then the legacie of her or them soe dyinge shalbe equallie divided and paid to & amongst the rest of my children then livinge at such tyme as it should have beene if she or they had lived

Item my will and minde is further that if any of my said three daughters shall contract in themselves and marrie without the consent and allowance of my wife and Supervisors or any two of them then that then she or they that shall soe doe shall loese the benefitt of one hundred pounds of her legacie wch is appointed to be paid at her age of one and twentie yeares and then as to that hundred pounds my former gift to her and them soe dyinge shalbe void and then I will the same be equallie divided amongst my sonnes

Item my will and minde is that if my sonne Thomas and his heires shall fail to paie the said Twentie shillings yearely to my Sister Stracey during her life within fourteen daies after the feast daie of St. Michaell th'archangell that then it shalbe lawfull for my said Sister and her assignes to enter into and upon the said barne before given to my said sonne Thomas and there to distraine and the distresse and distresses therefound to take leade drive and carrie awaie and the same to detaine and keepe untill she shall be fullie satsified and paid the said annuity or yearely rent of twentie shillinges and the arrrerages thereof if any be together with her reasonable costs and expences in that behalf sustayned

Item I give to my loveinge friends Mr. Hooker Mr. Nathaniell Rogers Mr. Daniell Rogers and Mr. Collins twentie shillinges apeece as a token of my love

Item I give to my sonne Thomas my great oyle Sisterne of lead soe as he give and deliver to my sonne John the litle sistern of lead for oyle wch I late bought and gave to my sonne Thomas

Item I give to my brother John Malden and my sister his wife twentie shillings apeece

Item I give unto henry Stracey my kinsman five pounds to be paid him within sixe moneths next after my decease

Item my will and minde is that if any losses shall happen by any of my debts or wares soe that my stocke shall not be sufficient to paie the legacies herein given that then such losses shalbe equallie borne and abated out of the legacies wch I have given to my children

Item I give to my brothers John Reeve and Willm Stacey fortie shillinges apeece and To my brother Jeremy Reeve twentie shillings as a token of my love

All the rest & residue of my goods chattalls debts plate money and household stuffe whatsoever bequeathed I doe give and bequeath to my said wife for and towards the payment of my debts and legacies & perfomance of this my last will and testament upon this condicon nevertheless that within one moneth the next after my decease she shall enter bond of two thounsand pounds to my said brothers John Reeve and Willm Stacy with condicon to prove this my will within two moneths after my decease and to paie all the legacies hereingiven and bequeathed according to this my will and alsoe to performe all things in this my will contayned And further alsoe that if she shall agree to marrie againe with any man that he the daie before his marriage with her shall enter the like bond of two thousand pounds with such sufficient suerties as shalbe thought fitt by my said brothers John Reeve and Willm Stacy or the Survivor of them wth the like condicon respectively and my brothr Stacy to keepe the said bonds And then I make my said brothers John Reeve and William Stacy Supervisors of said my will to see the same performed in all things Provided allwaies that if my Wife doe not enter bond as aforesaid Then I doe make my said brothers John Reeve and William Stacy Executors of this my last will and testament who I doe earnestly entrust to take the same upon them and to see this my will in all things to be performed and my minde is that they shall allow themselves out of my estate all theire charges and expenses anywaies to be laid out thereabouts And thus revoking all former wills by mee made I pronounce this to be my last will and testament beinge written in sixe sheetes of paper

In witnes wherof I have hereunto sett my hand and seale the daie and yeare first abovewritten

Thos. Fitch

Signed sealed and published in the presence of W. Lyngwood, cla: (heridge) John Read

Probatum fuit Testamentum suprascriptum ayud Londn coram venerabili vivo Domine Marten Milite logum Doctore curie Prerogative magistro custode.[1]

---

1. P.R.O. B 11/163 Transcribed by Edith Fitch Swapp.

About the Author

J ohn[10] Townsend Fitch is a sixteenth generation descendant of William Fitch of Wicken Bonhunt. He spent most of his professional career in the continuing education of practicing engineers through the media of television and videotape.

Now retired, he devotes his time to Fitch family history. Long interested in the subject, he began his research on this first volume burdened by the same misinformation and illusions that have clouded the work of earlier family historians. It was not until he made the first of several trips to England that he began to disentangle the true story of the family from the myths and mistakes that have grown up around it.

John Fitch was born in Shanghai, China, son of missionary parents. He was educated at Northwood School in Lake Placid and at the Massachusetts Institute of Technology, where he majored in electrical engineering. He served on the staff of M.I.T. for thirteen years before becoming Executive Director of the Association for Media-based Continuing Education for Engineers, a post he held until retirement in 1987. He is the author of several papers on continuing education and the producer of numerous science education films.

He and his wife, a retired school teacher, live in Cambridge, Massachusetts. They have six grown children and seven grandchildren. John[12] Fitch, to whom this book is dedicated, is the oldest.

Made in the USA
Coppell, TX
24 January 2021